In the Eyes of the Law

In the Eyes of the Law

WOMEN, MARRIAGE, AND PROPERTY IN NINETEENTH-CENTURY NEW YORK

NORMA BASCH

Cornell University Press

ITHACA AND LONDON

Cornell University Press gratefully acknowledges a grant from the Andrew W. Mellon Foundation that aided in bringing this book to publication.

First published 1982 by Cornell University Press.
Published in the United Kingdom by Cornell University Press Ltd., Ely House, 37 Dover Street, London W1X 4HQ.

International Standard Book Number 0-8014-1466-0
Library of Congress Catalog Card Number 82-2454
Printed in the United States of America
Librarians: Library of Congress cataloging information appears on the last page of the book.

The paper in this book is acid-free, and meets the guidelines for permanence and durability of the Committee on Production Guidelines for Book Longevity of the Council on Library Resources.

To Carl E. Prince

MENTOR, SCHOLAR, TEACHER,

FEMINIST, AND FRIEND

Contents

Preface

When I began research for this book, I set out to explore the historical contours of what I perceived to be a dramatic shift in the status of American women. For centuries Anglo-American law had rendered wives dependent on and subservient to their husbands by denying them legal identities and by depriving them of control of property. I was convinced that the complex of mid-nineteenth-century statutes which endowed wives with independent legal personalities and gave them the right to own their own property obliterated the very foundations of the patriarchal family. Through an in-depth investigation of these legal reforms in New York, I aimed to place this silent revolution, as it has been called, in the context of the history of American women.

It soon became clear to me, however, that in New York the passage of the married women's property acts was neither silent nor revolutionary. Conflict permeated the public discussions, ambiguity clouded the intent of the Legislature, and conservatism suffused the interpretations of the courts. Large remnants of the wife's former inferior status survived the legislative assaults of the nineteenth century. Despite state-by-state variations in marital property reform, the case of New York seemed sufficiently representative to suggest some inherent limits in much of this legislation. Gradually the scope of my research and the shape of my analysis changed. It became important to understand how and why the law did not change.

Relying on both legal and nonlegal sources, I cast a wide net around a tangible body of legal reforms. Women occupied the center of my angle of vision. I drew on jurisprudence, the legislative record, and appellate court cases, the traditional and notably all-male sources of legal history, because these are critical documents in the history of ideas, profoundly reflecting and affecting attitudes and beliefs about women. Such nonlegal sources as popular periodical literature and the literature of the antebellum women's movement demonstrated that opponents and proponents of legal reform viewed the liberation of married women from their common law disabilities as the pivotal first step toward a larger and more fundamental equality between the sexes.

This book is more than a chronicle of the married women's property acts in the state of New York. It is an exploration of nineteenth-century social and ideological conflict over the appropriate roles for American women in marriage, in the economy, and in the political life of the nation. It is the story of legal changes forged grudgingly, slowly, and in bits and pieces, and of legal continuities sustained in subtle, complex, and powerful ways. It is a study in power and powerlessness. If it should shed some light on the legal problems of women today, I hope that it will be presentist in the nonpejorative sense of the word.

Encouragement and support for this book came from many quarters, and I have benefited enormously from the criticism and comments of mentors, colleagues, and students. A Woodrow Wilson Grant in Women's Studies funded by the Lever Brothers Foundation and the Helena Rubinstein Foundation provided research funds. My thanks go to Thomas Bender and Daniel Walkowitz of New York University for their cogent criticism of an early version of this work. I am especially grateful to the editors of *Feminist Studies,* who made important suggestions for a 1979 article on the same theme and who encouraged me to rethink some assumptions. Materials from the De Peyster Family Papers, the De Peyster Chancery Papers, and the Beekman Family Papers are published with the permission of the New-York Historical Society.

Colleagues in law and legal history were patient, generous, and extraordinarily helpful in filling in the gaps in my background and in suggesting improvements in the manuscript. Special thanks go to Michael Grossberg of Case Western Reserve

University, Nancy Erickson of the Ohio State University College of Law, and Marlene Stein Wortman of the Institute for Research in History. As their suggestions were not always taken, they are in no way responsible for the flaws in this book. Without them, however, flaws undoubtedly would have been more numerous.

My gratitude goes to the members of my family. Shelly Basch taught me to use a law library, proofread innumerable versions of the manuscript, took over a sizable portion of our domestic chores, and translated the concept of equality in marriage into a reality. Rachel Basch typed portions of the revisions and supported this endeavor with an enthusiasm and pride that were an endless source of pleasure to me. Fred Basch endured day-to-day deprivations with flexibility and good humor, and brightened the bleaker moments with his lively conversation and good food. The process of altering our traditional family roles was painful for each of us at times but benefited all of us.

I am grateful to Lois Van Epps, who typed the manuscript, and to Bernhard Kendler and Barbara H. Salazar of Cornell University Press, who respectively supported its publication and edited it with intelligence and care.

My profoundest thanks go to Carl Prince for his professional criticism, his friendly advice, and most of all his abiding faith in me.

NORMA BASCH

Rutgers, The State University
University College
Newark, New Jersey

Abbreviations

DAB	*Dictionary of American Biography,* ed. Dumas Malone. 22 vols. New York: Charles Scribner's Sons, 1935.
HWS	*History of Woman Suffrage,* ed. Elizabeth Cady Stanton, Susan B. Anthony, Matilda Joslyn Gage, and Ida Husted Harper. 6 vols. New York: Fowlers & Wells, 1881–1922.
JNYA	*Journal of the New York Assembly.*
JNYS	*Journal of the New York Senate.*
LNY	*Laws of New York.*
NAW	*Notable American Women,* ed. Edward T. James, Janet Wilson James, and Paul S. Boyer. 3 vols. Cambridge: Harvard University Press, 1971.
NYAD	*New York Assembly Documents.*
NYHS	The New-York Historical Society, New York, New York.
NYSD	*New York Senate Documents.*
RSSNY	*Revised Statutes of the State of New York.*
Stanton-Blatch Letters	*Elizabeth Cady Stanton as Revealed in Her Letters, Diary, and Reminiscences,* ed. Theodore Stanton and Harriot Stanton Blatch. 2 vols. New York: Harper, 1922.
USMDR	*United States Magazine and Democratic Review.*

In the Eyes of the Law

CHAPTER 1

Married Women's Property Rights: An Introduction

In *Thaler v. Thaler,* a 1977 New York divorce case in which alimony was awarded to the husband, the judge had occasion to summarize the nineteenth-century shift in the legal status of married women. At common law, he asserted, "the husband and wife were one and the husband was the one.... But with the advent of the married woman's property acts ... any previous justification for this one-way support duty faded."[1] In the same year, however, an unemployed Brooklyn construction worker aired his reservations about his wife's employment by evoking the old common law image of marriage. "When you get married," he said, "you figure it's gonna be like one. Only it's always the husband's one."[2] The first of these comments suggests the subject of this book: challenges to the common law doctrine of marital unity during a pivotal era of American law, roughly 1820-60.[3] The second reflects its emphasis: the uncanny persis-

[1]Thaler v. Thaler, *New York Law Journal,* January 21, 1977, p. 14.

[2]Anna Quindlen, "Relationships vs. Intimacy," *New York Times,* November 28, 1977, p. 36.

[3]Some significant assessments of the period include Roscoe Pound, *The Formative Era of American Law* (New York, 1950); Charles M. Haar, ed., *The Golden Age of American Law* (New York, 1965); Maxwell Bloomfield, *American Lawyers in a Changing Society, 1776-1875* (Cambridge, Mass., 1976); Lawrence Friedman, *A History of American Law* (New York, 1973); and Morton J. Horwitz, *The Transformation of American Law, 1780-1860* (Cambridge, Mass., 1977). Perry Miller placed the jurisprudence of the era in the context of American intellectual history in *The Life of the Mind in America from the Revolution to the Civil War* (New York, 1965). For important scholarship on legislative activity in the period, see Louis Hartz, *Economic Policy and Democratic Thought: Pennsylvania, 1776-1880* (Cambridge, Mass., 1948), and J. Willard Hurst, *Law and the Conditions of Freedom in the Nineteenth Century United States* (Madison, Wis., 1956).

tence of that doctrine far beyond its Christian and common law origins.

The married women's property acts were a diverse group of statutes passed by most American states in the middle decades of the nineteenth century. As the judge in *Thaler v. Thaler* asserted, the ostensible purpose of the statutes was to erode the traditional common law disabilities of married women by granting them the power to own and control their own property. What gave rise to these statutes, and what effects did they have on the lives of nineteenth-century women? What place do they hold in the history of American women?

History in general and legal history in particular cannot be compartmentalized in tidy chronological units. *Thaler v. Thaler* suggests the usefulness of the long view. So, of course, does the comment by the Brooklyn construction worker. But for its lack of elegance, it might have emerged from the pen of Sir William Blackstone. We cannot begin, then, in the 1840s, with the statutes themselves, or even in the 1820s, with the discussions that anticipated them. We cannot understand in full historical context the impulse, resistence, and conflict that accompanied the passage of the married women's property acts unless we first understand the legal status of married women in the Anglo-American legal tradition. Although the economic and social exigencies that confronted antebellum legislators when they drafted the first statutes were quite new, in some ways the legal issues that confronted them were centuries old, a part of the English heritage.

The legal heritage of most of America was distinctly English. Except for a few jurisdictions, the impress of the common law on American law was pervasive. Most states stipulated their adherence to the common law in early statutes or state constitutions. American law, moreover, was knitted to English law through a shared group of precedents, statutes, procedures, and theories. Despite widespread popular hostility to the complexity and professionalism exhibited by the English legal system, American lawyers cast their pleas and American jurists rendered their decisions in the formal language of their English predecessors. And as one nineteenth-century American specialist in domestic relations law observed, in no other area was the correspondence between the two legal systems closer than in the law of husband

and wife.[4] At the core of that law was the doctrine of marital unity.

From the time of the Norman Conquest, the common law developed a complex body of theory based on the simple presumption that "in the eyes of the law" the husband and wife were one person—the husband. Common law jurisprudence perpetuated this legal fiction as a convenient device for ordering the legal and economic relationship of the two parties to the marriage and of the married couple with third parties. At marriage a wife assumed her husband's name and his rank; she came under her husband's wing or protective cover in a condition designated as coverture. As a result of this condition, a husband and wife could not contract with one another, nor could they testify in court for or against one another. More important, coverture imposed serious procedural and substantive disabilities on the wife. She could neither sue nor be sued in her own name, she was limited in making contracts and wills, and all of her personal property as well as the management of her real property went to her husband.

The doctrine of marital unity not only mandated the wife's subservience to her husband, but it also held the distinction of obliterating her legal identity. At common law a wife was a nonentity in most situations; her husband subsumed her legal personality. The law created an equation in which one plus one equaled one by erasing the female one. To be sure, husband-wife was only one relationship among others in which the "superior" protected and legally represented the "inferior." Reflecting a finely calibrated social and political hierarchy, the common law in its early stages was not interested in the family per se.[5] As long as the family was intact, the common law treated only its head, the master of master-servant, the guardian of guardian-ward, and the baron of baron-feme.

Many commentators, therefore, stress the rational material

[4]Julius Goebel, Jr., *Cases and Materials on the Development of Legal Institutions* (Brattleboro, Vt., 1946), pp. 1-2; Bloomfield, *American Lawyers,* pp. 32-58; Joel Prentice Bishop, *The Law of Married Women* (1875), cited in John D. Johnston, Jr., "Sex and Property: The Common Law Tradition, the Law School Curriculum and Developments Toward Equality," *New York University Law Review* 47 (1972):1062.

[5]Goebel, *Cases and Materials,* p. 442.

basis of the wife's legal status in the feudal structure.[6] No cogent explanation, however, exists for the differences between the development of Anglo-Norman law in comparison with a continental model of community property, which gave the husband great authority over the wife but supported in a variety of systems the idea of a community of goods.[7] The controversial issue is not the wife's inferiority under Anglo-Norman law—male dominance was an accepted principle in the Western world—but rather the weakness of her family's influence in comparison with that of the wife's family in community-property systems, which also functioned within a feudal structure.

The English husband-baron of the thirteenth century enjoyed more power over marital property than his northern French counterpart. Coverture, which operated in both systems, was weaker in France. For the most part, the two systems managed to produce comparable results, few of which could be construed as favorable to the wife, but they involved fundamentally different modes of thinking about marital property. At the core of the continental model was the idea of shared property, at least with respect to what was acquired during marriage, although separate property was recognized as well. At the core of the common law model was the idea of separate property. What is weak in the common law model is the notion that the wife is entitled to a share of the profits of the marriage because she is a working partner in that marriage. Dower, the wife's share as a survivor at common law, falls more readily into the category of maintenance.

If we look ahead from the thirteenth century, we can see that the introduction of the common law into England had important

[6]Florence Griswold Buckstaff, "Married Women's Property in Anglo-Saxon and Anglo-Norman Law and the Origin of the Common-Law Dower," *Annals of the American Academy of Political and Social Science* 4 (1893–94):233–64; Sir Frederick Pollack and Frederic William Maitland, *The History of English Law,* 2d ed., 2 vols. (1898; reprinted London, 1968), 2:406. For the protection inherent in feudal statuses, see Roscoe Pound, *The Spirit of the Common Law* (Francestown, N.Y., 1921), p. 27.

[7]For a comparison of common law and community-property models in the thirteenth century, I have relied on Charles Donahue, Jr., "What Causes Fundamental Legal Ideas?: Marital Property in England and France in the Thirteenth Century," *Michigan Law Review* 78(1979):59–88. Donahue concludes that differences probably came from the "irrational force of legal ideas operating away from the influence of conscious policy choice."

consequences for the modern wage earner's wife who brought little or nothing in the way of separate property to her marriage. If we look backward, we can see that the legal status of wives in England was considerably better before the introduction of the common law, a phenomenon that controverts theories that locate the changing legal status of married women on a path of steady improvement.[8]

The doctrine of marital unity, which shaped the wife's legal disabilities, was not unique to the common law. The wife's inferior status had a religious and metaphysical foundation in Western culture. Both the Old and New Testaments supported the wife's subordinate status, and the doctrine of marital unity had a specific canonical equivalent in the doctrine of the unity of the flesh.[9] This doctrine shaped decisions in the ecclesiastical courts. In England by the twelfth century, cases of adultery, bigamy, separation, and the few complete divorces the church allowed came within the jurisdiction of ecclesiastical courts. In matters related to the law of husband and wife, ecclesiastical courts and common law courts, despite early jurisdictional clashes, complemented each other harmoniously; they simply divided their respective jurisdictions according to the nature of the particular problem. The common law generally reserved for itself the right to adjudicate land-related problems. The church courts tended to deal with the succession of "movables" as well as areas touching the sexual morality of the family.[10] They set the rules on the degree of consanguinity permitted between the marrying couple. In cases concerning legitimacy, the common law declared that the child who was capable of inheriting was the child whom the church deemed to be legitimate. Similarly, in cases concerning dower, the common law abided by the church's estimate of whether or not a marriage was valid.[11]

On the other hand, the English legal heritage, which placed harsh restrictions on the wife and allowed spacious powers to the

[8]See Buckstaff, "Married Women's Property"; Pollack and Maitland, *History of English Law,* 2:403; and Courtney Stanhope Kenny, *The History of the Law of England as to the Effect of Marriage on Property and on the Wife's Legal Capacity* (London, 1879), pp. 8–11.

[9]On the role of the church and its effects on married women's status, see Mary Daly, *The Church and the Second Sex* (New York, 1975), pp. 74–106.

[10]Johnston, "Sex and Property," pp. 1050–51.

[11]Pollack and Maitland, *History of English Law,* 2:367–68, 374–77.

husband, had an alternate side. Situations arose to confound the secular doctrine of absolute marital unity, which was merely a legal fiction, a premise on which to base conclusions rather than an article of faith. First of all, the common law afforded a certain amount of leeway in the wife's activities; she could buy "necessaries" and enter into contracts as long as she represented her lord. Thus out of necessity a primitive theory of agency developed. Second, the common law recognized the wife's contingent interest in her husband's realty through its championship of dower, and it functioned during marriage to protect her potential interests as a widow. By allowing the wife a life interest in one-third of her husband's realty if she survived him, the common law did have some limited notion of a community of goods. Third, the common law accommodated the woman who resided in a center of trade and participated in local commerce, either as a matter of custom or through "sole-trader statutes." Thus a married woman might contract business debts and engage in trade if she had her husband's permission. Finally, the common law recognized some specific emergencies in which a married woman would need to act as if she were a single woman, such as when her husband "abjured the realm," or when he was judged to be civilly dead. In several situations the common law either removed or eased the wife's disabilities.[12]

The ecclesiastical courts also mitigated the wife's position in England. These courts, which controlled separation, had to treat the wife as a separate legal entity. Although once the marriage was consummated, a complete divorce was almost impossible, a divorce from bed and board was available, especially in cases of adultery. Consequently, in permitting such a separation and stipulating the financial terms of settlement, the church dealt with the wife as a separate person.[13]

The most significant body of precedents modifying the wife's legal status, however, came with the development of equity. Originating in the concept of fairness as opposed to legal strictness, equity emerged as a separate jurisdiction that offered special remedies when none were available at law. Beginning in the thirteenth century with special petitions for relief to the king's

[12]Ibid., pp. 434–36.
[13]Goebel, *Cases and Materials,* p. 494.

chancellor, equity grew into a whole system with its own forms, pleadings, and precedents and with its own jurisprudence.[14] The earliest petitioners before the king's chancellor prayed for the relief that was foreclosed to them through the ordinary course of justice. In pathetic terms, they lamented that they were too poor, too sick, too old, too powerless, or too disadvantaged by the rigidities of the law. As the administration of equity became more formal and took place in a separate court of chancery, special categories of persons and distinct areas of law fell within its province; eventually it came to deal with married women and their property.

Equity, however, was neither antithetical to nor independent of the common law; rather it was ancillary, filling in gaps left by the rigidity of the common law.[15] Nonetheless, equity ultimately produced a body of precedents that undercut the doctrine of marital unity and ameliorated the disabilities of wives. By the seventeenth century, English equity recognized antenuptial contracts and trusts, devices whereby a wife could keep property apart from her husband for her separate use. Next came recognition of the wife's equity to a settlement, and a husband who wished to reach his wife's assets when they were subject to the jurisdiction of the court was obliged by the court to make special arrangements for her support. By the eighteenth century, equity's fully developed precedents enabled a prospective wife with considerable assets and skilled legal advice to strike a bargain in advance of marriage for economic autonomy far beyond the limits of the common law.[16]

Another important breach in the doctrine of marital unity came with the Protestant Reformation and the abandonment of marriage as a sacrament. Luther and Calvin retained the admonition that the husband was the head of the marriage, but they expanded the wife's separate identity and moral responsibility in

[14] Frederic William Maitland, *Equity* (Cambridge, 1926), pp. 2–5.

[15] Ibid., p. 19. Maitland points out that the common law and equity should not be considered rival systems. "Equity was not a self-sufficient system; at every point it presupposed the existence of common law. Common law was a self-sufficient system." On the development of equity, see also William S. Holdsworth, *A History of English Law,* 14 vols. (London, 1903), 1:395–468, 5:278–338.

[16] Johnston, "Sex and Property," p. 1057.

the process of championing the personal spiritual regeneration of the individual. Although the liberal ideas of the Reformation with respect to marriage made little impact on the English ecclesiastical courts and marriage remained within their jurisdiction, they permeated the more radical Protestant sects. These ideas made their way to the American colonies with the Puritans and other dissenting sects.

Nevertheless, it is a mistake to assume that the legal status of married women was miraculously transformed when it crossed the Atlantic. The legal status of married women in colonial America remains somewhat ambiguous, varying geographically from colony to colony and chronologically over more than a century and a half of development.[17] The effects of New World environmental and social conditions on transplanted English legal institutions are far from clear. The question of whether frontier conditions, a shortage of labor, the presence of dissenting religious sects, uneven sex ratios, and non-English influences improved the legal status of wives has not been answered yet in a comprehensive way, especially for the seventeenth century.[18] Despite the sanguine view set forth by Richard Morris in his pioneering work on the subject, there can be no doubt that in the English colonies of North America, the English common law

[17]Richard B. Morris stresses the improved legal status of colonial wives in *Studies in the History of American Law with Special References to the Seventeenth and Eighteenth Centuries* (New York, 1930). Other works on the status of colonial women include Julia Cherry Spruill, *Women's Life and Work in the Southern Colonies* (1938; reprinted New York, 1972); John Demos, *A Little Commonwealth: Family Life in Plymouth Colony* (London, 1970); Elizabeth W. Anthony Dexter, *Colonial Women of Affairs: A Study of Women in Business and the Professions in America before 1776* (Boston, 1924); George Lee Haskins, *Law and Authority in Early Massachusetts: A Study in Tradition and Design* (New York, 1960); and Marylynn Salmon, "Equality or Submersion? Feme Covert Status in Early Pennsylvania," in *Women of America: A History,* ed. Carol Ruth Berkin and Mary Beth Norton (Boston, 1979), pp. 93–113. For a comparative approach, see Roger Thompson, *Women in Stuart England and America: A Comparative Study* (London, 1974). For a comparison between the colonial and postrevolutionary periods, see Joan Hoff Wilson, "The Illusion of Change: Women and the American Revolution," in *The American Revolution: Explorations in the History of American Radicalism,* ed. Alfred F. Young (DeKalb, Ill., 1976), pp. 383–445.

[18]Lois Green Carr and Lorena S. Walsh meticulously document the economic and legal advantages some Maryland women derived from early social and demographic disruptions. See "The Planter's Wife: The Experience of White Women in Seventeenth-Century Maryland," *William and Mary Quarterly,* 3d ser., 34 (1977):542–71.

model of marital property, along with its ameliorating exceptions, did take root, grow, and flourish until it eventually crowded out most informal non-English practices.

Colonial departures from English legal practices were not always advantageous to wives. In the most comprehensive study to date on the legal status of wives in the colonial and early national periods, Marylynn Salmon points out that wives fared better in jurisdictions that closely replicated English law than in those that were innovative. In Puritan Connecticut and Quaker Pennsylvania, bastions of religious dissent from the English perspective, wives did not enjoy some fundamental common law protections in conveyancing and dower.[19]

To be sure, a shortage of labor and greater social mobility in the early stages of colonization afforded some wives wide scope for economic activity. Married women in colonial America acted as sole traders by custom or through provincial legislative statutes. Sometimes private legislative acts extended particular powers to individual women. We know that colonial wives held licenses as tavern operators, managed large landed estates, made use of marriage settlements, and had the protection of dower, which was often calculated quite liberally with respect to waste.[20] There is evidence that the Dutch women of New York acted as agents for their husbands in courts of law, made joint wills with their husbands well into the eighteenth century, and made antenuptial agreements without trusts.[21] Few colonial practices, however, were radical departures from English law, with the exception of some Dutch practices, and these were superseded eventually by English law. Furthermore, the trust, the device used most widely by parents on behalf of their married daughters, usually allowed them a life interest with no powers.

The major American departure from English practices was procedural and involved the sale of land. The sale of land at common law always was complicated by the wife's inability to convey her own land and by her potential claim to dower in her husband's land. In England the solution to this problem con-

[19]Marylynn Salmon, "The Property Rights of Women in Early America: A Comparative Study," Ph.D. dissertation, Bryn Mawr College, 1980.

[20]Ibid., pp. 287–94.

[21]Morris, *Studies in the History of American Law,* pp. 131–32; Goebel, *Cases and Materials,* p. 538.

sisted in using the legal fiction of the fine and recovery, a formal procedure that took place in a court.[22] In many American jurisdictions in the colonial period, a deed executed by both spouses and the wife's separate examination before a minor official, such as a justice of the peace, were sufficient to validate the sale of the wife's property or to remove the cloud of dower from the sale of the husband's. The separate examination, frequently cited as a legal victory for American women, was essentially a convenient way to get around cumbersome procedures in a society where land was an important commodity. Its origins were in the older procedure of the fine, which required the wife's separate examination in a court of law. The simple joint deed, like many other American innovations, was procedural rather than substantive. Abundant land devoid of feudal connections was an important source of economic growth and social mobility, and had to be bought and sold with ease. When the separate examination was ignored, however, as it was at times in many jurisdictions, the simple joint deed actually stripped the wife of an older protection. When it was observed, it theoretically ensured the wife's consent to the sale free from her husband's coercion, but if coercion were really a factor, it seems unlikely that a wife could bar her husband from selling land.

Accounts that herald the legal freedom of American wives during the colonial period, in comparison with their English counterparts, are probably overdrawn. Many comparisons involve descriptions of American practices in relation to English legal abstractions and therefore create a distortion by ignoring variations in English practices. In terms of what the common law allowed to married women, there were few differences between England and America, and in some ways the sway of common law restrictions was even greater in America. Informal American practices eroded some fundamental common law rights, and while equity offered an alternate path to English families of wealth and legal sophistication, in some American

[22]The fine is a "final concord" that is the result of fictitious litigation in court establishing the clear legitimacy of the conveyance. Less formal conveyances, such as the simple joint deed, were certainly known in England. See Pollack and Maitland, *History of English Law,* 2:101 and 413, n. 1.

jurisdictions it was poorly developed.[23] In states that hewed closely to the English model after the Revolution, as New York did, equitable remedies could be unwieldy and costly.

The Revolution itself, which unleashed an aggressively egalitarian ideology antithetical to the very concept of coverture, and which encouraged rising political expectations on the part of women, managed to leave coverture intact. The revolt against the father, the king—a metaphor Thomas Paine exploited with devasting effectiveness in *Common Sense*—set off no concomitant revolt against the father, the political head of the family, at least not immediately. Early statutes made it clear that women, married or single, were not to be part of the new political order. Wives of Loyalists with property at stake might be considered independent political agents when it suited Patriot purposes, but such recognition was a temporary wartime strategy.[24]

After the Revolution and in the first three or four decades of the nineteenth century, the legal separateness of the wife in specific situations was sharpened somewhat in both statutes and judicial decisions. Some statutes recognized long-established exceptions to coverture. For example, in 1787 Massachusetts passed a statute that enabled abandoned wives to become sole traders without the formality of a special petition. Other statutes decreased the length of time that was required to pass before a spouse who had disappeared could be presumed dead. Statutes of this type recognized that women who were the victims of the dislocations of war or who had been abandoned by their husbands were a potential burden to the community and needed to be freed from their common law disabilities in order to earn a living or to remarry. They were not departures from the com-

[23]On the development of equity in early America, see Stanley Katz, "The Politics of Law in Colonial America: Controversies over Chancery Courts and Equity Law in the Eighteenth Century," in *Colonial America: Essays in Politics and Social Development*, ed. Stanley Katz (Boston, 1976), pp. 401–22. For the inherent indignities to which equity subjected married women, see Leo Kanowitz, *Women and the Law: The Unfinished Revolution* (1969; reprinted Albuquerque, 1975), pp. 39–40.

[24]Linda K. Kerber, *Women of the Republic: Intellect and Ideology in Revolutionary America* (Chapel Hill, N.C., 1980), pp. 9–12, 119–55; Mary Beth Norton, *Liberty's Daughters: The Revolutionary Experience of American Women, 1750–1800* (Boston, 1980), pp. 191–93; Wilson, "Illusion of Change," pp. 414–19. Wilson finds a marked deterioration in the legal status of women following the Revolution.

mon law, which recognized the need for a wife to function in special situations as if she were single. At the same time, courts in some jurisdictions made the creation of a married woman's separate estate easier by eliminating the need for a trust. A woman could create a separate estate in advance of marriage without conveying property to a trustee.[25]

We can speculate that the majority of women did not fit these special categories. They were neither abandoned nor sufficiently wealthy or legally sophisticated to create a separate estate. Most wives continued to live with the harsh disabilities and limited rights of coverture. Furthermore, dower, one of the most fundamental of those rights, was eroded during the same period. A North Carolina statute of 1784, abolishing entail and primogeniture, reduced the widow's portion if a child's share were to be divided between two or more children. In the first two decades of the nineteenth century, the judiciary diminished the scope of dower in some states and even menaced it as a legal right.[26]

When antebellum legislators contemplated drafting married women's statutes, a marital prototype fabricated out of centuries of custom, precedent, and statute permeated their thinking. That is not to say that the law had been static; on the contrary, it had been enormously flexible. Still, some basic principles that had been evident in thirteenth-century England were evident in nineteenth-century America. The long view of married women in the Anglo-American legal tradition reveals a powerful mainstream of crushing substantive and procedural disabilities propelled by the legal fiction of marital unity. It also reveals a strong undercurrent that weakened the doctrine of absolute marital unity. It is fair to say, in summing up this tradition, that in the eyes of the law, most of the time, the husband and wife were one person—the husband. In special situations the law would avert its eyes and allow the wife to enjoy the status of an honorary single woman or feme sole, as in the case of her separate estate, but in all other respects it viewed her as a married

[25] Kerber, *Women of the Republic*, pp. 149–50; on abandonment, see Michael Grossberg, "Law and the Family in Nineteenth Century America," Ph.D. dissertation, Brandeis University, 1980, p. 130; on the equitable estate without a trust, see Salmon, "Property Rights of Women," pp. 210–20.

[26] Kerber, *Women of the Republic*, pp. 146–47; on the application of the principle of waste in dower, see Horwitz, *Transformation of American Law*, pp. 56–58.

woman, a feme covert. Furthermore, in order to attain some of the rights of a single woman, she was consistently dependent on others: on her husband for an antenuptial agreement, on relatives for a trust estate, and on the state in abandonment, separation, and divorce.

Consider the resilience and strength of the concept of marital unity. Clearly that ancient metaphor for marriage which submerged the person of the wife under the person of the husband had amazing staying power. The concept functioned in a diversity of historical contexts. Its religious origins lay in the one-flesh doctrine of Christianity, its empirical roots in the customs of medieval Normandy. Its introduction into English law after the Norman Conquest signaled a decline in the status of English wives which reached a nadir in the early capitalism of the sixteenth and seventeenth centuries. It was part of the baggage that English colonists carried to the New World. But what is most striking about the long course of the concept of marital unity is its ability to serve the legal needs of three shifting social structures: the kin-oriented family of the late Middle Ages, the patriarchal nuclear family of early capitalism, and even the more companionate nuclear family of the late eighteenth century.[27]

By the middle of the nineteenth century, however, the legal fiction of marital unity was under attack; statutory challenges to the old common law prototype began to appear. Beginning with Mississippi in 1839, American states began to pass statutes that allowed married women to own the property they brought to marriage or acquired afterward by gift or bequest. The Mississippi statute further stipulated that slaves owned by the wife at the time of marriage or acquired afterward should be her property, but their control and management, along with the profits from their labor, were reserved to the husband. A Michigan statute of 1844 exempted the wife's property from the husband's debts, a measure that suggests links between marital property reform and the need to clarify debtor-creditor relations. A Massachusetts bill of 1845 limited the wife's separate estate to the provisions of an antenuptial agreement, thereby recognizing lib-

[27]Considerable controversy exists over the chronology of these shifts. I have relied on Lawrence Stone, "The Rise of the Nuclear Family in Early Modern England: The Patriarchal Stage," in *The Family in History*, ed. Charles E. Rosenberg (Philadelphia, 1975), pp. 19–31.

eral equity precedents but also requiring a written agreement for the creation of a separate estate.[28] A married woman's clause that was part of the Texas Constitution of 1845 was vague and stipulated that "laws shall also be passed providing for the registration of the wife's separate property." Married women's clauses were placed in the state constitutions of California in 1849, Oregon in 1857, and Kansas in 1859. A Wisconsin constitution of 1847 containing a similar clause, however, went down to defeat by the voters.[29] The boldest of the statutes, the New York Earnings Act of 1860, gave wives the right to sue and be sued and included their wages as part of their separate estate.[30]

By 1865 twenty-nine states had passed some form of married women's property law.[31] The nation did not complete this process of piecemeal reform until the end of the nineteenth century. Statutes, of course, continued to be passed in the twentieth century, but the first phase of altering the American marital property system was a nineteenth-century phenomenon. The most historically revealing segment of this long process was undoubtedly the antebellum era, when the first major statutes engendered considerable public controversy and established the models for other jurisdictions.

For an exploration of the underlying dynamics of the married women's property acts, the experience of a single state in this pivotal era seems to offer the most promising focus. Nineteenth-century New York offers the researcher diversity and size, the two qualities that have made it a laboratory for studies of Jacksonian democracy. In the antebellum era, New York sustained the shocks of industrialization, urbanization, and the westward-moving frontier. With the important exception of slavery, New York history in the three decades before the Civil War encompassed or presaged the major historical forces at

[28] *Laws of Mississippi, 1839,* chap. 46; *Michigan Acts, 1844,* no. 66; *Acts and Resolutions of Maine, 1844,* chap. 117; *Acts and Resolutions of the Massachusetts General Court, 1845,* chap. 205.

[29] Goebel, *Cases and Materials,* pp. 555–56.

[30] *LNY, 1860,* chap. 90.

[31] Kay Ellen Thurman, "The Married Women's Property Acts," L.L.M. dissertation, University of Wisconsin Law School, 1966, p. 4. See also Elizabeth Bowles Warbasse, "The Changing Legal Rights of Married Women, 1800–1861," Ph.D. dissertation, Radcliffe College, 1960, a path-breaking study of the married women's property acts.

work in nineteenth-century America. Seventeen percent of the white population of the thirty states and territories in 1840 resided in New York.[32]

Furthermore, New York was a legally significant jurisdiction. Its jurists enjoyed national prominence, its decisions were cited frequently in other states, and its married women's statutes achieved international attention. The state was also a base for reform movements, including codification, abolition, temperance, religious revivalism, and most important, feminism. New York feminists entered the public arena before the Seneca Falls convention of 1848, lobbied persistently, and left behind the documents that relate their movement to the married women's acts.[33]

My original interest in the married women's property acts arose from the apparent paradox of this legislation in the midst of the declining political and economic status of nineteenth-century American women relative to American men.[34] The paradox generated many questions. How did the legislation correlate with the separation of home and work, with the meticulous definition of gender roles, with the cult of domesticity, with the emphasis on the psychological functions of the nuclear family?[35] Was it possible that scholarship on nineteenth-century American women had exaggerated the decline in women's status by failing to take into account the liberalizing impact of the married women's acts? Or was it possible that a revolution in the legal status of women was insignificant in comparison with their larger political and economic disabilities?

[32]Lee Benson, *The Concept of Jacksonian Democracy: New York as a Test Case* (Princeton, 1961), p. 3.

[33]For links between the married women's acts and the women's movement, see Keith Melder, "The Beginnings of the Women's Rights Movement in the United States," Ph.D. dissertation, Yale University, 1963, pp. 28–30; Peggy A. Rabkin, "The Origins of Law Reform: The Social Significance of the Nineteenth-Century Codification Movement and Its Contribution to the Passage of the Early Married Women's Property Acts," *Buffalo Law Review* 24 (1974–75):683–760.

[34]For the major article on women's declining status, see Gerda Lerner, "The Lady and the Mill Girl: Changes in the Status of Women in the Age of Jackson," *Midcontinent American Studies Journal* 10 (1969):5–15.

[35]Literature on the cult of domesticity in relation to wider social changes is voluminous. Two important examples are Barbara Welter, "The Cult of True Womanhood, 1820–1860," *American Quarterly* 18 (1966):151–74, and Ann Douglas, *The Feminization of American Culture* (New York, 1977).

The analytical challenge of correlating the improvement in the legal position of married women with larger social changes was modified by recent scholarship that subtly undermined the concept of women's declining status. Colonial historians began to challenge "the myth of a golden age" for preindustrial women.[36] At the same time, specialists in the nineteenth century embarked on a highly sophisticated exploration of the compensatory and even protofeminist strategies of a female subculture in which middle-class white women redefined and expanded their roles within the framework of domesticity.[37] This scholarship implicitly raised a new set of questions about the married women's property acts. What were the links between the improvement in the legal status of women within the family and women's efforts to carve out new roles in an industrial economy? Was it not reasonable to assume that the legal revolution in domestic relations laws which swept the nation in the nineteenth century was the distinct public and political reflection of women's growing private power within the domestic sphere?

Preliminary research in legal sources, however, suggested that my basic premise was erroneous. The revolution that the married women's acts seemed to herald simply did not take place. The public debate surrounding the passage of the statutes revealed that the ideological potential for a legal revolution was there. Nevertheless, it became clear that the restructuring of the marital property system represented the juncture of conflicting demands. The changes created by the statutes were either limited or in some areas even illusory. Accordingly, the analytical challenge gradually shifted from an effort to understand the changes wrought by the legislation to an effort to understand the continuities that survived.

Secondary sources that influenced the shape of this work were numerous, but the catalyst was Mary Beard's highly speculative

[36]Mary Beth Norton, "American History," *Signs* 5 (1979):335–36.

[37]See especially Carroll Smith-Rosenberg, "Beauty, the Beast and the Militant Woman: A Case Study in Sex Roles and Social Stress in Jacksonian America," *American Quarterly* 23 (1971):562–84; Kathryn Kish Sklar, *Catherine Beecher: A Study in American Domesticity* (New Haven, 1973); Nancy Cott, *The Bonds of Womanhood: "Woman's Sphere" in New England, 1780–1835* (New Haven, 1977); and Ellen Carol DuBois, Mari Jo Buhle, Temma Kaplan, Gerda Lerner, and Carroll Smith-Rosenberg, "Politics and Culture in Women's History: A Symposium," *Feminist Studies* 6 (1980):26–64.

and wide-ranging 1946 work, *Woman as Force in History*. The only previous historical study to explore the evolving status of American wives was Richard Morris' work in colonial law. Professional appreciation of Beard's work, however, awaited the growth of women's history. After mixed reviews at the time of publication, the historical profession virtually ignored *Woman as Force in History*. In a brief note on Mary Beard's death in 1958, the *American Historical Review* misstated its title and offered no comment on its place in historical scholarship. With the burgeoning of women's history, however, *Woman as Force in History* began to excite a flurry of interest.[38]

Beard's astonishing range and grasp of history supported a thesis of special interest to revisionists in women's history. Scholars who despaired of the sterility of the woman-as-victim theme and who at the same time questioned androcentric interpretations of historical significance had high praise for Beard's early exploration of these two problems.[39] Like her historian-hero, Henry Adams, Beard ridiculed the notion that women have been outside the flow of history.[40] She debunked the characterization of women as a caste, bound together in eternal subordination and oppression regardless of social rank. Stressing the significance of the family in history, *Woman as Force in History* anticipated the modern feminist impulse to study women's historical roles from the perspective of a nonmale structure of values while it simultaneously carried correctives to nineteenth-century feminist polemics.

Emphasis on the prescience of Beard's stance, however, has overshadowed the substance of her thesis. Beard's thesis is the modern starting point for the exploration of the married women's statutes. The structure and development of Beard's work rested on her assertion that the classic expression of women's

[38]Carl Degler, "*Woman as Force in History* by Mary Beard," *Daedalus* 103 (1974):67–73; Berenice Carroll, "On Mary Beard's *Woman as Force in History:* A Critique," in *Liberating Women's History,* ed. Berenice Carroll (Urbana, Ill., 1976), pp. 26–41. Beard was also the subject of a major panel at the Berkshire Conference on the History of Women at Mount Holyoke College, August 23, 1978.

[39]Regina Morantz explores the futility of the woman-as-victim theme in "The Lady and Her Physician," in *Clio's Consciousness Raised,* ed. Mary S. Hartman and Lois Banner (New York, 1974), pp. 50–51.

[40]Beard, *Woman as Force in History: A Study in Tradition and Realities* (New York, 1946), pp. 215–28.

subjection originated in the "mythology" of married women's common law disabilities as it appeared in Blackstone's *Commentaries.* This mythology, she claimed, was picked up by intelligent women who should have known better. Drawing on the crude outlines of the common law in Blackstone, they warped historical reality by depicting men everywhere and at all times as the tyrannical masters of women. For Beard, M. Carey Thomas, president of Bryn Mawr and early-twentieth-century suffragist, exemplified the feminists who manipulated the common law to produce an image of women in static subjection. Thomas contended, for example, that women had been waiting for justice "since the time of the the caveman. . . . Forever behind a woman is the mediaeval English common law which places upon her the stigma of inferiority and bondage."[41]

Thomas' ahistorical leap from the era of the caveman to medieval England was just the sort of distortion that Beard believed precluded the development of women's history. If women were so frail and weak, so invisible and powerless, and most of all so unchanging, how could they have a history at all? Beard set out to test the theory of subjection against long history and found it wanting by discovering some women at all times who exerted power in the family and in the public arena.

Since the quintessential source for the "haunting idea" of female subjection was Blackstone's *Commentaries* (1765–69), Beard traced the perpetuation of the myth of subjection as it evolved from Blackstone through the nineteenth century. Beginning with Mary Wollstonecraft's *A Vindication of the Rights of Woman* (1792), Beard asserted that Wollstonecraft "vitalized" the idea that at marriage a woman was civilly dead, even though she had no special interest in law. Next, the doctrine of subjection assumed its historical political form at Seneca Falls in 1848 with the Declaration of Sentiments. Then, with Harriet Taylor serving as the bridge between the feminists in America and their English counterparts, the American movement influenced John Stuart Mill to write his famous treatise, *The Subjection of Women* (1869). Marxists were the next group to seize upon the doctrine, according to Beard, with Frederick Engels' *The Origin of the Family, Private Property and the State* (1884) doing for the proletariat

[41]Ibid., p. 32.

what Blackstone did for the patricians and Wollstonecraft for the bourgeoisie. Later propagators of the myth included Sigmund Freud, Charlotte Perkins Gilman, and Simone de Beauvoir.[42]

Beard showed how each variation on Blackstone's theme, although it temporarily fitted some political party or grand ideology, made subjection the image of women throughout history. Thus what was politically useful turned out to have been disastrous for the writing of history. Beard, moreover, singled out the antebellum period in America as central to the development of the mythology of subjection. Nowhere was the sway of Blackstone greater, she insisted, than in America at this time. Even after Joseph Story and James Kent corrected Blackstone in their erudite treatises on equity and the common law, American feminists and the rank-and-file "Blackstone lawyers" continued to parrot Blackstone's dicta. Beard accused male historians of putting the finishing touches on the myth by writing women out of historical existence. But of all the multifarious groups and ideologies that perpetuated the myth of women's eternal subjection, she singled out the early feminists as giving it its most "complete and categorical form."[43]

For evidence of the paucity of Blackstone's scholarship and the magnitude of his distortions, Beard drew on equity. She stressed the flexibility of arrangements recognized in equity and the variety of agreements men and women made with each other as spouses, parents, and siblings. Equity, she contended, which liberated millions of American wives, should have been the slogan of the women's movement instead of equality. In other words, fairness between the sexes should not have been synonymous with legal sameness. She designated women's plea for equality before the law as an empty slogan that stemmed from a tendency to see the male as the measure of all things.[44] She claimed that equality of rights was an atomistic concept that split families and communities into individuals in pursuit of wealth. It had little significance for husbands and wives who struggled "to survive and provide safeguards for each other and

[42] Ibid., pp. 105–13.
[43] Ibid., pp. 119–32.
[44] Carroll, "On Mary Beard's *Woman as Force in History,*" p. 33; Beard, *Woman as Force in History,* p. 163.

for their children, under the law or in spite of it."[45] Although Beard admitted the married women's acts reached more women than equity, especially when they included a provision for the wife's earnings, she noted the difficulty of drafting a statute to cover all the tangles and contingencies of marital property. Posing a series of questions raised by the adjudication of the American statutes, Beard implied that the legislation extended the rights of wives without increasing their obligations or reducing their husbands' obligations, and thereby created a new set of inequities.[46]

Beginning, as the feminists did, with Blackstone, Beard constructed a glittering counterpolemic to the feminist position. Yet, as Carl Degler pointed out, she was far more feminist than antifeminist.[47] The theoretical impotence of married women at common law enraged her in the same way it enraged feminists of the nineteenth century. Her constant use of such words as "nothing," "nonentity," "ghostly," and "shadowy" exemplified her preoccupation with female invisibility. Although Beard failed to come to grips with coverture even as a demeaning metaphor that created psychological impediments for women, her sense of being demeaned by it and her desire to eradicate it permeated her work.

Some obvious flaws mar Beard's work. First, she merged opponents and proponents of female subjection together without adequately crediting the feminists with sharing her aim to obliterate Blackstonian stereotypes. Second, she placed entirely too much weight on Blackstone, who did not single-handedly create the outlines of the common law. Third, she exaggerated the power of equity by depicting it as a thoroughly independent legal system, equal in weight and antithetical in direction to the common law. Finally, in contrast to her perceptive critique of women's immutability, Beard evinced a belief in the immutability of marriage. Therefore she minimized married women's common law disabilities by claiming that women were disabled because of the nature of marriage as a social institution, not because of their sex per se. Because she assumed marriage ir-

[45]Beard, *Woman as Force in History,* p. 98.
[46]Ibid., pp. 178–80.
[47]Degler, "*Woman as Force in History,*" pp. 68–69.

revocably bound the interests of a man and woman together, an assumption in common law, Beard failed to take into account situations in which husbands and wives had diverging or conflicting interests. If marriage was the inexorable relationship she insisted it was, then it mandated a certain immutability in the roles of women and men.

Despite its flaws, however, *Woman as Force in History*, is still an extraordinary work; it is provocative, imaginative, scholarly, and enormously bold for its time. It projected a model for women's history when there was little on which to draw. It anticipated a methodological debate in women's history by some thirty years. It demonstrated a broad mastery of European and American history. More specifically, it devoted three chapters to Blackstone, the status of women at common law in America, and the married women's statutes. Implicitly at least, as Ann Lane noted, Beard issued a challenge for more particularized research that ought to be taken up by historians.[48]

Other significant analyses of the connections between women's social roles and marital property law remain in the works of the political theorists Beard named in her discussion of the mythology of subjection. Among them is John Stuart Mill, who probably best defined and polished the liberal nineteenth-century feminist position. It is Engels' theoretical foundation, however, that is the most directly antithetical to Beard's. Beard did not find the division of labor on sexual lines necessarily oppressive. For Beard, the family and women's place within it provided some women in all ages with important roles of power. In contrast, Engels in *The Origin of the Family, Private Property and the State* rooted the sexual division of labor in the beginnings of private property and exploitive class relations. Engels evaluated the monogamous patriarchal family—genuine monogamy demanded only of women—as an oppressive arrangement that ensured the legitimacy of children for patrilineal descent while turning women into the first exploited class.[49] According to Engels, there was nothing natural or irrevocable in the patrilineal

[48]Ann J. Lane, ed., *Mary Ritter Beard: A Sourcebook* (New York, 1977), p. 66.

[49]Frederick Engels, *The Origin of the Family, Private Property and the State in the Light of the Researches of Lewis H. Morgan*, ed. Eleanor Burke Leacock (New York, 1972), p. 129.

design. In fact, he designated patriarchy as unnatural with respect to human love and sexuality.

In some ways Beard's view of marriage is closer to that of the structural anthropologists whose influence on historical writing crystallized after *Woman as Force in History*. Claude Lévi-Strauss, for example, depicts marriage as a fixed and timeless pattern of exchanges, occurring in complex as well as simple cultures. Even while recognizing the apparent emancipation of modern couples from their families, he finds the tribal and reciprocal aspects of marriage immutable, appearing at all times in all cultures. The exchange, he notes, may be explicit or implicit, with women perpetually being among the things of value that are exchanged. We continue to ask for the hand of a bride, give her away in marriage, and celebrate the alliance with gift giving.[50] While Beard emphatically did not share the view that women were ever handed around like chattel except in situations where men were also, she shared Lévi-Strauss's idea of a core immutability in the institution of marriage.

The theories of the Marxists and the structuralists are a rich source for historical speculation, but anyone interested in studying the historical connections between married women's status at common law and the larger role of women in the society has to begin with Beard. She set the terms; she raised doubts about the effectiveness of the statutes; she emphasized the gap between common law theory and common practice; she created the idea of a mythology originating in Blackstone's *Commentaries;* and she took the early feminists to task for perpetuating the idea of women's historical impotence.

In addition to the work of Beard, the other major influence that informs this work is the ideological ferment of contemporary feminism. The similarities between the demands of current feminists and those of their nineteenth-century counterparts to improve the legal status of married women are too striking to be ignored. The contemporary use of the title Ms. and the increase in the numbers of women who retain their maiden names after marriage in symbolic refusal to be labeled as married and subsumed under a husband's identity echo with the strategies

[50]Claude Lévi-Strauss, *The Elementary Structures of Kinship,* rev. ed. (Boston, 1969), pp. 65, 478–79.

employed by Lucy Stone more than a century earlier. The controversy over sex as a legal classification which has been generated by the drive for the Equal Rights Amendment and the debate over the wife's value as a homemaker in relation to her social security benefits revitalize nineteenth-century issues. The reluctance of the law to interfere in cases of wife beating despite a stance as protector of the wife is a pattern etched deep in the recesses of the common law. These distinctly feminist concerns, raised now in a context radically different from that of the nineteenth century, attest to the need to evaluate the origins and consequences of nineteenth-century legal reform from a feminist perspective.

Difficulty arises in delineating the application of feminist ideology to history. Despite an urgent quest for a conceptual framework in women's history, such a framework does not exist.[51] Yet unquestionably a feminist perspective guides the selection of historical subjects and the formation of historical questions, as it obviously has done here. In the absence of anything more precise, I have relied on Hilda Smith's definition of a feminist historical perspective: a way of seeing women as a distinct sociological group "for which there are established patterns of behavior, special legislative restrictions, and customarily defined roles."[52] This perspective does not diminish the significance of class; rather it underscores the significance of sex. Sex and marital status were the critical classifications in domestic relations law. To say that the law did not distinguish between the lady and the mill girl is not to assume that it impinged on their lives in the same way.[53]

In the long and piecemeal reform of the marital property system, class interests were pervasive. Marriage was, among other things, an arrangement of property. It is not surprising that the earliest exceptions to the common law were carved out for and by families with enormous financial resources. Nor is it

[51]See Barbara Sicherman, "American History," *Signs* 1 (1975):461–85, and Joan Kelly-Gadol, "The Social Relations of the Sexes: Methodological Implications of Women's History," *Signs* 1 (1976):809–23.

[52]Hilda Smith, "Feminism and the Methodology of Women's History," in *Liberating Women's History,* ed. Carroll, p. 370.

[53]For the way domestic relations laws touched the poor in comparison with the rest of the population, see Bloomfield, *American Lawyers,* pp. 122–35.

surprising that the codification of those exceptions, the nineteenth-century married women's acts, represented the demands of an acquisitive and propertied middle class. With some justification historians have designated married women's property rights as the realization of an exclusively middle-class goal.

But although the mainstream of the nineteenth-century drive for marital property reform reflected the economic goals of an emergent bourgeoisie, both female and male, the ramifications of that drive were far broader. The inclusion of women's wages in the statutes was one example of its breadth. The drive for marital property reform also encompassed a constellation of ideas that extended beyond class interests to gender interests. Marriage, after all, was also a social arrangement between the sexes in which the distribution of property was inextricably connected to the allocation of power. Consequently, to challenge the common law marital prototype was to challenge the patriarchal organization of the family. If one defines patriarchy in its purest form as the reduction of women to the status of property owned and controlled by men, then one can find many of its components in Anglo-American domestic relations law.[54] In the context of the nineteenth century, the right of wives to own property entailed their right not to be property.

The nineteenth-century challenge to the marital prototype in the common law was historically significant in itself, but the legislation it produced did not create a new prototype; it modified the old one. At the end of the nineteenth century, New York wives were not fully free from the confines of coverture. If there is a single theme that emerges loud and clear in the ensuing chapters, it is the theme of legal continuity played against a counterpoint of social and economic upheaval. Because the married women's property acts drew on older judicial precedents, they could not create substantial changes. Furthermore, any genuinely radical potential they might have held was eroded in the appellate courts. In short, the legal fiction of marital unity survived the legislative assaults of the nineteenth century. The issue of why statutes were passed and what changes they actually

[54]On the desire of men to own women, see Keith Thomas, "The Double Standard," *Journal of the History of Ideas* 20 (1959):195–216.

effected provides the counterpoint to the main theme. Three concerns were distinct in the public discourse over the statutes: the need for structural reform of the law, the need to adapt law to economic change, and the need to come to terms with what contemporaries called "the woman question."

In New York the thrust for codification and the larger movement to reform the legal system were closely related to the statutes. The persistent attack on the elitism, high fees, and inefficiency of the state's equity courts and the trend toward more statute law and less judge-made law took place simultaneously with the drive for a married women's statute. The egalitarian rhetoric of Jacksonian democracy infused the whole movement for legal reform. Judges were to be elected by the people, not appointed. Laws were to be made by legislators, the people's representatives. Marital property laws were to be uniform, and diverse equitable exceptions were to be codified.

The need to adapt law to structural changes in the economy, especially in such a commercially sophisticated jurisdiction as New York, was another pressing concern. The world of husbands and wives in antebellum New York was far removed from the agricultural world of baron and feme in medieval England. New Yorkers lived amidst an intricate network of speculation, credit, insurance, stocks, and wages which was subject to cycles of boom and bust. Even those in the most rural segments of the state were affected by its tremors. New institutions engendered new legal questions. Could a married woman own a savings account in her own name? Could she become the beneficiary of her husband's life insurance?

The increasing scope and complexity of the marketplace created an intricate pyramid of credit that still depended on mutual trust and personal associations at the lowest levels, but which was becoming depersonalized and bureaucratic.[55] Credit was more and more a matter of assets and liabilities. To what extent and in what particular circumstances was the property of a wife subject to her husband's debts? The law of baron and feme would not suffice, not would its equitable exceptions. Al-

[55]On changes in the debtor-creditor relationship, see Peter J. Coleman, *Debtors and Creditors in America: Insolvency, Imprisonment for Debt, and Bankruptcy, 1607–1900* (Madison, Wis., 1974), pp. 283–85.

though the English chancery court had gradually refashioned the law by carving out exceptions in the form of the married woman's equitable estate, actually refashioning the relationship of elite married women with their husbands and with third parties, it seemed imperative to some nineteenth-century legislators to clarify the relationship of all married women with their husbands and third parties.

Coming to terms with the woman question, the question of what was the appropriate role for women in the family and in the larger polity, was not the primary motivation behind the earliest legislation. Yet it was not possible to consider a married women's statute without confronting the woman question. By the last quarter of the eighteenth century, the traditional hierarchical model of marriage, with its emphasis on the husband's dominance and the wife's subordination, was giving way to an ideal of greater complementarity in the roles of husbands and wives. Women, as wives and mothers, had an important role to play in supporting their husbands' efforts and in rearing children to become proper citizens. As industrial capitalism pushed production out of the home in the first half of the nineteenth century, emphasis on the wife's special role was intensified, sentimentalized, and transformed into the cult of domesticity. Women, as wives and mothers, occupied a lofty sphere that was complementary to but clearly separate from the world of men.[56]

The cult of domesticity, as a popular ideal, blurred the degree to which many women, at some point in their lives, left home to enter the workplace, and it ignored the amount of production that continued to take place in the home. Nevertheless, it reflected a significant shift in the economic status of women; by the outbreak of the Civil War, women were more at the margins of production than they had been at any other time in American history. At the same time, their authority within the family expanded. If antebellum women played an important role in the family, how could the law continue to relegate them to the status of children or servants? Supporters of a married women's stat-

[56]On the rise of a more complementary and less hierarchical model of marriage in the late eighteenth century, see Nancy Cott, "Divorce and the Changing Status of Women in Eighteenth-Century Massachusetts," in *The American Family in Social-Historical Perspective*, ed. Michael Gordon, 2d ed. (New York, 1978), pp. 115–31.

ute consistently asked this question to expose the gap between the enlarged position of women within the family and their subordinate legal status.[57]

It was not possible, however, to limit debate to the family; the property rights of married women were a political issue as well. The antebellum drive for married women's property rights constituted a bridge between spheres, a link between the private space of home and family and the public space of politics and the marketplace. Women's participation in the drive formed a critical intermediary stage between the Republican Motherhood that women fashioned for themselves after the Revolution and the independent suffragism they forged after the Civil War.[58] The very absence of property rights and the very persistence of other gender-based inequities in marriage laws during the first third of the nineteenth century demonstrated the determination of the state, the all-male state, to preserve the legal aspects of patriarchy in its most fundamental unit of social organization—the family. This notion emerged at the radical edge of antebellum feminist thought in conjunction with the campaign for statutory reforms. Thus as it became controversial, the common law collectivized women and encouraged them to connect their dependency in the private sphere to their powerlessness in the political arena.

[57]For an overview of the transition from the late eighteenth-century ideal of womanhood to the antebellum cult of domesticity, see Mary Ryan, *Womanhood in America: From Colonial Times to the Present,* 2d ed. (New York, 1979), pp. 61–117.

[58]On Republican Motherhood, see Kerber, *Women of the Republic;* on independent suffragism, see Ellen Carol DuBois, *Feminism and Suffrage: The Emergence of an Independent Women's Movement in America, 1848–1869* (Ithaca, N.Y., 1978).

CHAPTER 2

Baron and Feme: The Theory

Some particularly long-lived structures become the stable elements of generation after generation; they resist the course of history and therefore determine its flow.

—Ferdinand Braudel

The legislative impulse to alter the legal status of married women in New York began in the 1830s, took tangible statutory form in the 1840s, and culminated in the legislation of 1860. Since it simultaneously challenged and was shaped by national jurisprudence, it has to be viewed within the context of that jurisprudence. The world of antebellum legal thought illumines the tensions and continuities in Anglo-American domestic relations law.

In the eyes of the law the husband and wife were one person—the husband. In many situations, of course, they were two persons; nobody recognized this fact more fully or delineated it with greater precision than American jurists. Still, the old presumption of marital unity dominated American legal writing throughout the first half of the nineteenth century. Marital unity, after all, was only a legal fiction, a metaphor that had certain legal results. American treatise writers riddled it with exceptions, twisted it into new forms, and explained it away with a variety of rationales. Innumerable situations arose in which they could attest to the legal power and contractual capacity of American wives. Yet they maintained the fiction. It was an integral part of every common lawyer's education, and like all legal fictions, it had an autonomy of its own.

The significant historical issue is the impact of this fiction that was at the center of public controversy over change. The legal fiction of marital unity, as Mary Beard pointed out, was not descriptive. It reduced a complex legal relationship to a crude metaphor. It was perhaps prescriptive in that it perpetuated an authoritative model for husbands and wives and a popular metaphor for marriage. One can imagine it exerted some influence over nonlawyers unfamiliar with its exceptions and likely to meet it in its simplest form. Unquestionably, however, it was restrictive. It imposed on the law a way of thinking about wives that was difficult to eradicate. It classified married women so comprehensively that exceptions were just that. No single precedent or statute could compete with the hegemony of the ancient legal fiction.

The fiction permeated the literature of the law in the first half of the nineteenth century. Tapping Reeve, James Kent, Joseph Story, and Joel Prentice Bishop, the first jurists to deal with American domestic relations law in treatises and commentaries, transmuted the fiction to fit modern requirements and endowed it with the appropriate exceptions, but they maintained its validity and supported its desirability. No nineteenth-century jurist, however, presented it with greater cogency or authority than Sir William Blackstone, and no nineteenth-century jurist surpassed him in sustained popularity. A comparison of his treatment of marriage with that of American jurists suggests some fundamental similarities.

We begin with Blackstone not because he is the preeminent expert on the common law, but because he was its most popular theoretician. Colonials welcomed Blackstone's work with its first appearance in the New World. On the brink of separation, they eagerly bought up all available English editions, although Blackstone vehemently opposed American revolutionary ambitions. In response to the popularity of the *Commentaries,* Robert Bell, a Philadelphian, published the first American edition of 1,000 copies in 1771 and 1772, and followed it with an equally successful edition in 1773. From the early national period through the Civil War, when most lawyers received their professional training under an apprenticeship system, the *Commentaries* formed some part of their legal education. For the poorly trained, Blackstone provided more than a theoretical approach to the law; he was all they knew.[1]

[1]Gareth Jones, ed., *The Sovereignty of the Law: Selections from Blackstone's Commentaries on the Laws of England* (Cambridge, Mass., 1941), p. xlvii; Daniel Boorstin, *The Mysterious Science of the Law: An Essay on Blackstone's Commentaries* (Cambridge, Mass., 1941), p. 1.

Blackstone's influence on American legal education ranged from the "Blackstone lawyer" of Mary Beard's description to the giants of American jurisprudence. John Marshall's father was a subscriber to the first American edition, and it is likely that the son was initiated to Blackstone under his father's tutelage at the age of seventeen or eighteen. One of the myths surrounding the chief justice has him relying on a combination of Blackstone and mother wit in Supreme Court decisions, and then calling on Joseph Story to furnish more specific authorities.[2] Both James Kent and Joseph Story, two eminent figures in the development of American legal education, gave Blackstone their wholehearted approval. Kent, in fact, decided to become a lawyer at the age of fifteen when he first read Blackstone's *Commentaries,* and as a young law student he continued to read portions of the work over and over.[3]

As law schools came into being, the *Commentaries* informed the very structure of the curriculum, and often served as one of the assigned texts. Tapping Reeve, founder of the first law school in America, at Litchfield, Connecticut, in 1784, taught on a lecture plan modeled after the *Commentaries.* Understandably, a judiciary raised on Blackstone cited Blackstone. William G. Hammond, one of Blackstone's nineteenth-century editors, estimated that between 1787 and 1890, American judges cited Blackstone more than any other single authority.[4]

Although Blackstone was an essential text for the more erudite members of the bar as well as for those whose legal education began and ended with a brief apprenticeship, his acceptance was far from total in either England or America. Criticism emanated as much from a deep hostility to the common law tradition

[2]Stanley G. Kutler, ed., *John Marshall* (Englewood Cliffs, N.J., 1972), pp. 1–2; Julius Goebel, Jr., "The Common Law and the Constitution," in *Chief Justice John Marshall: A Reappraisal,* ed. W. Melville Jones (Ithaca, N.Y., 1970), pp. 101–2. Goebel insists that Marshall was thoroughly at home in the literature of the law.

[3]The following statement is recorded in Kent's memoranda: "When the college [Yale] was broken up and dispersed in July, 1779, by the British, I retired to a country village, and finding Blackstone's *Commentaries,* I read the four volumes. Parts of the work struck my taste, and the work inspired me at the age of 15, with awe, and I fondly determined to be a lawyer." See William Kent, *Memoirs of Chancellor Kent* (n.p., 1898), pp. 17–18.

[4]Friedman, *History of American Law,* p. 279; Sir William Blackstone, *Commentaries on the Laws of England,* ed. W. G. Hammond, 4 vols. (San Francisco, 1898), 1:ix.

with which Blackstone was equated as it did from a distrust of his explication of that tradition. In England the foremost among his opponents was Jeremy Bentham. Bentham, the founding father of the codification movement, attacked the common law as judge-made law that was intellectually irrational and politically dangerous.[5] In America the Revolution marred the unqualified acceptance of Blackstone. Men who would not submit to a king did not have to submit to his laws.

Attacks on the feudalism of the common law led to attacks on the legal fiction of marital unity. As Gordon Wood contends, by the 1780s Americans held a fairly modern conception of statutory law which did not necessarily require precedents to be old or English. Buoyed by the achievement of a written constitution, American codifiers attacked the feudal vestiges of the common law. From the Revolution until after the Civil War, they held out the promise of a precise and comprehensive body of legislation calculated to reduce what they believed was judges' power to make law by placing that power in the hands of the people's representatives—their legislators. In the words of one popular organ of Jacksonian democracy, the common law was "an absurd jumble of arbitrary rules." It was "at best, a rude, uncertain, inconsistent, and dangerous jumble of precedents."[6] Bentham's American proponents included the Irish-born William Sampson, the more moderate Edward Livingston, and in later years David Dudley Field. Some American codifiers led the battle for married women's property statutes.

Generally, however, the *Commentaries* enjoyed popularity in and out of the legal profession. Blackstone reached American nonlawyers in the same way he had intended to reach the eighteenth-century English gentry. By designing his work for the intelligent amateur, he created a legal manual for country squires and urban entrepreneurs, and a legal history for intellectuals. The *Commentaries* complemented a native American distrust of professionalism with the promise of unlocking the secrets of an arcane discipline. Suspicion of lawyers was a persistent theme in American culture. One antebellum writer attacked

[5]Rabkin, "Origins of Law Reform," pp. 695–97.

[6]Gordon S. Wood, *The Creation of the American Republic, 1776–1787* (Chapel Hill, N.C., 1969), pp. 299, 302; "Edward Livingston and His Code," *USMDR* 9 (July 1841):11, and 9 (September 1841):213.

the plans of some fledgling bar associations to fix fees with the claim that it would result in giving a man the services of "a drudge" at the price of "a man of genius and learning."[7] While an engaging style ensured the *Commentaries* a place in the libraries of the American gentry, innumerable abridgments were available to do-it-yourselfers without the time, inclination, or ability to explore the byways of English law.[8]

One source of Blackstone's popularity was his sheer ability as a writer. In his capable hands the common law of England came alive. In contrast to Joseph Story, for example, who drew on his immense erudition to qualify every statement in the minutest detail, leaving the reader with a welter of conflicting facts and theories, Blackstone was the soul of brevity, clarity, and simplicity. As Daniel Boorstin demonstrates, Blackstone wrote from within an ordered eighteenth-century thought system that gave his work its coherent structure and its quasi-scientific spirit.[9] Furthermore, his a priori assertions about the nature of things, including the nature of marriage and property, suited the individualistic, competitive thrust of the American economy.

Nevertheless, Blackstone contained his subject too neatly. His spare tenets and crisp maxims had profound effects on the popular American perception of marital property law. Telescoping centuries of custom, statute, and precedent, he imposed clarity upon chaos and created a disarmingly simple image of the law of husband and wife. As Mary Beard asserted, he failed to give a full picture of the inroads that equity made on the theory of conjugal unity.[10] His compression of time and simplification

[7]"Bar Associations," *New Yorker* 5 (September 1838):399, quoted from *Southern Literary Messenger* (n.d.). The *New Yorker*, edited by Horace Greeley and Park Benjamin, became the *Weekly Tribune*. For an attack on the adversary system and the profession in general, see "The Legerdemain of Lawcraft," *USMDR* 23 (August 1848):134–38.

[8]For a partial list of the innumerable editions, abridgments, and abridgments of abridgments of Blackstone's *Commentaries*, consult Catherine Spicer Eller, *The William Blackstone Collection in the Yale Law Library: A Bibliographic Catalogue* (New Haven, 1938). The *Commentaries* were first published in 1765–69. Variations on the *Commentaries* included *A Comic Blackstone* and one for young people in the form of letters written by a father to his daughter.

[9]Boorstin, *Mysterious Science of the Law*. Boorstin makes this point throughout, but as his title indicates, he is convinced that Blackstone was as mystical as he was rational, and that his world was as full of faith as of reason.

[10]Beard, *Woman as Force in History*, pp. 144–45. Blackstone, however, *does* deal with equity in a limited way.

of complexity, the very qualities that contributed to his readability, also contributed to a picture of the law of husband and wife as a timeless, seamless web.

In tracing the law of husband and wife, Blackstone manipulated logic and natural law to demonstrate the truth of what he already believed. Consciously selecting the term "husband and wife" over "baron and feme" from "the elder law books," Blackstone upheld the propriety of selected baron-feme principles with demonstrations of their universality and their correspondence to the laws of nature. His natural law emphasis served to enhance the static quality of his representation. If the best human laws conformed to the law of nature, which he imagined to exist in an original form of pure and rational simplicity, he had only to declare what the law of nature was, and then demonstrate the correspondences between the common law and natural law.[11]

Insofar as Blackstone's underlying goal was to preserve the legal and social institutions of England in his own time, he pressed natural law into a highly conservative mold. Like the medieval canonists before him, he created a legal model of the family. It was around this model, which embodied a curious blend of feudal law and eighteenth-century rationalism, that nineteenth-century debate revolved, and it was this model that shaped and in fact warped the public perception of the common law. Most important, more than any other jurist Blackstone was responsible for separating the right to property, which republicans equated with individual liberty, from the legal status of married women.

Blackstone's general classifications are vivid indications of the legal status of married women. Although those sections of the *Commentaries* that treat life, liberty, and property contain the building blocks for a vigorous republican ideology, other sections describe relationships of ineluctable dominance and dependence. The law of husband and wife appears in a subsystem of private, relative rights which includes other relationships of social superiors and inferiors, such as parent-child, master-

[11]Boorstin, *Mysterious Science of the Law,* p. 70. For the relationship between competitive self-assertion and natural law, see Roscoe Pound, *An Introduction to the Philosophy of Law* (New Haven, 1922), pp. 15–16.

servant, and guardian-ward. The rights and duties of the husband and wife are derived from a set of feudal conditions and assumptions that contribute to the logic of the organization. Married women are enclosed within the hierarchy of the family, where their status is quasi-servile in relation to their lords. Similarly those "in lifetime servitude," Blackstone's euphemism for chattel slavery, are included in the master-servant category.[12] This organization discourages comparisons of the legal rights of various subordinates with the basic rights of English men. While slavery was enough of an issue in Blackstone's day to compel him to try to deal with the ideological incongruities between slavery and the common law, women's rights were not. Blackstone did not have to confront the question of whether or not the rights of English men were the rights of English women as well. It was not an issue.

Nevertheless, aside from a preference for males in descent, there is little in Blackstone's treatment of private law that explicitly places single women in an inferior legal position. A man and a woman approach marriage as theoretical equals. They are potential parties to a civil contract. Like any other contracting parties, they must be willing and able, and they must have contracted in fact in order for the marriage to be valid.[13] The concept of marriage as an ordinary contract between equals, however, has radical implications. If marriage is only a simple contract, then the contracting parties may set the terms to suit their individual wants and desires or terminate their agreement by mutual consent.

Blackstone quickly dispels the notion that marriage is a contract like any other; marriage once contracted is a status. As part of their new legal situation, the married pair have become one person, with the wife's legal identity incorporated within her husband's:

> The very being or legal existence of the woman is suspended during the marriage, or at least is incorporated and consolidated into that of the husband; under whose wing, protection

[12]Sir William Blackstone, *Commentaries on the Laws of England in Four Books,* ed. Thomas Cooley, 2 vols., 4th ed. (Chicago, 1899), 1:359–62. All citations refer to this edition unless otherwise noted.

[13]Ibid., 1:374–75.

> and cover, she performs everything; and is therefore called in our law-french a *feme covert, faemina viro co-operta;* and it is said to be *covert-baron,* or under the protection and influence of her husband, her *baron,* or lord; and her condition during her marriage is called her *coverture.*[14]

Here is the controversial doctrine of coverture in the form most frequently quoted in nineteenth-century America. As Blackstone points out, "Upon this principle of union of person in husband and wife, depend almost all the legal rights, duties, and disabilities that either of them acquire by the marriage."[15] The Anglo-Norman language eloquently points up the change created by marriage. The two former equals have become baron and feme, or the protector and the protected.

Blackstone's treatment of this change is purely expository at this point; his tone is matter-of-fact. He eschews elaborate moral or legal justifications for coverture, and he circumvents the religious foundation of the doctrine. Coverture, he insists, is the direct result of the legal fiction of marital unity, a fiction that he employs as a shorthand device to enable his readers to understand the consequences of marriage. It is his job to explain what those consequences are, not why they exist.

All legal fictions, however, have underlying premises and motives.[16] Blackstone places his rationale for coverture in his discussion of descent and succession. According to Blackstone, marriage has one critical socioeconomic function: the creation of lawful heirs.[17] This statement illuminates his entire discussion of family law. With this single premise he erects clear standards for the evaluation of family law which are distinctly earthbound and material rather than religious or metaphysical. Of course in

[14]Ibid., 1:387. Italics are Blackstone's. Blackstone stressed that marriage was nothing more than a civil contract so that he could refute the idea that it was in any way sacred. According to David E. Engdahl, Blackstone wished to place marriage squarely within the province of secular law; differences between marriage and other contracts were emphasized in the nineteenth century, when marriage increasingly was called a status. See "Proposal for a Benign Revolution in Marriage Law and Marriage Conflicts Law," *Iowa Law Review* 55 (1960):57.

[15]Blackstone, *Commentaries,* 1:387.

[16]See Lon Fuller, *Legal Fictions* (Stanford, Calif., 1967), pp. 51–58, for a perceptive analysis of legal fictions. Fuller maintains that a legal fiction is a way of reconciling a specific legal result with a particular premise or postulate.

[17]Blackstone, *Commentaries,* 1:358, 402.

Blackstone's larger intellectual orbit such a purpose corresponds with the eternal laws of nature. In more concrete terms, however, human law is good to the extent that it serves this purpose. Blackstone's consideration of marriage is essentially teleological; his standard for what is good is efficiency, not morality.[18] The laws of marriage are good to the extent that they support the production of lawful heirs, and Blackstone proclaims that no other system of law serves this purpose so efficiently as the common law of England.

In Roman law, he points out, a man may remain a bastard until the age of forty, and then be legitimized, thereby frustrating the main inducement of marriage—to have legitimate children. Roman law in this instance is aberrant, since it deviates from the main purpose of marriage. English law concerning bastards is infinitely more efficient. If a child is begotten of single parents, there is time to marry, but a bastard is considered fatherless so far as inheritance is concerned. He loses basic rights "for he can *inherit* nothing, being looked upon as the son of nobody, and is sometimes called *filius nullius,* sometimes *filius populi.*" He may gain a surname by reputation, but he has none by inheritance.[19]

Blackstone sees marriage as an arrangement for the propertied and their issue, who are assets in this context. They are the conduits for the perpetuation of family wealth and identity. Nevertheless, those without property, he insists, have to marry also so that their children will not become burdens on society. Because the children of the poor are potential liabilities, the main end of marriage in "the lower ranks" is to "ascertain and fix upon some certain person" the care, protection, maintenance, and education of children.[20] In both cases Blackstone's concern is with property. In his view, property is the juncture at which the law significantly impinges on marriage. Unlike nineteenth-century American jurists who would endow marriage with sweeping moral attributes, Blackstone shuns broader

[18]Christine Pierce treats the effects of natural law and teleology on women's status. See "Natural Law Language and Women," in *Women in Sexist Society: Studies in Power and Powerlessness,* ed. Vivian Gornick and Barbara K. Moran (New York, 1972), pp. 242–58.

[19]Blackstone, *Commentaries,* 1:401, 405.

[20]Ibid., pp. 394–95.

interpretations. He concentrates on assets, liabilities, and legitimate descent.

Having established the doctrine of marital unity, Blackstone delineates its results. Working in a closed logical system with martial unity as a starting point, he sketches the substantive disabilities that coverture imposes on the wife. Such personal property as the household furniture, money, and jewels that the wife brings to marriage belongs to the husband absolutely. Choses in action—rights not now in possession but potentially recoverable in a lawsuit—can be reduced to the husband's possession, thus going the way of personal property. Management of the wife's realty goes to the husband. Consequently there is little point to the wife's making a will, although technically she can do so with her husband's permission.[21]

Perhaps no area of the *Commentaries* was later construed as more demeaning to women than the section dealing with married women's loss of testamentary power. Blackstone avers that a married woman's will at common law is an exercise in futility. Persons prohibited from devising include, in Blackstone's words, those "grown childish by reason of old age or distemper, such as have their senses besotted with drunkenness," and those "who have always wanted the common inlets of understanding."[22]

Coverture also carries a web of procedural disabilities. If the wife is injured in her person or property, she can bring an action for redress only with her husband's permission and in his name as well as her own. She cannot be sued in a separate action unless her husband is named as a defendant. Spouses cannot contract with each other, because to do so would constitute a recognition of the wife's separate legal existence. In a trial a husband and wife cannot give evidence for or against each other.[23]

Although the wife's procedural disabilities, if rigidly defined, would seem to relegate her to total passivity in commerce, Blackstone insists this is not the case. Building on the doctrine of agency, he demonstrates that the wife's regular household duties ensure her right to contract on behalf of the family. The husband at common law is bound to provide his wife with "neces-

[21]Ibid., p. 825.
[22]Ibid., pp. 824–26.
[23]Ibid., pp. 389–91.

saries," so that when she contracts debts for necessaries with third parties, he is obliged to pay them. The husband is even responsible for his wife's debts incurred before marriage, "for he has adopted her and her circumstances together." On the other hand, he is not liable after the marriage for anything beyond necessities. Yet Blackstone claims that coverture allows the wife considerable leeway in her contracts with third parties. She can participate actively on her husband's behalf in almost all areas of commerce, and even act in some cases as his attorney, because in this capacity she acts in "representation of her lord."[24]

Blackstone emphasizes that as part of the equipoise of the common law, the person with enormous responsibilities is the person with enormous powers. Thus the husband, who is responsible for his wife's debts before marriage and for her maintenance during marriage, and for whom the wife acts as an agent, is responsible in some degree for his wife's behavior. Just as he has a right to correct apprentices or children for whom he is bound to answer, so must he have similar rights in regard to his wife. For this reason "the old law" gave husbands the power to restrain wives by domestic chastisement. Blackstone asserts that wife beating still exists only in "the lower ranks," where husbands lay claim to "their ancient privilege."[25]

The husband has a right to his wife's services and to all she may acquire by her personal activity. This is a proprietary right, and if she is injured, he may recover for loss of consortium. This recourse, however, is available only if the wrong is done to the wife. In keeping with its feudal roots, the common law takes notice of the injury to the superior of the two parties. "[T]he inferior hath no kind of property in the company, care or assistance of the superior as the superior is held to have in those of the inferior and therefore the inferior can suffer no loss or injury."[26]

Although the disabilities of coverture finally end when the marriage ends, the internal logic of coverture persists beyond marriage to influence the disposition of marital property. Curtesy, the husband's interest in his wife's realty, is considerably

[24]Ibid., pp. 388–89.
[25]Ibid., p. 392.
[26]Cited in Kanowitz, *Women and the Law,* pp. 82–83.

greater than dower, the wife's corresponding interest in her husband's realty. On the death of the wife, the husband is limited to her realty because he has been entitled to all of her personalty during marriage. If the wife has lands and has at least one surviving child, the husband holds her lands as a tenant by the curtesy of England. Blackstone underscores the feudal origins of curtesy, which emanates from the husband's right to do homage to the lord for his wife's lands. As the natural guardian of his children, the husband is entitled to the profits of the lands in order to maintain the children under his guardianship. At his death, if no children survive him, the lands revert to the wife's family, one of the few instances in which the common law recognizes the significance of the wife's kin.[27]

If the wife survives the husband, as a tenant in dower she is entitled to the use of one-third of the lands and tenements he possessed during marriage. A husband may exceed the provisions of dower by substituting a settlement in lieu of dower in his will, but he may not exclude his wife from her dower right.[28] She has the right to elect dower over the terms of his will. Dower is the minimum the common law guarantees to widows. Paraphernalia is an interesting addition to what the wife may retain; it includes those special articles of clothing and ornaments suitable to her station in life.[29]

In sum, Blackstone has drawn a marital prototype. The husband adopts his wife together with her assets and liabilities. Taking responsibility for her maintenance and protection, he enjoys her property and the products of her labor. The wife assumes her husband's name and by extension his rank in the social order. Giving up her own surname and coming under his wing or protective cover, she acquires a cloak of legal invisibility. Her legal personality is submerged in her husband's. With their identities fused and their assets combined, the husband and wife are in an incomparable position to produce legitimate heirs, thereby

[27]Blackstone, *Commentaries,* 1:531, 774–75.

[28]One exception that Blackstone notes is a jointure, an estate settled on a wife before marriage in lieu of dower. He points out that "in estates of considerable consequence tenancy in dower happens very seldom, for the claim of a wife to her dower at the common law . . . became a great clog to alienations, and was therefore inconvenient to families" (ibid., pp. 540–41).

[29]Ibid., pp. 775–76.

Table 1. Common law rights and duties of wife and husband during coverture

Wife	Husband
Entitled to support.	May sue on behalf of his wife without her consent.
Cannot contract except for necessaries and as her husband's agent.	Owns wife's personalty outright.
Cannot sue or be sued in her own name.	Can reduce wife's choses in action to his possession.
Cannot make a will except with her husband's consent.	Controls management of wife's realty.
Cannot alienate her realty except with her husband's consent.	May charge wife's realty, but may not devise it.
	Responsible for wife's necessaries.
	Responsible for maintenance of children.
	Responsible for wife's debts incurred before marriage.
	Cannot alienate wife's dower without her consent (cannot alienate his own realty without her consent).

fulfilling the true function of marriage. Tables 1 and 2 outline the basic rights and duties of this marital prototype.

Blackstone presented these common law principles of marriage in a well-organized, widely consulted, and comparatively modern work.[30] He justified their perpetuation as a compelling incentive for the production of lawful heirs; at the same time he endowed them with a larger metaphysical validity by implying that they corresponded with the higher laws of nature. Finally, employing circular logic, he validated one law in terms of another, turned subject into predicate, merged cause with effect, and discouraged logically inductive alternatives. His concise depiction of coverture belied the legal and social changes that were taking place in his own time. Equity, which he treated perfunctorily, was ameliorating the rigidity of the marriage contract he described. The patriarchal nuclear family he championed was giving way to a more modern companionate ideal. He en-

[30]Blackstone's organization followed his own 1754 outline for *Analysis of Law,* which was based, in turn, on Matthew Hale's *Analysis of the Civil Part of the Law.* The law focuses on rights, which it recognizes, and wrongs, which it prohibits. Rights may pertain to persons or to things; wrongs may be private or public. Blackstone devoted one volume to each of these four categories. Discussing the extent to which Blackstone copied Hale, Jeremy Bentham called the *Commentaries* "a paltry but effectual artifice" (Bentham, *A Comment on the Commentaries: A Criticism of William Blackstone,* ed. Charles Warren Everett [London, 1928]).

Table 2. Common law rights of dower (surviving wife) and curtesy (surviving husband)

Dower	Curtesy
Wife entitled to tenancy in one-third of husband's realty as long as she does not remarry.	Husband entitled to tenancy in all of wife's realty for as long as he lives.
Wife entitled to her paraphernalia.	At his death, wife's realty reverts to her family if there are no living children.
Wife may lose custody of children by husband's will.	Husband has custody of children.

dowed American culture with an outdated view of English domestic relations law. Still it was a highly influential view, and it reduced the wife to complete economic dependence and legal invisibility.

In nineteenth-century America lawyers quoted Blackstone as a matter of course. Yet his pronouncements on marriage did not pass from the *Commentaries* into American legal theory without engendering some controversy. Editors who updated Blackstone year after year with descriptions of statutes and precedents in various jurisdictions ultimately created a series of glosses through which one can trace the diverging path of American domestic relations law. English editors contributed to the revisions as well, so that by the late nineteenth century, an edition such as Thomas Cooley's, first published in 1883, contained a rich compilation of leading American and English glosses. From the 1830s on, moreover, legal journals, becoming increasingly specific and utilitarian, noted exceptions to Blackstone's broadly stated principles. American legal periodicals cited English and American equity decisions that controverted many common law principles, and devoted attention to the practical problems of married women's legal disabilities. The emphasis was usually on debtor-creditor relations, fraud, and the problem of third parties with respect to marital property.

Furthermore, specific statements by Blackstone consistently sparked editorial outrage. At the end of his discussion of married women's legal disabilities, for example, Blackstone asserted with equanimity that "even the disabilities which the wife lies under are for the most part intended for her protection and benefit. So great a favorite is the female sex of the laws of England."[31] Edward Christian, an editor of some late-eighteenth- and early-nineteenth-century English editions, took exception to this statement in a lengthy footnote, and his comments were picked up by most American editors. Christian urged the reader to compare this section of the *Commentaries* with other portions that outlined a savage common law bias against women. At one time in England, Christian pointed out, the killing of a feme by her baron was regarded as a simple murder, but the killing of a baron by his feme was regarded as regicide and was punishable by being drawn and burned alive.[32] To Americans such bleak precedents exemplified all that was dark and oppressive in their English legal heritage and dramatized the extent to which they considered themselves emancipated from it. To Blackstonian assertions that "the law regards the fair sex with peculiar favor," one lawyer quoted by the *New York Legal Observer* noted that "such politeness on the part of the law is like amiability from a hyena."[33]

Recoiling from Blackstone's blatantly patriarchal bias, American editors of the *Commentaries* sometimes expressed the need for change in marital property law while at the same time they exhibited ambivalence about how much change was either safe or desirable. In an 1847 edition of the *Commentaries* John F. Hargrave acknowledged that while the permanent interests of American society required strict enforcement of marital obligations, ideally such enforcement should occur in a legal system somehow "unshackled from the harsh unending rules of the common law." Change was necessary, but an inversion of gender roles was to be avoided at all costs. "Where will it all take us?"

[31]Blackstone, *Commentaries,* 1:392.

[32]Blackstone, *Commentaries on the Laws of England,* ed. Edward Christian, 4 vols., 15th ed. (London, 1809), 1:444–46. Christian asserted, "Nothing, I apprehend, would more conciliate the good will of the student in favour of the laws of England, than the persuasion that they had shewn partiality to the female sex. But I am not so much in love with my subject as to be inclined to leave it in possession of a glory which it may not justly deserve." Christian, moreover, extended his discussion to the political realm, claiming that with regard to the property of women, "there is taxation without representation." Christian's notes were published as a fifth volume to an 1801 Boston edition of the *Commentaries.* On Christian's editions, see Eller, *William Blackstone Collection,* p. 42.

[33]"Facetiousness of the Law: Husband and Wife," *New York Legal Observer* 3 (March 1845):155–56.

Hargrave asked. "To women on juries, in the militia, serving on posses?"[34] In addition to ambivalence in regard to change in marital laws, another tendency that sharply differentiated the pioneers in American legal education from Blackstone was their stress on practical problems. Blackstone was an exemplary source for the student mastering the first principles of the law, but he could not direct the young lawyer in the specifics of his daily problems.

A stress on practical problems and an ambivalence in regard to common law solutions characterized the first American treatise on marriage, *The Law of Baron and Femme* (1816) by Tapping Reeve. Reeve particularized common law generalities in his Litchfield law school lectures. On the other hand, as evidence of the influence of Anglo-Norman language on the common law, it is worth noting that Reeve employed the old terms "baron" and "feme" almost as though they gave his work legitimacy, but changed "feme" to the modern French "femme." He closely followed Blackstone's organization and included in his work the law of parent and child, guardian and ward, and master and servant, but he discarded the legal fiction of marital unity as a device to explain the wife's legal status.

Reeve's approach entailed the expansion and detailed explication of the principle of agency. Where Blackstone merely suggested that a wife might act as her husband's agent in court, Reeve proclaimed, "It is an indisputable rule, that the wife can act as an attorney to her husband." If a husband might be absent for a year or more, Reeve insisted, "there necessarily resides in the wife a more ordinary power" to make contracts. Emphasizing the need for cheap and simple procedures, he applauded the use of the joint deed in conveyances.[35]

Despite his practicality and his stated desire to write a textbook for future practitioners, Reeve divided his attention between law as it was and law as he believed it ought to be. This division created confusion, but it also highlighted Reeve's discomfort with certain aspects of the law of husband and wife. At given points he was forced to tell his students what the law was while

[34]Blackstone, *Commentaries on the Laws of England*, ed. John Hargrave, 4 vols. (New York, 1847), 1:452, n. 15.

[35]Tapping Reeve, *The Law of Baron and Femme,* 3d ed. (Albany, 1862), pp. 98, 156–60.

he criticized its logic. Nowhere was he more critical than with regard to the wife's loss of testamentary power. He did not see how it was possible for a single woman to make a will that was suddenly nullified by her marriage. "Has marriage," he asked, "caused her to lose her ability or her volition? . . . [S]he who was sufficiently discreet to devise when unmarried, is not by marriage rendered less discreet." Was it not enough, he protested, that marriage already gave so much to the husband at the expense of the wife? Why should she die intestate as well? Surely a mother as a testator should have the power to reward or punish children for their behavior. Economic sanctions grounded on moral considerations should belong to the mothers of the republic as well as to the fathers.[36]

One might speculate that Reeve's embarrassment over the husband's vast powers came in part from his own immersion in the ideology and rhetoric of the American Revolution, which depicted power as incessantly encroaching on legitimate boundaries. Reeve had been active in revolutionary politics, had served on a committee of correspondence appointed by the Connecticut Assembly in 1776 to arouse revolutionary sentiments, and had held a commission in the Continental Army.[37] Not only did the wife's servile status relative to her husband probably conflict with his Whiggish sensibilities, but also her childlike status with respect to her husband's discipline conflicted with contemporary celebrations of motherhood. Consumed by practical considerations that required a wife to act separately and buttressed by a long tradition of equity, Reeve flatly denied the legal fiction of marital unity.

Nevertheless, he managed to arrive at equally patriarchal results by inverting the fiction and by emphasizing the principle of male coercion. Where Blackstone said that the wife came under the husband's power and protection because when they were married they became one person in the eyes of the law, Reeve said they were two people in an irrevocable relationship in which the wife was always the weaker of the two. Reeve, in other words, made the results of coverture his premise.

Reeve saw coercion as a reality in relations between the sexes;

[36]Ibid., pp. 229–32.
[37]*DAB*, vol. 8, pt. 1, pp. 468–69.

it was psychological as well as physical, and it incapacitated the wife.[38] Where before marriage the wife was "sui juris," capable and competent to contract, "in the moments of her warm confidence in the honorable and generous intentions of her suitor," she may not have been able to guard her own rights.[39] For good or ill, the wife was in the husband's power. Marriage, therefore, was not a civil contract between equals, but a relationship between the stronger sex and the weaker sex which the common law in its wisdom recognized. The married woman's common law disabilities, then, were checks to protect her against her husband. A husband and wife could not contract with each other, not because they were one person, but because they were two persons, and the stronger one, the husband, might coerce the weaker one, the wife, into an agreement.

Reeve's coercion argument seemed to justify the giving of the management of the wife's realty and the ownership of her personalty to the husband since the wife was in his power anyway. Nevertheless, he did discuss equity and the widespread use of trusts and marriage settlements as a way of protecting the wife's property. He favored American recognition of liberal English equity precedents. Here also his deep belief in the husband's innate power was evident. There was little doubt in his mind that equity precedents resulted from the wife's need for protection from her husband, rather than from third parties. Reeve implied, moreover, that the husband's exclusive responsibility to support the marriage was a consequence of his naturally superior power; it was not a legal consequence of the marriage contract, as Blackstone asserted. Blackstone counterpoised the husband's heavy liabilities with his corresponding rights, creating a typical common law balance. Reeve insisted that fairness had nothing to do with the law. A wife could bring enormous assets to her marriage or nothing at all; in either case the husband was liable for her support.[40]

Whatever embarrassment Reeve exhibited over some facets of

[38]Because of his belief in the reality of coercion, Reeve found the wife's separate examination a dubious protection for the wife. If the husband were coercive and the wife weak, the law was an empty ritual. See Reeve, *Law of Baron and Femme,* p. 231.

[39]Ibid., p. 64.

[40]Ibid., p. 53.

the common law, he continued to support many of its basic principles. He exposed some of the incongruities of coverture, gave ample space to developments in equity, and updated much that was archaic in Blackstone. But he arrived at comparable results. His abandonment of the legal fiction of marital unity enabled him to emphasize the wife's capacity to contract, but his justification of the protective qualities of coverture led him to support most of the essentials in Blackstone's outline.

Reeve's work was less influential and enjoyed less sustained popularity than Blackstone's *Commentaries* or Kent's *Commentaries* (1826–30). If the antebellum lawyer relied on one legal work other than Blackstone's, it was Kent's. In fact, America produced a Blackstone of its own in the person of James Kent. Charles Sumner, for example, evaluated Kent's work as the essential manual for the American practitioner. Edward Everett found it to be the one source the English consulted for American law. It was equally influential in formal American legal training. The Harvard Law School catalogue of 1834 described two parallel courses, one to be completed in two years, the other of indeterminate length and with an extensive supplementary reading list. Among the works that were required reading for all students were Blackstone's and Kent's *Commentaries.* These two works presumably incorporated the vocabulary, methodology, and general knowledge every student had to master to pursue the profession.[41]

Like Reeve, Kent particularized the application of common law principles in modern commercial dilemmas with specific bits of advice to his reader. Not the least of the problems was a complex pyramid of credit of which wives were a part. While a woman was married and living with her husband, third persons had to be wary of making contracts with her, for "they give credit at their peril." If a wife were imprudent, the husband was not bound to pay for her imprudence. Kent was cautioning the potential creditor or his attorney to be aware of the problems inherent in the wife's contractual limitations. Fraud perpetrated by the couple was always a possibility. Acting as her husband's

[41]Charles Sumner to James Kent, April 5, 1836, in *Memoirs of Chancellor Kent,* p. 203; Edward Everett to James Kent, October 31, 1845, in ibid., pp. 204–5; Haar, ed., *Golden Age of American Law,* pp. 67–70.

agent, a wife could incur a debt for which her husband denied responsibility.[42]

Unlike Reeve, Kent created a general compilation of American law patterned after the broad range of Blackstone's *Commentaries.* Therefore his approach to the common law and his rationale for its validity and authority in America were significant. In contrast to the pure natural law premises on which Blackstone relied, Kent shifted his own emphasis to the evolutionary nature of the common law. This shift enabled him to celebrate its suitability to dynamic American needs. The renowned flexibility of the common law, Kent argued, would satisfy the free and commercial spirit of the United States.[43] American legal variations were merely a matter of simpler, cheaper, and more convenient substitutions; they remained within the canons of the older law. Thus Americans had dropped the complexities of the wife's conveyance of a deed by fine, substituting instead her signature accompanied by her separate examination. Her husband's signature was evidence that he was present to protect his wife from imposition. These procedural changes were modern versions of the basic common law principle of the wife's protection. Kent found the wife in this case doubly protected: first from her husband's coercion, and second by her husband from third parties.[44]

The tone of Kent's argument on behalf of coverture differed significantly from Blackstone's. Compared to Blackstone's straightforward, material defense of coverture, Kent's was convoluted and nonmaterial. Kent began, for example, to attribute intensely moral qualities to the role of child rearing. Influenced by the theological utilitarianism of William Paley's *Principles of Moral and Political Philosophy,* Kent invested his discussion of marriage with religious overtones and elevated marriage to heights far beyond Blackstone's simple contract. Marriage had acquired intangible, sacred characteristics; Kent's expectations of marriage as a social institution were idealized: "We may justly

[42]James Kent, *Commentaries on American Law,* ed. George F. Comstock, 4 vols., 11th ed. (Boston, 1867), 2:134.

[43]Perry Miller, *Life of the Mind,* pp. 126–27. On the ties between the bar and powerful entrepreneurial interests, see Horwitz, *Transformation of American Law,* pp. 257–59.

[44]Kent, *Commentaries on American Law,* 2:139–41.

place to the credit of the institution of marriage a great share of the blessings which flow from refinement of manners, the education of children, the sense of justice, and the cultivation of the liberal arts." For Kent, marriage was considerably more than a conduit for wealth and the production of legitimate heirs.[45]

Where Blackstone seldom was obliged to discuss women's abilities, Kent constructed lengthy testimonies to female talent and intelligence. He denied that women were in any way incapable, indiscreet, or inferior. The wife's disabilities at common law did not rise from her "want of discretion" but "because she is placed under the power and protection of her husband."[46] The woman lost her ability to make contracts and to sue and be sued because the unity of spouses was an integral part of the marriage contract. In America, according to Kent, the fiction of marital unity prevailed as a part of a historic legal heritage, and although it was not to be interpreted too literally, it continued to operate as a common law principle.

Kent was not an avowed enemy of community-property principles, but he was against superimposing them on American law. Comparisons of women under common law with those under the French civil law were common in Kent's time. Kent, a scholar fluent in French, drew on French jurisprudence when he was a New York Supreme Court judge riding circuit between 1799 and 1804. A Federalist among Republicans, who he claimed knew nothing of French law but "were very kindly disposed to every thing that was French," Kent made extensive use of French authorities to "enrich" American commercial law. In his *Commentaries* he noted almost wistfully that community-property systems managed to confer considerable "equality and dignity" on women. Yet he was opposed to codifiers' schemes to disrupt Anglo-American legal continuity with crude legislative tinkering.[47]

Furthermore, as Mary Beard asserted, Kent filled in the omissions in equity jurisprudence left by Blackstone, and showed

[45]Ibid., p. 139. Paley was a Yorkshire theologian whose *Principles* (1785) became a standard college text in America. Kent initiated his law lectures at Columbia with Paley's work. For Paley's influence on Kent, see Bloomfield, *American Lawyers,* pp. 105–6.

[46]Kent, *Commentaries on American Law,* 2:137–38.

[47]Kent, *Memoirs,* p. 117; *Commentaries on American Law,* 2:187.

how the economic restrictions resulting from coverture might be set aside by private contract. He quoted the estimate of "a learned lawyer" who claimed that "half of the property in England was vested in nominal owners, so extensive were trusts growing out of marriage settlements." Always cautious, Kent admonished his readers to be wary of the wording of such agreements, but he admitted that a carefully drafted instrument could give a married woman with a separate estate the complete powers of a single woman. Under the proper instrument, a wife might dispose of her estate without even the assent of her trustee.[48]

Kent's treatment of married women in equity, however, mirrored the sentimentality and paternalism that characterized his treatment of women at common law. Trusts and settlements were devices that protected the wife from "being overwhelmed by the misfortunes, or unkindness, or vices of her husband." Such trusts "usually proceed from the foresight of friends," or from "the warm and anxious affection of parents; and if fairly made, they ought to be supported according to the true intent and meaning of the instrument by which they are created."[49]

Nonetheless, these inroads on the theory of conjugal unity emphasized the protection of the wife's interests against the husband, and constituted an admission that their interests were not always harmonious. They also recognized that the husband as head of the household was not always able to carry out his heavy responsibilities. Yet the notion persists in Kent that these situations comprised notable exceptions or special problems, and that any deep incursions on the husband's power might threaten marriage as a social institution and ultimately the structure of the whole society. Kent strenuously defended marriage as a patriarchal institution that mandated the supremacy of the husband and the dependence of the wife. The husband was the guardian of the wife, "and bound to protect and maintain her." Consequently "the law has given him a reasonable control over her person, and he may even put gentle restraints upon her liberty." Kent was convinced that the "husband is the best judge of the wants of the family, and the means of supplying them;

[48]Kent, *Commentaries on American Law,* 2:157–58, 181.
[49]Ibid., pp. 157–58.

and if he shifts his domicile, the wife is bound to follow him wherever he chooses to go."[50]

Both Kent and Reeve recognized situations in which the wife had to act as a separate legal personality, and both discussed the degree to which equity ameliorated common law strictures on married women. The practical advantages to wives in equity will be discussed in Chapter 3, but its limitations as a counterforce to the theory of baron and feme are worthy of consideration here. Nobody outlined the theoretical limitations of equity more sharply or with greater erudition and authority than Joseph Story in his *Commentaries of Equity Jurisprudence* (1835). Like Kent, Story exerted his influence as a teacher and a judge. His series of pioneering works on American law helped to establish the dominance of the common law in the United States. A United States Supreme Court justice and the first Dane professor at Harvard Law School, Story was a major figure in this formative era of American law. In fact, by common consent, the two most significant figures in American jurisprudence in the first half of the nineteenth century were Joseph Story and James Kent.[51]

Like Kent, Story envisioned marital unity as a historical fiction, an elastic base from which new precedents might evolve, but which at the same time would prevent radical upheavals. In his *Commentaries on Equity Jurisprudence* Story depicted equity as a complementary or supportive court with its roots firmly fixed in the legal history of England. One could not consider equity without considering the common law; it was a component of an elaborate legal web not easily compartmentalized. Thus while Story noted that equity recognized trusts for married women, antenuptial agreements, and in some cases postnuptial agreements, he consistently balanced the principles of the common law against equity. Among the factors that inhibited equity from overturning common law principles were the type of device or instrument by which a married woman owned her separate estate, the danger of fraud against third parties, and most important, the husband's common law marital rights. Equity, for example, would not restrain a husband who had already re-

[50]Ibid., p. 180.

[51]Friedman, *History of American Law,* p. 288; Morgan Dowd, "The Influence of Story and Kent on the Development of the Common Law," *American Journal of Legal History* 17 (1973):221–22.

duced his wife's estate to possession, even if it were an equitable estate, because his action was within the just exercise of his common law marital rights.[52]

Story also affirmed the husband's traditional common law right to the custody of his children while he took note of the exceptions being carved out in the courts. His discussion of guardianship exemplified antebellum ambivalence in regard to the purely patriarchal model of marriage. Story stated, "As between husband and wife, the custody of the children generally belongs to the husband." A husband could even designate a guardian other than the mother in his will. There were some serious problems with this common law principle, however. On the one hand, the husband's right to his children was a logical result of the common law marital prototype. If his issue were extensions of his personality and conduits for his property, the wife functioned only as the bearer of his seed. On the other hand, the unique child-rearing abilities that antebellum culture attributed to women were in conflict with this older patriarchal concept. Story pointed out that equity would tend to confer a daughter of "very tender years" upon the mother.[53]

Story's discussion of the foundations of equity, moreover, highlighted the ways in which the principles of equity were as patriarchal as those of the common law. He emphasized that equity jurisdiction originated in the concept of the king of England as *parens patriae,* the father of the country. Persons under various disabilities could make special appeals or prayers to his sovereign powers of guardianship. Those who came under equity's jurisdiction, he pointed out, included infants, lunatics, and married women, the same group of legal incompetents prohibited at common law from making a will.[54]

In other words, equity did not alter common law classifications; rather it ministered to the difficulties created by those classifications. Consequently in his discussion of married women's

[52]Joseph Story, *Commentaries on Equity Jurisprudence,* 2 vols. (Boston, 1839), 2:662.

[53]Ibid., pp. 596–97; on custody, see Jamil S. Zainaldin, "The Emergence of a Modern American Family Law: Child Custody, Adoption, and the Courts, 1796–1851," *Northwestern University Law Review* 73 (1979):1038–89.

[54]Story, *Commentaries on Equity Jurisprudence,* 2:581–85; he cites Blackstone's *Commentaries,* 3:427.

property, Story was compelled to weigh equity against the common law, and the latter consistently outweighed the former. Equity precedents were islands in the sea of the common law. Accordingly Story conscientiously qualified Blackstone's bold pronouncement on marital unity to state that "in most cases" the wife's legal identity was merged with her husband's.[55]

To appreciate fully the pervasive influence of the principles of baron and feme, however, we have to go beyond Kent and Story. They represented a conservative legal elite; they reflected "the legal mind" to which Perry Miller referred in his essay on nineteenth-century American law.[56] They used their profound technical proficiency and their wide-ranging knowledge of alternate legal systems to champion the common law as the best system for orderly social progress in America. Their approach was erudite and their attention to detail was meticulous. One could read their works and at least get a sense of the flexibility that was possible in arrangements of marital property, but this was not always the case with student manuals and do-it-yourself legal guides. Writers of abridgments pressed Blackstone's already reductive description of the law of husband and wife into the simplest axioms and corollaries. It is reasonable to assume that these guides had a greater effect on the public in general than a four-volume work such as Kent's or Blackstone's *Commentaries,* or a complex explication of equity by Joseph Story. These attenuated works depicted the common law in its narrowest and most rigid form.

John Anthon's slender 1809 abridgment of Blackstone's *Commentaries* reiterated and reinforced Blackstone's comparison of married women with servants and children. Similarly, Asa Kinne reduced Kent's *Commentaries* to question-and-answer form in an 1844 abridgment: "What is the general rule as to the rights and liabilities of the husband?" he asked. "That he becomes upon the marriage entitled to all the goods and chattels of the wife," he responded, "and to the rent and profits of her land." Demeaning descriptions of the wife's loss of testamentary power and her inclusion in the list of other legal incompetents were repeated with deadly regularity. Anthon enumerated the members of this

[55]Story, *Commentaries on Equity Jurisprudence,* 2:621.
[56]Miller, *Life of the Mind.*

group as "persons non compos," "idiots," and such "as want sufficient liberty and free will, as captives and feme coverts." Classifying this group in a more modern form, Benjamin Hall, author of *The Land Owner's Manual* (1847), proclaimed that in New York "all persons except idiots, persons of unsound mind, married women, and infants" might devise realty in a will.[57]

It is impossible to assess with any precision the impress of the common law theory of marriage on popular thought. Nonlegal literature often merged a Christian rationale for the doctrine of marital unity with a common law one. There is considerable evidence, however, that the parroting of common law classifications and designations for married women went beyond legal abridgments to popular books and magazines. An 1856 *Putnam's* article, for example, reaffirmed the ancient principles of baron and feme: "The English common law makes the husband the guardian and master of the wife who stands to him in the relation of a child or a servant."[58]

Of course in discussing the husband-wife relationship, sophisticated treatise writers muted master-servant and parent-child analogies. Clearly they were adjusting their analyses to a more companionate vision of marriage that was at odds with such flagrantly deferential relationships. Also there was some recognition, especially by Reeve, of the wife's economic and psychological need to be viewed by the law as an individual in her own right. Marriage, in this newer view, was enlarged beyond the socioeconomic arrangement for the production of lawful heirs which Blackstone described to a sacred national institution for the rearing of moral citizens. Nonetheless, greater emphasis on the innate weakness and vulnerability of the wife provided a fresh facade for the older and more forthright rationale for her subordinate status. And even the erudite explications of the ways in which equity had ameliorated the wife's common

[57] John Anthon, *An Analytical Abridgement of the Commentaries of Sir William Blackstone* (New York, 1809), pp. 46–51, 145; Asa Kinne, *The Most Important Part of Kent's Commentaries Reduced to Questions and Answers*, 3d ed. (New York, 1844), pp. 75–76; Benjamin Hall, *The Land Owner's Manual* (Auburn, N.Y., 1847), p. 105.

[58] "Men's Rights," *Putnam's Monthly Magazine* 7 (February 1856):208–9. This article was written to protest the married women's statutes; the repetition of the common law categories is noteworthy.

law disabilities provided a cogent justification for keeping the essentials of the baron-feme relationship intact.

This sampling of common law abstractions that spanned more than half a century and were set forth by a handful of male legal theorists tells us little about the lives of flesh-and-blood American women. In no sense were these abstractions descriptive. They cannot give us an accurate picture of women's changing economic roles or the variations that were possible in those roles. An ambitious wife could pool her resources, her abilities, and her labor with her husband's to participate actively in a shared economic venture. In a union of this type she was not acting "in representation of her lord," but rather as a business partner. A trusting, affectionate husband could bequeath to his wife the management of a vast estate, thereby enriching her and empowering her far beyond the limits of her dower. These common law abstractions only set forth elementary principles.

Inasmuch as these abstractions outlined formally agreed-upon gender roles, they were to a degree prescriptive, setting boundaries that individuals conformed to or deviated from. If one measure of the force and authority of prescriptive material is the respectability of the writer, few individuals in America could pass the test of respectability more readily than Blackstone, Kent, and Story.[59] People did not read their work with the regularity with which they read the Bible or popular magazines, yet it seems fair to assume that common law prescriptions for wives and husbands made a contribution to the body of ideas that supported wifely subservience and dependence.

Prescriptions, to be sure, did not pass unchanged from Blackstone into American jurisprudence. Blackstonian sex-role definitions engendered some embarrassment. Certain aspects of the older version of the common law were in conflict with the sanctification of motherhood, others with democratic sen-

[59]Two discussions of methodology in the use of prescriptive literature have influenced my use of this material; Carroll Smith-Rosenberg and Charles Rosenberg, "The Female Animal: Medical and Biological Views of Woman and Her Role in Nineteenth-Century America," *Journal of American History* 60 (1973):333, and Hilda Smith, "Feminism and Methodology of Women's History, in *Liberating Women's History*, ed. Carroll, pp. 375, 377. Smith equates the prescriptive weight of sources with the respectability and acceptability of the writer.

sibilities, and still others with the practical needs of a market economy. Similarities between Blackstone and American jurists, however, were striking. The law of baron and feme meshed neatly with the antebellum stereotype of the self-sacrificing helpmeet as well as her alternate, the lady who stood as a glittering ornament to her husband's success. In either case the wife's place in the economy was mediated by the husband.

More important, as a linguistic device, the legal fiction of marital unity was inherently restrictive.[60] It established a way of thinking about wives and marriage that was difficult to alter without dismissing the entire fiction. As part of the common law heritage, it was a metaphor of enormous power. It could be manipulated in many ways, but as a starting point, it exerted linguistic hegemony over all who used it. Reeve inverted the fiction of marital unity, turning its results into a justification for its existence while he lavished praise on American womanhood. Kent and Story, interpreting it as a historical fiction and a moderating force in the midst of economic and social flux, insisted that as a practical matter equity could adjust and ease the inconveniences resulting from coverture.

But under the haze of sentimental rhetoric sanctifying marriage and elevating womanhood, American jurists imbued the fiction with patriarchal dimensions that were more subtle but perhaps more ominous. Not only did they frame the fiction in condescension, but they informed it with the conviction that the married woman's status at common law was confluent with her inner nature, with her physical and psychological makeup. In some ways they extended both its depth and its range as a legal abstraction. Thus the idea that the husband and wife were one person—the husband—survived the dislocations of colonization and revolution. It survived its feudal origins and early modern connections to penetrate nineteenth-century American thought. It left its mark directly on American law and at least indirectly on the lives of wives and husbands.

[60]Fuller, *Legal Fictions,* p. 11. For the significance of language in law, see also Pollack and Maitland, *History of English Law,* 1:81, 85, 87. They argue that one momentous result of the Norman Conquest was its effect on the language of English lawyers.

CHAPTER 3

Husbands and Wives: The Reality

And, for that dowry, I'll assure her of
Her widowhood, be it that she survives me,
In all my land and leases whatsoever.
Let specialties be therefore drawn between us,
That covenants may be kept on either hand.
—William Shakespeare, *The Taming of the Shrew*

The abstract husband and wife of the common law are not difficult to envision. Innumerable authorities delineated their elementary rights and duties with such consistency that their depiction approached the simplicity of an icon. The real husbands and wives of nineteenth-century New York are another matter. The recognition of trusts, antenuptial agreements, and the wife's equity to a settlement altered the legal relations of wives to their husbands and to the outside world. Out of the state's bustling chancery courts came a body of precedents that significantly modified the baron-feme model of marital property.[1]

[1] In its first state constitution, New York recognized the office of the chancellor and by implication the separate jurisdiction of equity. Equity remained a single and separate jurisdiction until 1823, when, in accordance with the state constitution of 1821, the Legislature conferred equity jurisdiction on eight circuit judges. The circuit judges, eventually called "vice-chancellors," adjudicated cases in both law and equity. Appeals in equity went to the chancellor. In 1831, because of the growing business of the courts of equity, a separate vice-chancellor with jurisdiction over equity only was appointed for the First District and sat in New York City. In 1839 an assistant vice-chancellor was added to the First District and a separate vice-chancellor for equity only was appointed for the Fourth District in Rochester. The Constitutional Convention of 1846 voted for the complete merger of law and equity jurisdictions, and by the end of 1847 the appellate court of chancery and its lower courts ceased to exist. See *Constitution of the State of New York, 1777*, art. 28; *Constitution of the State of New York, 1821*, art. 5, sec. 5; Charles Z. Lincoln, *The Constitutional History of New York*, 5 vols. (Rochester, N.Y., 1906), 2:70; Alden Chester, ed., *A Legal and Judicial History of New York*, 3 vols. (New

As Morton Horwitz has pointed out, from the Revolution through the 1830s, an avidly procommercial judiciary transformed the law of contract from an equitable conception of contract concerned with the underlying fairness of the exchange to a "will theory of contract" devoted to enforcing the terms and intentions of the contracting parties.[2] Ironically, New York chancellors, the judges in the jurisdiction created to dispense equity, adopted a "will theory" with respect to marriage contracts. In one sense they were fulfilling the traditional role of equity by easing the rigidity of the common law; in another sense they were subverting the traditional role of equity by ignoring the underlying fairness of the contract that was made. Nevertheless, an alternate legal model of marriage was emerging, and some women were bound to benefit by it. In this new model, marriage might be a bargain between contracting parties, and the terms of their bargain, at least with respect to marital property, were to be recognized.

Historically, marriage had been, among other things, a bargain. The process through which Anglo-American law bent or even ignored uniform marital property rules to accommodate the needs of the bargaining parties, and thereby created a new body of law, is worth considering. For centuries English families of wealth and standing consolidated their positions through the marriages of sons and daughters. Some daughters who brought wealth to marriage were able to bargain for special privileges for themselves or for their families of origin. Legal instruments to effect the bargain became increasingly sophisticated from the sixteenth century onward.

In *The Taming of the Shrew,* Petruchio's address to Baptista, his future father-in-law, promising Kate a widowhood in all his land and leases should she survive him, documents Shakespeare's familiarity with personalized marriage contracts. Their agreement is still crude; technically, it is a jointure, an agreement in lieu of dower that will take effect on the death of the husband. Although it generously exceeds the terms of common law dower, it gives the fiery Kate no autonomy during the marriage.

York, 1911), 1:331; "Barbour's Reports on Cases in Chancery," *Hunt's Merchants' Magazine* 17 (October 1847):392; Friedman, *History of American Law,* p. 130.

[2]Horwitz, *Transformation of American Law,* pp. 180–85.

Her best prospect lies in outliving her husband, and even then she is limited to a life estate. The important transition in the marriage bargain came with the seventeenth-century recognition of the married woman's trust.

If ever there was a legal revolution in the status of married women—a dubious proposition at best—it began with the recognition of the married woman's separate estate created by a trust. The married woman's trust first collided with the husband's marital rights and then initiated a series of legal steps that culminated in the married women's acts. In a simple trust, in the abstract language of jurists, *A* conveys property to *B,* who administers it on behalf of *C. A* is the settlor or trustor, *B* the guardian or trustee, and *C* the beneficiary or cestui que trust, the one who trusts. *B*'s ownership is considered legal while *C*'s is considered equitable. To translate this situation into human possibilities, a trust allowed a father to endow his daughter with property while keeping it out of the hands of his son-in-law by conveying nominal ownership to a trusted friend, who administered it for the benefit of the daughter. A woman with assets and with the permission of her intended husband could create a similar trust for herself in anticipation of marriage. With the next step it became possible to reserve to the woman the powers that ordinarily went to the trustee, thereby making the trust itself function as a kind of legal fiction. If a woman who anticipated marriage and desired control over her property entered into an antenuptial contract that spelled out the precise extent of her property and the exact nature of her powers, and if her husband agreed to those terms, why was it necessary to bother with the conveyance to a third party? Some judges or chancellors decided it was not, and found the terms of an antenuptial contract binding. The next step eliminated even this last procedure with statutes—the married women's acts—stipulating that the property a woman brought to her marriage was hers.

This explanation is the bare bones of more than three centuries of complex legal development. Our knowledge of the precise chronology and jurisdictional variations of this development is fragmentary. According to Sir William Holdsworth, recognition of the wife's separate estate came at the end of the sixteenth century. In cases where the husband was at sea or had abandoned the wife, the English court of chancery began to recognize the right of a wife to convey her property to a trustee in order to protect it. By the early seventeenth century a married woman's estate created with a trust was recognized regardless of the marital circumstances, and by the end of that century it was possible to create a trust that gave the married woman some of the powers of a single woman over her separate property. The next step, the simple antenuptial agreement without a trust, was first recognized by the English court of chancery in 1769.[3] New York chancery validated this development, as we shall see, in 1818 in *Bradish v. Gibbs;* the state's 1848 statute recognized the existence of a married woman's separate estate without even the formality of an antenuptial agreement, and an 1849 amendment to that act gave women some powers to go with ownership.[4]

The legal evolution of the wife's separate estate was jagged. The law was capable of taking one step backward before taking two forward. Between 1815 and 1828, New York equity established liberal precedents with respect to the married woman's separate estate; after 1828 the uses and trusts provisions of the Revised Statutes clouded those precedents and diminished the range of options available to wives.[5] The application of the "will theory" in the 1828–48 period was no longer so clear.

Unfortunately, the number of women who enjoyed the benefits of a separate estate must elude us because New York, unlike some other states, did not require the official registration of marriage settlements.[6] Nevertheless, the range of equitable op-

[3]Holdsworth, *History of English Law,* 5:309–15. Pennsylvania formally recognized the simple antenuptial agreement in 1783, and Maryland did the same in 1792. See Salmon, "The Property Rights of Women," pp. 210–19.

[4]*LNY, 1848,* chap. 200; *LNY, 1849,* chap. 375.

[5]See *RSSNY, 1829,* 3 vols. (Albany, 1829), 1:727–30, secs. 45–72, on uses and trusts. The Legislature passed the statutes on December 10, 1828. The 1836 revisions included no significant changes in the uses and trusts provisions as they applied to married women. The 1836 edition contains extracts from the revisers' original 1828 report to the Legislature. See *RSSNY, 1836* (Albany, 1836), 1:582–83, for the rationale behind the uses and trusts provisions.

[6]On Virginia, for example, see Suzanne Dee Lebsock, "Women and Economics in Virginia: Petersburg, 1784–1820," Ph.D. dissertation, University of Virginia, 1977. For Joseph Story's general 1821 assessment of equity in the United States, see "An Address Delivered before the Members of the Suffolk Bar . . . at Boston," *American Jurist and Law Magazine* 1 (April 1829):21–22; see also Warbasse, "Changing Legal Rights," p. 39; Beard, *Woman as Force in History,* p. 135.

tions women might enjoy is easily accessible in the voluminous chancery reports of the era.[7] Under the leadership of Kent, who served as chancellor from 1814 until 1823, the married woman's separate equitable estate became more clearly defined. Underscoring the burst of activity that took place with his appointment, Kent asserted, "For the nine years I was in that office there was not a single decision, opinion, or dictum of either of my two predecessors cited by me, or even suggested." Kent approached the court "as if it had been a new institution."[8]

Since the Legislature eventually attempted to follow the patterns of the separate equitable estate in its married women's statutes, the chancery record is important. In the three decades before the 1848 statute, New York chancellors inadvertently influenced the course of statutory reform and shaped judicial decisions on marital property in the state long after 1848. The question posed here is the one raised by Mary Beard: in the context of the married woman's legal status, what was the power of equity relative to the common law?[9] More specifically, what options did equity offer the women of New York before marriage and after marriage?

The most important mode of circumventing the common law was the marriage settlement. If there were special circumstances, such as children from a previous marriage, a large inheritance expected during marriage, or a substantial dowry, a settlement could delineate what was his and hers and provide for contingencies. Generally a settlement served one or more of the

[7]Evidence consists of all the printed chancery reports for the state from 1815 through 1847, a manuscript collection of records and master's notes in the First Judicial District from 1829 to 1839, some family papers and lawyers' formbooks, and a sampling of Westchester County wills. The comprehensive reporting of New York chancery cases began in 1815 with Kent's chancellorship. The De Peyster Chancery Papers include the notes, petitions, bills, schedules, and decrees collected by Frederic De Peyster, a master in the First District, and are filed in alphabetical order by the names of the litigants and petitioners at the New-York Historical Society.

[8]Quoted in Chester, ed., *Legal and Judicial History,* 1:354. Kent's predecessors were Robert R. Livingston, who served from 1777 to 1801, and John Lansing, Jr., who served from 1801 to 1814. After being forced into retirement, Kent was succeeded by Nathan Sanford in 1823, Samuel Jones in 1826, and Reuben Walworth, who served from 1828 until the demise of the court (ibid., pp. 330–31).

[9]Beard, *Woman as Force in History,* pp. 135–55.

following purposes: it kept property out of the husband's reach; it kept property out of the reach of the husband's creditors; it gave the wife powers unavailable to her at common law; it provided an economic inducement for marriage; it freed the husband from the encumbrance of dower. Property set aside for the wife ranged from a substantial dowry of real and personal property to specific items of jewelry or even a few household utensils.[10] Powers reserved to the wife ran anywhere from full autonomy over her property to complete dependence on a designated trustee.

If the main objective was to insulate the wife's property from the husband, the active trust—the conveyance of the wife's property to a trustee who actively managed it for her benefit—was the most secure arrangement. As one might expect, an antenuptial contract drawn up simultaneously with a trust presented New York families of wealth and standing with an attractive alternative to the common law arrangement of marital property. Typical of such an agreement was the antenuptial settlement executed in 1844 by Frederic De Peyster, Frederic G. Foster, and Emily Hone, in which De Peyster was named as a trustee for Emily Hone before she married Foster. A daughter of Philip Hone, one of New York City's most prominent citizens, Emily brought a dowry in the form of a trust that provided her and her husband with income while keeping the principal out of her husband's hands.[11] One possible motive was the traditional one of supporting the interests of the wife's kin against the husband. While the demand for married love detached the couple psychologically from their parents, the antenuptial agreement and trust arranged by a father for his daughter reaffirmed the importance of the family of her birth against the newly formed one.[12] A more modern possibility was the formation of a com-

[10]For forms available in popular lawbooks, see John S. Jenkins, *The New Clerk's Assistant or Book of Practical Forms* (Auburn, N.Y., 1853); David Wright, *Executor's, Administrator's and Guardian's Guide,* 3d ed. (Auburn, N.Y., 1852); George Bishop, *Every Woman Her Own Lawyer* (New York, 1858). For a highly sophisticated collection of professional forms, see John Watts De Peyster, "Law Precedents," ca. 1838, NYHS. This manuscript collection of a working lawyer's forms include a wide variety of trusts and antenuptial agreements.

[11]Frederic De Peyster to Emily Hone with nuptial settlement of marriage, November 11, 1844, in De Peyster Family Papers, 6:93, NYHS.

[12]Stone, "Rise of the Nuclear Family," pp. 19–20, 24–25.

mercial alliance with the advantage of keeping the wife's assets free from the husband's creditors.

New York chancellors clearly recognized the married woman's separate estate created by an active trust throughout the 1815–48 period. They also recognized the passive trust, the device that reserved powers to the married woman. In *Methodist Episcopal Church v. Jaques* (1815), Mary Alexander, a widow posessed of an estate valued at $22,000, created a trust for her own use and that of her husband in an antenuptial agreement. Her trust deed conveyed all her estate real and personal to one H. Cruger until her marriage should take place, and after that for such purposes as she and her husband should designate by deed with two witnesses. After her marriage she conveyed her property in trust to Robert Jaques, a relative of her husband, stipulating that at her death one-third of the surplus after expenses was to go to the Methodist Episcopal church, one-third to relatives, and one-third to her husband. The trustees of the church demanded an accounting, claiming that the husband, "by artful contrivances," had used the income from the realty for personal expenses and had appropriated her personal property.[13]

It is apparent that the first trust she created was fictional in a legal sense. The trust deed, although signed by Cruger and properly witnessed, never left her possession, and Cruger never actively managed her property. Her second trust was created after her marriage on the basis of the powers reserved to her in the original trust and antenuptial contract. Chancellor Kent affirmed the validity of the arrangement. Coercion was considered as a possibility and rejected. Although Kent noted that "Mrs. Jaques was very indulgent to her husband," he honored the specific terms of the antenuptial contract. In accordance with this principle, he ruled that no allowances were to be made for the support of the couple out of the rents of the trust because support was the husband's common law duty, and neither the original antenuptial agreement nor the second trust stipulated otherwise.[14] More important, he established the principle that the wife enjoyed powers over her separate estate only to the extent that they were spelled out in the deed that created the

[13]Methodist Episcopal Church v. Jaques, 1 Johns. Ch. 450 (1815).
[14]Ibid., pp. 456–57.

estate. To the extent that Mary Jaques spelled out those powers, they were recognized.

Kent's position would have necessitated the same careful delineation of powers in any trust deed in order for a married woman to exert control over her separate property. On an appeal in 1820, the Court of Errors modified Kent's position on powers and held that a married woman was to be considered a single woman with respect to her separate estate as long as the deed of settlement did not restrain her in any way.[15] The difference between the two positions was enormous. The Court of Errors opened the way for a married woman to control her separate property with a much simpler kind of agreement.

Delivering the opinion for the Court of Errors, Judge Jonas Platt devoted considerable energy to lamenting the growing use of marriage settlements and the weakening of the doctrine of marital unity. Settlements, he warned, gave the wife "the amphibious character of a *feme covert* and a *feme sole.*" They were the "excessive refinements" of modern civilization, "an adulteration of that holy union," and were often nothing more than a form of "legalized prostitution." But settlements were here to stay, and it was dangerous, he asserted, to view the husband as the wife's worst enemy. He held that Jaques was entitled to use the interest from the estate for family expenses because that was his wife's intention regardless of the limited terms of the original settlement. It was a mistake, he concluded, to restrict the wife to a single mode of disposition as spelled out in the settlement, and it was reasonable to allow her to substitute one mode of disposition for another unless she was specifically restricted from doing so in the marriage settlement. In his *Commentaries,* Kent later pointed out that the Court of Errors had gone beyond English chancery decisions on the wife's powers, but he admitted that English equity was far from clear on the wife's powers.[16]

[15]Jaques v. Methodist Episcopal Church, 17 Johns. 548 (1820). The Court for the Trial of Impeachments and Correction of Errors, the court of last resort in the state, consisted of the lieutenant governor, the Senate, the chancellor, and the judges of the state's Supreme Court. The judges and the chancellor did not sit on cases they had adjudicated, but the Senate reviewed its own legislation. The court was abolished in 1847 and was replaced by the Court of Appeals. See Chester, ed., *Legal and Judicial History,* 1:381.

[16]Jaques v. Methodist Episcopal Church, 17 Johns. 582, 584, 590–91; Kent, *Commentaries,* 2:165.

In *Bradish v. Gibbs* (1818), Chancellor Kent held that the creation of a trust, even a trust that functioned as a legal fiction, was not necessary. In 1814 Helen Elizabeth Gibbs entered into a marriage contract with her fiancé stipulating that any profits and sales from her estate made during her marriage were for her own separate use. She was to have full power during her coverture to dispose of her property according to her pleasure, by will or by any instrument in writing. Her transactions were to be considered as valid as if she were a feme sole. A separate schedule listed her property, including a house in New York City purchased at the time of her marriage for $23,500. If her husband died before her, said the deed, her property was to vest in her absolutely, as if no marriage had taken place.[17]

Helen Gibbs Bradish's husband was forced to sue his wife's relatives to get them to convey title to the house and lot that she had left him. At issue was her ability to devise her realty. The attorney for her relatives argued that her will was invalid because her real estate had not been conveyed to trustees. Kent found the will valid and the reservation of testamentary power to the wife quite safe from the husband's coercion because a will was "revocable at the pleasure of the wife."[18] In upholding the validity of her antenuptial contract without a trust, Chancellor Kent made it possible for a woman to create a separate estate in a fairly simple fashion. To be sure, she needed her future husband's permission, but such an agreement might exclude him from his common law marital rights over her property. The will theory of contracts was extended to marriage contracts.

Obviously New York equity was validating legal devices that were in wide use. Relying almost exclusively on English equity cases at first, Kent was attempting to build a body of New York precedents that clarified some controversial issues. What was validated between 1815 and 1820 was, first, the passive trust, which might give the wife extensive powers; second, the simple antenuptial agreement without a trust, which established a married woman's separate estate; and third, against Kent's better judgment, the principle that in relation to her separate estate a married woman was like a single woman as long as the deed that

[17]Bradish v. Gibbs, 8 Johns. Ch. 523 (1818).
[18]Ibid., pp. 550–51.

created that estate did not specifically restrict her. Ostensibly, a woman with assets, a little foresight, and the permission of her intended could create a separate estate for herself over which she had complete control with a simple antenuptial agreement.

The significance of the wife's economic independence obtained through an antenuptial agreement engendered controversy among lawyers throughout the period. The possibility that financial independence could encourage a wider independence and form a direct challenge to the husband's marital authority was a persistent issue. One law journal noted that antenuptial contracts obliterated "that just authority which nature and the laws give a man over his wife as well as the obedience and subjection which the rules of the gospel prescribe in the deportment of the woman." Reiterating Judge Jonas Platt's phrase, the writer asserted that marriage settlements gave the wife the "amphibious" character of a married woman and a single woman. What would happen, he speculated, if the couple contracted that the wife was not under her husband's control?[19] Many of the antenuptial contracts in the chancery reports, however, seem to have been designed to insulate the wife's property from the husband's creditors while placing some portion of it at the couple's disposal. Considerable flexibility was possible in these arrangements.[20]

The issue of the wife's powers, however, remained ambiguous, and the uses and trusts provisions of the Revised Statutes of 1828 created further ambiguity.[21] The Revised Statutes did not

[19]"Marriage Settlements," *American Law Magazine* 3 (April 1844):16–22; quotation on p. 19.

[20]See, for example, Danforth v. Wood, 11 Paige Ch. 9 (1844), where the wife's trustees with her assent sold her property and loaned her husband's partnership $1,800.

[21]For professional discussion of the Revised Statutes and the married woman's separate estate, see "Recent Revisions etc. of Statute Laws: New York," *American Jurist* 18 (October 1837):244–47; "Trust for the Separate Use," *New York Legal Observer* 1 (November 1842):113–15; "Property of Married Women," *New York Legal Observer* 2 (October 1843):284; "The Validity of Marriage Settlements in Exclusion of the Marital Rights of a Future Husband," *American Law Magazine* 3 (July 1844):273–97; "Accumulation from Property Settled to Separate Use," *New York Legal Observer* 3 (March 1844):3–4; "The Law of Real Property as Affected by the Revised Statutes of the State of New York," *American Law Magazine* 5 (April 1845):50–80; "Uses and Trusts as Affected by the Revised Statutes of the State of New York," *American Law Magazine* 6 (January 1846):268–81; "In Chancery: Cruger v. Douglas," *New York Legal Observer* 4 (February 1846):55.

destroy the concept of the wife's equitable estate, but they created confusion as to how such an estate might be fashioned safely. By abolishing passive or formal trusts—trusts in which property was transferred to a third party to circumvent the wife's common law disabilities but in which the wife exerted control over the property—they seemed to destroy the prospective wife's best option. To complicate the matter even further, the revisers declared that formal trusts were to be converted to the legal estates of the beneficial owner.[22] This provision had dire implications for the married woman's formal trust. If a married woman's equitable estate were to become a legal one, it would go to her husband as his common law marital right. Into this legal limbo went the antenuptial agreement that created a separate estate without a trust. Nevertheless, Reuben Walworth, who served as chancellor from 1828 to 1847, continued to recognize the separate equitable estate created by a simple antenuptial agreement or a passive trust. After the demise of his court in 1847, the new Court of Appeals followed suit.

In *Blanchard v. Blood* (1848), a case in which the prospective wife made a simple antenuptial agreement stipulating that all her real and personal estate should be "forever at her disposal notwithstanding the said marriage," the Court of Appeals relied on an old principle of equity to protect the estate. To be more precise, it protected her estate from her husband's creditors rather than from her husband. Where there is no trustee for the wife, said the decision, a court of equity will regard the husband as trustee.[23]

The chancery reports include post-1828 cases that recognize the passive trust that the revisers set out to eliminate. In *North American Coal v. Dyett* (1837), the court recognized the antenuptial agreement with a trust that Jesse Ann Dyett eventually used to set up her husband in a business. Her agreement stipulated that her husband was to receive the income from the trust for their joint use, but it was not to be liable for his debts. One provision stated that should the husband become insolvent, the

[22] *RSSNY, 1829,* 1:727, sec. 47, stated, "Every estate which is now held as an use executed under any former statute of this state is confirmed as a legal one."

[23] Blanchard v. Blood, 2 Barb. 352 (1848), a case that appeared after the demise of the chancery courts and before the married women's property act of 1848.

interest was then to be paid to Jesse Ann Dyett for her sole and separate use. In 1823 the trustees took a mortgage on the house and lot Jesse Ann Dyett owned in New York City to finance the purchase of a Dutchess County cotton factory that Dyett managed as an agent for the trust. The terms of their agreement necessitated the consent of both husband and wife for all of the trust's transactions.[24]

The husband did become insolvent, and in the course of managing her factory he incurred debts with North American Coal and other creditors. Chancellor Reuben Walworth held that the cotton factory was now part of the wife's trust estate and the debts were to be paid by the estate whether they were contracted by the wife or her agent. "The feme covert is, as to her separate estate considered as a feme sole," he insisted. "And even the assent or concurrence of the trustee is not necessary where no restriction upon her power is contained in the deed or instrument under which such separate estate is held."[25]

This principle, however, could not be applied to married women's estates created after the Revised Statutes. In *L'Amoureux v. Van Rensselaer* (1845), he held it was not possible for a wife to create a charge against a trust that came under the Revised Statutes. Because Catherine Van Rensselaer's trust was created after the passage of the Revised Statutes, he reasoned that she had "no right to charge the trust property even for necessary repairs thereon, without the authority of the trustee."[26]

Further ambiguity arose over the ability of a married woman to make a will of personal property. The Revised Statutes specifically excluded married women from those legally competent to make wills of either real or personal property, but they also reserved to married women "a beneficial power" to convey or devise realty. Could a married woman who enjoyed testamentary powers in a trust created after the Revised Statutes make a will of personal property? *Strong v. Wilkin* held in 1845 that she could if the trust specifically gave her that power. This decision, however, is a far cry from the liberal interpretation of the wife's

[24]North American Coal Co. v. Dyett, 7 Paige Ch. 9 (1837); for a liberal reading of the wife's powers, see also Knowles v. McCamly, 10 Paige Ch. 342 (1843).

[25]North American Coal Co. v. Dyett, 7 Paige Ch. 14.

[26]L'Amoureux v. Van Rensselaer, 1 Barb. Ch. 34, 37–38 (1845).

powers that the Court of Errors had set forth in 1820 in *Jaques v. Methodist Episcopal Church.* In order to legitimate a simple reserve of testamentary power, Walworth was forced to thread his way through the Revised Statutes and conclude that this was "not strictly a will" but rather "an appointment."[27]

Furthermore, absolute clarity in setting the wife's estate apart from the husband's control was advisable in gifts and legacies. If a father created a trust for his daughter's use and neglected to make specific provisions for her marriage, the use of it could go to the husband as his marital right.[28] Stock phrases such as "for her separate use and enjoyment apart from her husband" were employed, but unanticipated problems persisted. In one case, a woman who received furniture from an aunt and purchased other furniture with the income from realty that was specifically set aside for her separate use found her husband could mortgage all of her furniture as security for his debts. The chancellor decided that the furniture was not given for the wife's separate use, nor was the income from the realty, but only the realty itself. Since there was no agreement between the couple setting apart the wife's property, all the furniture was therefore the husband's property and subject to his debts.[29]

The classic caretaker trust, the active trust, if it were meticulously drafted, could avoid such problems and fell within the guidelines of the Revised Statutes. But it offered nothing to the wife in the way of contractual powers or economic responsibility. As Leo Kanowitz has asserted, it was a device associated with infants and idiots.[30] There were other problems as well. In an age when professional trust companies did not exist, mismanagement of trusts was always a possibility. Sometimes large balances accumulated without being paid out; at other times the interests were exposed to hazardous speculation. Ann Eliza Campbell, for example, claimed her trust was grossly misman-

[27]Strong v. Wilkin, 1 Barb. Ch. 9, 13–14 (1845). On realty, see *Revised Statutes, 1829,* 1:732, sec. 80, which stated, "A general and beneficial power may be given to a married woman to dispose during her marriage and without the concurrence of her husband of lands conveyed or devised to her in fee." See also ibid., 1:735, sec. 110, which stated that a married woman might "execute a power."

[28]Kent, *Commentaries on American Law,* 2:157–58; Story, *Commentaries on Equity Jurisprudence,* 2:633.

[29]Shirley v. Shirley, 9 Paige Ch. 363 (1841).

[30]Kanowitz, *Women and the Law,* pp. 39–40.

aged by Frederic De Peyster, father of the master of the First District. Writing to the son, she said, "In October last I visited the City for the express purpose of obtaining the little that was due me previous to my marriage which your Father had in his possession for years."[31]

The chancery records suggest that after the Revised Statutes, the creation of a married woman's separate estate was fraught with problems regardless of the legal instrument that was used. Furthermore, it was no longer possible to create a trust in which the wife's powers were implied or in which a wife could personally charge her separate estate; it was still possible to reserve to the wife the power to convey, bequeath, or devise property, but the reserve of those powers had to be spelled out. The chancery records also demonstrate that the married woman's separate estate set apart by a simple antenuptial agreement continued to be recognized as an equitable estate despite the uses and trusts provisions of the statutes. Walworth, who rendered all appellate equity decisions in this period, did not permit the statutes to transform the wife's separate estate into a legal one that would therefore fall within the common law rules for marital property. If there were an instrument creating a separate estate and no trustee, then the husband would be viewed as the wife's trustee. The concept of the marriage bargain was sustained to the extent that it was still possible to insulate the wife's property from the husband's creditors, but the prospective wife's ability to bargain for powers over her property was seriously undermined.

The creation of a married woman's separate estate, however, was not the only function of the marriage bargain. It is clear that the chancellors throughout the period under consideration were fully prepared to view marriage in general as a transaction in which the couple brought various assets and liabilities to the bargaining table. A woman could use her property to attract a husband who would not otherwise be available to her. A potential husband could function in the same fashion. The marriage itself was a valuable consideration.

The court frankly acknowledged in *Fry v. Fry* that marriage

[31] Ann Eliza Campbell to Frederic De Peyster, February 4, 1835, in De Peyster Family Papers, 3:23, NYHS. The son responded that he was not responsible for his deceased father's trusteeships (Frederic De Peyster to Robert E. Campbell, February 13, 1835, in ibid., p. 22).

might be a transaction between unequals in which property could balance the scales. In this case the material assets of the wife compensated for her physical liabilities. Mrs. Fry, a grossly overweight young woman, conveyed all of her real estate to her husband in an antenuptial agreement. According to the common law, he would have the use and management of it during marriage anyway, but if he died first, it would return to the wife. By this agreement, however, the wife restricted herself to dower in the event of his death. In 1837, disillusioned by her bargain after a few years of marriage, Mrs. Fry attempted to prevent her husband from collecting a $3,000 cash legacy due her which would have gone to him as his common law marital right. Chancellor Walworth admitted that Fry might have taken advantage of his wife's ignorance of her legal rights in the antenuptial contract, but he also asserted that "she has been for several years so corpulent as to weigh nearly 300 pounds, . . . a circumstance from which it probably may be inferred that she would not readily have obtained a husband without a corresponding weight of purse."[32]

If Fry had committed adultry or had left his wife, the chancellor might have insisted on a settlement of some kind for the wife in return for the fortune she brought. In this case, however, in which she claimed she had been mentally incompetent and unable to understand the terms of her original settlement and was now living apart from her husband, it was decided that she had violated the marriage contract. The court ruled that her husband was entitled to collect her legacy.

Fry v. Fry indicates the possibility of disadvantages for potential wives. Because the antenuptial agreement allowed the couple to set their own terms, within certain limits, a woman could give up advantages as well as gain them. This was particularly true in the case of jointures, settlements in lieu of dower. A jointure freed the husband from the responsibility of dower in advance of marriage and enabled him to alienate his land without his wife's separate examination and signature. Men with extensive real estate holdings obviously might favor this kind of settlement, but it also could accommodate the full spectrum of motives underlying antenuptial contracts.

[32]Fry v. Fry, 7 Paige Ch. 461–62 (1839).

Sometimes jointures extended beyond arrangements for the forfeiture of dower. The antenuptial agreement arranged by the seventy-five-year-old Philip Jacobs with Elizabeth Brown's guardian demonstrates the groom's ability to dictate terms to his fiancée which precluded her enjoyment of the dower rights to which she was otherwise bound to be entitled soon enough. His settlement stipulated that at his death, his wife was to receive an annuity of $1,200 yearly plus the use of his household furniture and plate for as long as she remained unmarried. Jacobs was not about to allow a second husband to enjoy his property. He further stipulated that if she remarried, she was to receive a cash settlement of $1,000. Jacobs was nervous about his wife's sexual fidelity and her economic habits. He insisted that she was to remain "chaste" during marriage and was to contract no debts above the sum of $20 without his permission.[33] Presumably Elizabeth or her guardian found a $1,200 annuity the most promising marriage prospect available. Jacobs, for his part, managed to make the youthful Elizabeth an attractive offer without subjecting his estate to her dower right.

The agreement in lieu of dower was often a way of limiting a wife's potential interest in substantial fortunes by making a handsome settlement in advance of marriage. Less affluent husbands, however, also attempted to deprive wives of their minimal common law rights. Hazel Shepard, of Rensselaer County, agreed to give up her right to dower in return for her fiancée's promise that she should have dower in any future realty purchased "by their prudence and industry during their cohabitation." No such realty was ever purchased. After her husband's death, Hazel was forced to sue her son for a lot her husband had at first deeded her, a technical impossibility at common law, and subsequently sold at a low price to his son. The court ordered the son to release the land to his mother, deeming it only fair that Hazel get something after her years of marriage.[34]

[33] M'Cartee v. Teller, 2 Paige Ch. 511 (1831).

[34] Shepard v. Shepard, 7 Johns. Ch. 57 (1823). It seems that the husband was doubtful of his ability to convey realty to his wife, but a postnuptial bargain in consideration of the wife's dower right was fully recognized in equity. For conveyances between husband and wife, see Livingston v. Livingston, 2 Johns. Ch. 537 (1817); Garlick v. Strong, 3 Paige Ch. 440 (1832); Strong v. Wilkin, 1 Barb. Ch. 9 (1845); and Meriam v. Harsen, 2 Barb. Ch. 232 (1847).

While the common law rules for marriage ensured the unity of the married pair, the antenuptial agreement recognized and arranged for conflicting interests between the married pair. The feud between James Beekman, New York entrepreneur and widower of Lydia Beekman, with his sister-in-law Elizabeth Dunkin exposes just such a conflict. Lydia, who formerly had been married to a British army officer, had brought to her second marriage with Beekman, in 1800, a separate estate of some value. With the knowledge of her sister and brother, she agreed that she and Beekman were to enjoy the use of her estate jointly during their marriage, but that the principal was to go to her siblings after her death. The agreement was either oral or lost, but all interested parties were aware of its existence, if not in agreement about its terms.[35]

In 1833 Lydia made out a will leaving everything to her sister and brother and noted that James Beekman empowered her to dispose of her own estate "notwithstanding her coverture."[36] When Lydia died, Beekman protested he had been defrauded by her will, which violated their antenuptial agreement according him a life interest in her estate, with the principal going to her family after his death. The feud, in other words, centered on the terms of the original agreement and the powers Lydia had reserved for herself. An acrimonious exchange ensued. Beekman accused his sister-in-law of wresting away his wife's silver plate, and James Beekman and Elizabeth Dunkin articulated the advantages, problems, and tensions inherent in antenuptial agreements.

Elizabeth Dunkin gives us a rare personal account of the independence a separate estate could bring. Writing "from a proud feeling of integrity" that Beekman, she proclaimed, could never deprive her of, she pointed to the strength of her financial position, based on the income of a life estate created by her mother for her use, with the principal going to her daughter. "I who enjoy all the comforts of life with my children, from my own resources, which altho moderate, makes us more than comforta-

[35]Sworn statement by James Beekman of agreement between Lydia Beekman and James Beekman (n.d.), in Beekman Family Papers, Box 4, NYHS.

[36]Copy of will of Lydia Beekman, January 29, 1833; she referred to a document written by James Beekman on December 22, 1832, empowering her to make a will (both in ibid.).

ble, with my Daughter's aid from her Grand Mother," she protested, had no need to resort to petty theft. Elizabeth Dunkin claimed it was her understanding that "in consideration for love and affection," Beekman had given his wife full control over her own property.[37]

Asserting he was being cheated out of $2,400 a year in income, Beekman said his understanding with Lydia included the use of her estate as long as he lived if she predeceased him. What enraged Beekman even more, however, was his sister-in-law's inference that he counted on his wife for income. Beekman estimated that Lydia's estate was worth $10,643.29 at the time of their marriage, a sum he must have managed ably if in 1834 it would bring $2,400 a year in interest. He valued his own assets at the time of marriage, not even counting his real estate, at $42,000. Painstakingly Beekman calculated that his cash expenditures on Lydia, including her medical bills, came to more than $23,000.[38] From these figures he concluded it was patently obvious he had supported his wife handsomely and at great personal cost.

During this controversy and during his marriage, Beekman consulted an impressive and expensive array of attorneys. His papers include an opinion on the status of his wife's separate estate from Chancellor James Kent, for which he paid $25. In the feud Beekman was represented by I. S. Van Rensselaer, who took the case on a contingency fee of one-third of the income of the estate if Beekman recovered. Elizabeth Dunkin and her brother eventually settled with Beekman by paying him $3,500 to release all claims on Lydia's estate.[39]

Although there are missing pieces in the Beekman-Dunkin quarrel, the feud suggests some possible conclusions. The willingness of both parties to settle implies that Beekman's claim was weak but troublesome. More important, the stance taken by Elizabeth Dunkin against Beekman resonates with the pride she experienced as a result of having assets of her own. Beekman's

[37]Elizabeth Dunkin to James Beekman, December 9, 1833, in ibid.

[38]James Beekman to Elizabeth Dunkin, April 5, 1834, and schedule of Lydia Beekman's assets at the time of her marriage, both in ibid.

[39]Copy of bill from Chancellor James Kent to James Beekman for opinion; memorandum of settlement between James Beekman and Elizabeth Dunkin, executrix for the estate of Lydia Beekman, both in ibid.

position suggests that a separate estate such as the one Lydia brought to her marriage might be properly enjoyed by both spouses, but that it could not be construed as the basic support of the family without casting dishonor on the husband.

Trusts and antenuptial agreements, a wellspring of family feuds and extensive litigation, were clearly validated and staunchly supported by the New York chancellors in the period under consideration. Equity's recognition of the wife's separate estate subtly undercut the common law fiction of marital unity. In equity marriage was to some extent a contract between individuals. This perception of marriage as an individualized union was as much a result of the chancellors' agressive efforts to create commercial advantages for investors and speculators as it was an expression of equity's traditional role of protecting the wife. Nevertheless, some advantages to wives were a corollary. Thus for women with assets, with the proper instruments, and with the acquiescence and aid of parents or fiancés, equity significantly eased the rigidity of the common law. In an economy that increasingly segregated middle- and upper-class women from the material world and relegated them to the domestic sphere, these exceptions yielded a measure of security that would not have been possible at common law.

After marriage the spectrum of legal options available to women narrowed. The most significant bargaining tool after marriage consisted in the wife's refusal to give up her dower right in realty that her husband wanted to sell. New York equity recognized the wife's right to bargain for a settlement before she relinquished dower. In 1835, Mrs. Richard Searing declined to sign a deed giving up her dower right in the Saratoga farm her husband was selling until $2,000 was set aside for her separate use and deposited in a savings bank in her name. Her postnuptial agreement with her husband permitted her to draw this money out and invest it or loan it in her own name. Mrs. Searing, it should be noted—unlike the unnumerable wives who, after a perfunctory separate examination, signed most of the deeds in the state—was exceptionally aware of her options. She had an antenuptial agreement with her husband reserving for herself the power to invest and use $2,200 of the proceeds from the sale of her Vermont realty, part of which she had used to pay Searing's debts at the time of their marriage.[40]

New York equity, like English equity, recognized a variety of postnuptial bargains between husband and wife. A wife could bargain with her dower right or her separate estate. In equity the concept of the wife's separate property was strong and prevailed even when her property was not protected by a trust or antenuptial agreement. A husband could always settle on his wife the property she brought to the marriage or received afterward. He could settle his own property on her after marriage, but such a settlement required a valuable consideration and was scrutinized closely as a possible attempt to defraud creditors. Equity, then, permitted the generous or astute husband to insulate his wife's property from his creditors after marriage. The initiative in these postnuptial bargains had to be taken by the husband, however, if the wife had no clearly defined separate estate.

Postnuptial bargains were based on a principle known as the wife's equity to a settlement. This principle gave the wife some options in a court of equity because it recognized that she had at least an informal interest in the property she brought to marriage or received during marriage. It worked in three types of situations: when the court became involved in the wife's legacy, when the court became involved in suits with creditors or in the husband's insolvency, and in separations and divorces.

When the wife's property was subject to the jurisdiction of the court, it was within the court's discretion to give her all or part of it, depending on the circumstances.[41] When a husband petitioned the court with his wife for her legacy of $1,500 and a milk cow, the court gave her a choice; she could elect to have the court set aside a portion in trust for her use, or after a separate examination she could elect to waive her rights and turn the whole legacy over to her husband. Chancellor Kent stated that "as the husband and wife are suing for the wife's legacy, the wife is entitled to a reasonable provision out of the legacy, small as it

[40]Searing v. Searing, 9 Paige Ch. 283 (1841).

[41]Howard v. Moffat, 2 Johns. Ch. 206 (1816); Kenny v. Udall, 5 Johns. Ch. 464 (1821).

may be, before the decree in favor of her husband is pronounced."[42] But if a husband could get his wife's property as a result of his common law marital rights without the aid or intervention of the court, he was not compelled to make any special provision for his wife.[43]

The second situation in which the concept of the wife's equity to a settlement operated involved the right of a wife to sue her husband for a portion of her property against creditors. Here the wife's equity to a settlement actually provided the husband with the right to settle all or part of his wife's legacy on her in a postnuptial agreement because such a settlement was in keeping with equitable principles if his wife filed a suit against him to protect her claim against his creditors. In *Wickes v. Clarke,* for example, a case in which the husband already had appropriated much of his wife's estate, the court set aside a portion of what was left and arranged for an allowance for the wife.[44]

The question as to what was in the reach of creditors remained problematic throughout the period. John Sargent, a New York attorney who was trying to collect a debt owed to a client by a man who had moved to Taunton, Massachusetts, after marrying a wealthy woman, expressed doubt to a colleague about his chances of collecting. In a letter to a Massachusetts attorney, Sargent speculated that the debtor would probably repudiate the stock his wife owned on the grounds that he had given no reasonable consideration for it.[45] Sargent's letters in 1842–43 focus on bankruptcies and difficulties in collecting his own fees.

A wife whose husband pleaded insolvency could petition the chancery court for an allowance from her property, since the same court acted as a receiver in such cases. Caroline Dunscomb, for example, petitioned the court for an allowance from her property. The court pointed out that Caroline Dunscomb had secreted assets belonging to her husband and therefore to his

[42]Glen v. Fisher, 6 Johns. Ch. 33, 35–36 (1822).

[43]Kent, *Commentaries on American Laws,* 2:126; William E. Bullock, *A Treatise on the Law of Husband and Wife in the State of New York* (Albany, 1897), pp. 68–69.

[44]See Kent, *Commentaries on American Laws,* 2:16–22; Livingston v. Livingston, 2 Johns. Ch. 537 (1816); Wickes v. Clarke, 8 Paige Ch. 161 (1840). For the interests of wives against the interests of creditors, see also Haviland v. Meyers, 6 Johns. Ch. 24 (1822); Smith v. Kane, 2 Paige Ch. 303 (1830).

[45]John F. Sargent to W. A. F. Sprock, June 28, 1842, in NYHS.

creditors; if she would return them, it would direct a small allowance to her out of her portion.[46] The wife's equity to a settlement attached to her property in any situation in which her property was subject to the jurisdiction of the court.

The wife's equity to a settlement did not apply to cases in which the wife's property had been reduced to possession by her husband as his marital right so long as he had not violated the marriage contract. If, for example, the court decided the husband was guilty of adultery, he might forfeit his marital rights by his misbehavior.[47] But if he slowly squandered property of his wife's that was rightfully his, she had no recourse. In an 1837 case, *Van Duzer v. Van Duzer,* the court decided that the equity to a settlement did not extend to her realty. Since the husband controlled her realty as his common law right and was able to collect rents and profits, the chancellor ruled that he could sell his interest on execution of a judgment against him and his wife had no remedy, even though Van Duzer had ruined himself by gambling and left his wife and children without any means of support. This somewhat narrow application of equitable principles stemmed from the theory that the husband's obviously improper conduct was still not grounds for a divorce or separation, and therefore was not within the court's jurisdiction. "The general rule of law is well settled," the chancellor insisted, "that by the marriage the husband takes an immediate vested interest in his wife's freehold estate, for their joint lives at least, and an absolute right to all her personal property in possession, unless the same is in the hands of a trustee, or is protected by an antenuptial contract."[48]

The wife's equity to a settlement similarly offered limited relief in cases of abandonment, legal incompetency, separation, and divorce—situations in which the common law rights and duties of husbands and wives were suspended, altered, or erased. If her husband were declared legally insane, a wife could petition the court for the use of the property she had brought to the marriage. The chancery records, moreover, were studded with examples of disappearing spouses and bogus second mar-

[46]Mumford v. Murray, 1 Paige Ch. 620 (1820).
[47]Haviland v. Meyers, 6 Johns. Ch. 25 (1822).
[48]Van Duzer v. Van Duzer, 6 Paige Ch. 366, 370 (1837).

riages.[49] Sometimes a runaway wife or husband took up residence far away and remarried. More frequently, a husband went west or embarked on an extended sea voyage, then returned years later to find his wife living with another man.

These cases probably represented the tip of the iceberg. Although Christian theology and common law theory considered marriage an inviolable contract for life, it is likely that innumerable men and women whose property and sexual fidelity never came within the purview of the courts violated their marriage contracts with informal second unions. Aside from the social opprobrium connected with illegitimate sexual liaisons, the marriage contract was of greatest concern and interest to those persons who had an economic stake in the society. If a woman's husband failed to support her or abandoned her, he deprived her of her most valuable asset in the contract. Without money and a lawyer, she found it far simpler to marry again even if she were technically guilty of bigamy. To be sure, cultural prescriptions supporting the sanctity and inviolability of marriage inhibited illegal liaisons, but they may also have indicated contemporary anxiety about the existence of illegal unions.

Considerations of property, however, brought bogus marriages to the attention of the courts. A wife, for example, could appeal to a chancery court when a legacy was imminent to ensure herself against a wayward husband's claim. In this situation, she had to prove her husband was adulterous or guilty of "cruel and inhuman treatment," the only grounds respectively for divorce and separation. Maria Magee petitioned the court with her second husband for her legacy, claiming that her first husband, John Burhanse, had abandoned her on three separate occasions. She remarried, she said, after learning that Burhanse was dead. Burhanse, meanwhile, was very much alive and had remarried and was raising a second family. The court chastised Maria for not investigating conscientiously her husband's whereabouts before remarrying. In recognizing that Burhanse had forfeited his right to her legacy, however, it tacitly legitimized her second marriage. The court did not award the legacy directly to Maria

[49]See, for example, the following bills of complaint: Susan Balcom by her Next Friend Increase Pettit v. Charles Balcom, December 22, 1837; and Harriet Stoner v. Rudolph Stoner, April 22, 1837, in De Peyster Chancery Papers, NYHS. Balcom finally was arrested on charges of bigamy.

and her second husband of some twenty years, but placed it in the care of the register of the court as a trust. She received the income from it; the principal would be divided among her children after her death.[50] This case demonstrates the principle that shaped decisions about marital property in cases of abandonment, separation, and divorce. The behavior of each spouse was crucial. John Burhanse violated the marriage contract; he failed to treat Maria with "that protection and support to which she [was] entitled."[51] His behavior was cruel and inhuman and would have been grounds for a separation. His second marriage, considered a form of adultery, would have been grounds for a divorce.

Sometimes a husband came to court to be formally released from his marital obligations to an adulterous wife. Richard Jacob, who had married his wife, Jane, in New York City in 1824, went on a whaling voyage in 1827. When he returned three years later, he found his wife living with Ira Robbins and two children as if they were married. The court granted Jacob a divorce and released him from all financial obligations to his wife.[52]

A wife could petition the court for the status of a feme sole when her husband abandoned her or failed to support her. Elizabeth Beach petitioned the court in 1835 for a separation from bed and board because of cruel and inhuman treatment. Her husband, John, who did not appear, had no property, was of "idle and dissipated habits," and was completely incapable of contributing to her maintenance. The master recommended that Elizabeth be entitled to her own future earnings and property for the support and education of their only child, of whom she should have custody in order "to preserve it from his pernicious example."[53] Elizabeth managed to free herself from her common law disabilities, but she could not remarry. The court always warned parties to a separation that they were to remain chaste.

[50]Dumond v. Magee, 4 Johns. Ch. 317 (1820).

[51]Ibid., p. 362.

[52]Bill of complaint, Richard Jacob v. Jane Jacob, April 1834, in De Peyster Chancery Papers, NYHS.

[53]Master's report and opinion, Elizabeth Beach by her Next Friend v. John Beach, November 1835, in ibid.

The economically abandoned wife was in a superior position if she could prove her husband was adulterous, even if he had insufficient assets for alimony. After a divorce, she was free to remarry instead of being relegated to the limbo of permanent separation. Sarah Brown, claiming she had always "been left to depend upon her own industry and resources for her maintenance and Support without any assistance whatever from her said husband," was able to prove her husband's adultery to the court's satisfaction and get a divorce. "Wickedly disregarding the Solemnities of his Vows and the sanctity of the Marriage State," her husband "became infected with a loathsome disease called the venereal by means and in consequences of his commiting [sic] adultery with some other person or persons."[54]

Even if a wife brought property to a marriage, a divorce or separation did not ensure her equity to a settlement. The court closely examined her behavior. If she moved out of the home and was unable to prove grounds for separation or divorce, she was entitled to nothing. If, on the other hand, a wife continued to live with her husband after she knew of his adultery, the court interpreted her behavior as forgiveness. Only if the wife could prove that her husband had committed adultery and if her behavior was impeccable as well as unforgiving did he automatically forfeit his marital rights to her property. In this situation the wife's real estate reverted to her just as if she had survived him, and theoretically had no bearing on the separate issue of alimony.[55] When the husband committed adultery, the court closely scrutinized the wife's behavior. Had she held up her part of the marriage contract? In *Peckford v. Peckford* the court noted that Mrs. Peckford had been less than "discreet, prudent, and submissive," and that her indiscretions were such as to "produce remarks from her more discreet neighbors." By going to England against her husband's wishes, it seems, she had exposed him to the temptations that destroyed the marriage.[56] The same

[54]Bill of divorce, Sarah Ann Brown v. James Brown, October 26, 1836, in ibid.

[55]Kirby v. Kirby, 1 Paige Ch. 261 (1828), and Renwick v. Renwick, 10 Paige Ch. 419 (1843).

[56]Peckford v. Peckford, 1 Paige Ch. 274–75 (1828). Divorce was granted for adultery only; for the jurisdictional limits of divorce, see Burtis v. Burtis, Hopk. Ch. 557 (1825); Palmer v. Palmer, 1 Paige Ch. 276 (1828); and Fry v. Fry, 7 Paige Ch. 461 (1839).

assessment of the wife's behavior that determined alimony determined whether or not she could claim her equity to a settlement out of her own property.

The case of Mary and James Gill eloquently illustrates how each party to a suit for separation or divorce worked to demonstrate that the other had violated the proper code of behavior in marriage. It is also an index of the power of husbands and wives to injure each other. Married in 1808, James and Mary Gill lived for a time in Haverstraw and finally settled in Brooklyn, where they bought a house. After some twenty-seven years of marriage and three children—one a son at sea, a younger son, and a grown daughter—Mary Gill sued her husband, a sea captain who earned a good living, for separation from bed and board. She testified that his "tyrannical and cruel temper" and his "unmanly" conduct made living with him unsafe. She assembled a carefully documented catalogue of physical abuses at her husband's hands. On March 30, 1830, when she spilled tea on him, her husband, in the presence of their daughter, struck her "with such force on the head with his fist, as to break her comb in pieces"; on June 30 he struck her in the face and cut open her eye; in November of that year he tossed water on her and threw her out of the house so that she had to climb in a back window; in March 1831 he tore the cap off her head and tried to push her into the fire. Finally, in April, to avoid any public exposure of his predilection for wife beating, he "calculatingly" hit her on the back of the head.

One basis for the separation and settlement was her safety. Her life, she said, had been made a burden, and he had "rendered it utterly unsafe for [her] to live any longer with him." Another basis on which she waged her case was the ill effects of the father's profane language and cruel deportment on the children, especially the daughter. She concluded in her complaint that James Gill's actions were "contrary to equity and good conscience" and an utter subversion of the marriage contract. To support her right to a settlement, she pointed out that she had received an inheritance, the exact amount unknown to her but roughly $800, after the death of her mother and brother.

James Gill, for his part, attested to the way his wife subverted their marriage. Depicting himself as a hard-working cabinmaster gone from home for long periods of time, he claimed his wife spent money extravagantly in his absence. She neglected their children and went out visiting with her friends at unreasonable hours, taking the daughter with her. She often refused to tell him where she had been. When he was ashore, she devoted all of her time to abusing and irritating him while neglecting his comforts, and then boasted of having done so. She persistently demanded he take her to the theater in New York City, a luxury beyond his means. She worked maliciously to prejudice the children against him and encouraged them in acts of "disobedience and ingratitude," especially the daughter. And yet, being a generous man, he had no wish for her to leave or to break up the family. He admitted that on extreme provocation, he had seized her by the arm; on another occasion, when she pulled his hair, he slapped her. Once he shoved her out of the room and she scratched her eye on a nail in the doorjamb. She provoked violence with her own violence, he asserted, striking him in the face once with a blow so hard that she complained about the pain in her hand. Just as Mary Gill drew a picture of James as unmanly, James Gill drew a portrait of Mary as unwomanly.

William McCoun, the vice-chancellor in the First District, found James Gill's behavior cruel and inhuman and decreed that Mary was to be separated from his bed and board forever. The court estimated Gill's yearly income plus the interest of his property if it were sold. Gill's house minus a mortgage was worth $6,156.90, and the court calculated interest on that amount at 7 percent to be $430.98. Interest in a share he owned in a brig was estimated at $35. His wages, including $640 for eight months at sea and $120 for four months at home, were added to the interest from his property so that his whole yearly income was estimated to be $1,225.98. Of this yearly total, Mary was to get one-third, or $408.66. Yet even though the court recognized that Captain Gill was guilty of wife beating, it did not award his wife or compensate her in any special way for the $800 legacy she had contributed to the marriage. It was merged with Gill's total assets as personal property that went to him as his marital right.[57]

[57]Copy of bill of complaint, Mary Gill by her Next Friend Francis Williams v. James Gill, 1835, and copy of answer of James Gill, defendant; Schedule A, July 1, 1835, and copy of decree by William McCoun in Gill v. Gill, all in De Peyster Chancery Papers, NYHS.

If women's options in separations or divorces were limited, their options in widowhood were almost nonexistent. Petitions by widows who were duped or confused contain formal appeals to the protective, benevolent powers of equity.[58] Although courts fiercely protected the widow from being completely defrauded of her dower, they were less than protective in calculating and administering dower. New York held in 1807 that a widow could not benefit from improvements on property, and in 1814 that she could not benefit from the increased value of property. Thus when a heavily indebted husband sold property near the time of his death without his wife's permission, the court ruled the widow was entitled to her dower right. It computed her dower on the basis of the value of the property in 1817, when it was sold, and ordered dower paid from 1821, the date of the husband's death. The total yearly amount of the widow's annuity was $146.66. In this case the widow could not get the court to award payment quarterly instead of yearly, even though she was desperately in need of it.[59]

Equity sometimes eased the lot of widows through its jurisdiction over trusts. The trust was one device for taking care of the widow and providing her with income while keeping the principal intact for children. Sometimes assets were placed in two trusts, one for the benefit of the widow, the other for the benefit of minor children. A widow could protest to the court about the mismanagement of the trust or the parsimony of the trustees. The chancellor would take into account the desires of the testator, the size of the estate, the integrity of the trustees, and the social standing of the family.

Mary Ann Byrnes came before the vice-chancellor of the First District in 1835 to complain about the administration of her children's trust. Created at her husband's death in 1826, the

[58]See, for example, petition of Jane Yager, March 6, 1828, and master's notes, both in ibid. Shortage of cash plagued many large estates, and widows petitioned for the right to sell realty or adult children petitioned for partition of realty subject to their mother's dower right. See master's report in the Matter of the Petition of Mary Nicoll and Others, October 30, 1835; copy order, January 16, 1832, In the Matter of the Petition of Anna Watts; Adam Stanley v. Elizabeth Stanley, November 13, 1832, all in ibid.

[59]Hale v. James, 6 Johns. Ch. 258 (1822); on dower, see Humphrey v. Phinney, 2 Johns. 484 (1807), and Dorchester v. Coventry, 11 Johns. 510 (1814), as cited in Horwitz, *Transformation of American Law,* p. 58, n. 131.

trust yielded $8,400 per year in interest. The trustees allotted the two minors only $2,000 per year. The income, the mother insisted, was inadequate for her daughters, now ten and thirteen, and not in keeping with "the station of life which it is desirable they should assume." Silas Wood, executor and trustee, found it more than adequate. Alluding to a clause in Byrnes's will allowing the trustees to assume control of the children if the mother's guidance were unsatisfactory, he acknowledged that the mother was capable of parental control. Prominent friends came to court to verify the daughters' increased needs. Cornelius W. Lawrence, mayor of New York, advocated at least $3,000 yearly. "These Young Ladies," he testified, "are growing up to womanhood, and the expenses incident to their time of life and more enlarged education are consequently proportionately increasing and increasing." A proper lifestyle, he pointed out, had an important object: "to establish them respectably in life, to give them husbands, to which by proper care and previous education, their merits thus improved and established with the property they are entitled to, recommend them."[60]

The master's report recommended granting Mary Byrnes' petition.[61] Her position, however, exemplified the status of a widow who would be considered wealthy by any antebellum standard. She enjoyed the income from $20,000 for as long as she remained Byrnes's widow. She managed to exert her influence on the court by relying on prominent friends and by stressing that the trust for her daughters was no longer managed in accord with her husband's intentions. She was undoubtedly well cared for financially. Yet her protest subjected her to a review of her parental abilities, and she had no control of her daughters' legacy or her own.

Equitable options for women after marriage were limited. The principle of the wife's equity to a settlement made postnuptial bargains a possibility, but if a wife did not enjoy a separate estate, she had only her potential dower with which to bargain. If she acquired property after marriage, she was dependent on the

[60]Petition of Mary Ann Byrnes, March 20, 1835, in DePeyster Chancery Papers, NYHS.

[61]Master's report, April 2, 1835, in ibid.

largess of her husband or the discretion of the court for a settlement. In divorce or separation, she might recover her property. Nevertheless, an all-male judiciary was likely to view any subversion of traditional gender roles unsympathetically, punishing wayward wives with reduced settlements or none at all. When the chancery court insulated wives from profligate husbands and irate creditors, chancellors wore the mantle of paternalism, protecting wives against negligent husbands when necessary. Generally, however, chancellors were prepared to accept the husband as the wife's trustee if none had been appointed. The married woman's common law disabilities forced the chancery court to place her under the tutelage of males. If the husband were unable to perform his tutelary role, then the court itself would do so.

Finally, it should be noted that one of the most salient deficiencies of equity was its failure to abrogate the wife's procedural disabilities, a situation that was not fully corrected in New York until 1860. In equity as in law, a wife came under her husband's wing or protective cover. She was precluded from suing in her own name for anything except divorce.[62] She could sue with her husband or with a "next friend" or "prochein ami," but not by herself. Therefore even in a suit for separation, a wife was compelled to use a next friend. This procedural incapacity was not only symbolically important, separating married women from the legal process by placing them in the same category as children and other legal incompetents, but it had practical results also. When a husband's funds were insufficient or a suit for separation was unsuccessful, the burden of the cost of the suit fell on the next friend. If a wife sued with her husband to protect her separate estate, that suit was considered the husband's. Thus when a husband released the defendant from such a suit for the sum of $100, the court declared it was his right to bar further prosecution since the suit was his and in his name.[63] If there was a fraud on the rights of the wife, she was advised to file a new suit against her husband through a next friend.

[62]Even when the husband had been a confirmed drunkard, his assets had been assigned to a committee that was suspected of fraud, he had left the state for Illinois, and had left his family without support, a wife could not file a bill in her own name (Hay v. Warren, 8 Paige Ch. 609 [1841]).

[63]Dewall v. Covenhoven, 5 Paige Ch. 581 (1836).

The two petitions of Frances Carter before the chancellor of the First District eloquently demonstrate the paternalistic role the court of equity assumed in its relation to married women. Frances Carter petitioned the court in May 1829, "praying to be secured an equitable allowance out of two certain bonds and mortgages . . . being your Petitioner's patrimonial property," because her husband, John, was a "lunatic" and assigned to the asylum at Bloomingdale. Since no committee had been appointed at this time to administer his property, the chancellor made himself a temporary guardian ad litem for the husband. Frances' property was transferred to the assistant register, who then collected the interest and doled it out to Frances from time to time. John Carter died, and in 1831 Frances appeared in court with her new husband, Joshua Lowe, to petition with him for the same property, which was still in the register's hands though it had been left to her in a valid will by her husband. After a separate examination to establish the absence of coercion on the part of her second husband, the court placed the property in the hands of her new husband.[64] Starting with her father's bequest, Francis' property went from her father to her first husband to the court, and finally to her second husband. Her first appearance in court necessitated a prochein ami, her second appearance her new husband. She was as legally incapacitated in both instances as the husband who had been declared legally incompetent.

The negotiating power of women in advance of marriage and the wife's equity to a settlement depended on having assets. Wills reveal what some women brought to marriage relative to male siblings. They indicate the provisions some husbands made for wives above and beyond dower. Wills by widows indicate the extent to which some widows achieved financial independence.

The wills in this sample include all those probated in 1825 (43) and in 1850 (62) in Westchester, a county in which testators had a good mixture of assets.[65] Obviously, the vast majority of the

[64]Carter v. Carter, 1 Paige Ch. 463–64 (1829); copy of petition, May 5, 1829, and In the Matter of the Separate Property of Frances Lowe, December 18, 1831, both in De Peyster Chancery Papers, NYHS.

[65]Bordering New York City and still rural and agricultural in its northern reaches, Westchester probate records include estates running anywhere from

population died intestate, a fact that suggests that the probate process offered options for only a limited number of women. If less than 5 percent of the deaths in most counties in the middle of the century are represented in the surrogate records, then we can estimate how infinitesimal were the numbers of widows whom the probate process enriched above and beyond the statutory provisions of dower.[66] For most women, the rules for intestate succession, which provided the widow with one-third of the husband's personal property after his debts if there were children, were far more important.[67] Nevertheless, when wills present overwhelmingly well-defined patterns, they yield important clues to the role women played in the transmission of property.

In Westchester County in 1825, 12 wills, or 27 percent of the 43 wills probated, were drawn by women. Nine of those wills were made by widows, three by single women, and none by married women. At least one-fourth of all testators regardless of sex made an effort to divide their estates equally among children of both sexes, some of them actually stating it was their desire for their children to have equal shares. Often they deducted gifts that had been given at the time of a marriage or loans made to sons or sons-in-law. Almost half of the wills simply did not fit into the son-daughter comparison either because children were all of the same sex, there was only one child, or there was no child. The remaining wills favor sons over daughters. Realty, especially the family homestead, was likely to go to a son if it had

---

small farms and farming implements to substantial holdings in New York City realty and in stocks. The 1850 period was selected not only to reveal any possible changes in a twenty-five-year span and to view practices around the time of the married women's acts, but also to parallel Lawrence Friedman's study of wills in 1850 in Essex County, New Jersey. See "Patterns of Testation in the 19th Century: A Study of Essex County (New Jersey) Wills," *American Journal of Legal History* 8 (1964):34–53.

[66]Friedman estimates that 1850 wills in Essex accounted for 4.5 percent of the deaths in the county (ibid., p. 35).

[67]These provisions for personal property were very much part of the common law tradition and appear in nineteenth-century New York statutes. Intestate succession in personal property, however, is quite different from the provisions for dower, which attached to realty only. The husband was free to give away his personal property by gift or in a will without regard for his wife. These provisions applied to the surplus of personal property in his estate after his debts. Dower could not be defeated in this manner. See Pollack and Maitland, *History of English Law,* 2:405; *RSSNY, 1836,* 2:37.

not been sold or partitioned. Even direct cash bequests reflected a preference for sons over daughters. Henry Barker of White Plains gave four daughters $187 each and two sons $350 each. Jesse Cox gave his son two-thirds of his entire estate and his daughter one-third. Joseph Hyatt of Somers left most of his farm to one son, fifty acres to another son with whom he had quarreled, ten acres each and the use of the farmhouse to two unmarried daughters for as long as they remained single, and $25 each to two married daughters.[68]

The reluctance of testators to endow married daughters appears to have come not so much from a distrust of sons-in-law, who often served as executors with another relative, but rather from the assumption that their daughters were not in need. Although sons do better than daughters in general as legatees, concern for unmarried daughters who might remain unmarried is widespread. Some testators evinced a similar concern for sisters. Henry Disbrow stipulated that his daughters Sarah and Jane were to have a room in his house for as long as they remained single. Jesse Smith, a childless testator who left almost his entire estate to his wife, reserved a room in his house for his sister "as Long as she lives a single life."[69]

Drawing links between the common law, social realities, and patterns of testation is difficult. Concern for unmarried women, whose legal status in private law was comparable to that of men, probably reflects the limited job opportunities for women and the increasingly disadvantageous sex ratio. The preference for sons over daughters may reflect assumptions that testators shared with the common law about the inferior status of women, a realistic recognition of married women's common law disabilities, or both. Farmers endowed daughters with furniture, bedding, silver plate, and cash, but not with the family farm if there were sons. In this limited sampling few farm women received bequests of property large enough to permit them to bargain for an economically liberating antenuptial agreement. It should be pointed out, however, that many sons in this category seemed to bring little in the way of patrimony also.

68Probated Wills, Surrogate's Office, Westchester County Archives, White Plains, N.Y., 1825, Liber K, pp. 447–49, 457–58, 434–37.

69Ibid., pp. 388–93, 465–66.

Table 3. Number of trusts and life estates created by will for various categories of beneficiary, Westchester County, 1825

Beneficiary	Number
Parent	3
Children or grandchildren	7
Adult females (not testator's wife)	4
Testator's wife	13
Adult males	1

What is most revealing about the powerlessness of wives and widows is the number of trusts of life estates created for women in comparison with men (see Table 3). Discounting anomalies such as small trusts set up to take care of the family burial plot, trusts and life estates were created almost exclusively for the benefit of women and children.

Only one will in 1825 provided for a trust for adult males. The testator, John Burgess of Mount Pleasant, carefully explained that his two sons, Henry and Thomas, "would soon make off with theirs and do themselves no good."[70] No single testator reserved even rudimentary powers in a trust for an adult daughter, such as the power to make a will. Trusts were often used in young families when the testator was trying to support the whole family together. Often such bequests creating a trust to support the widow and children stopped when the widow died or remarried or when the youngest child came of age. Samuel Gedney of Mount Pleasant, for example, ordered all his property sold and "put out to interest on good landed security" for the support of his wife and children.[71] Of the thirteen life estates created for wives, five cut the wife off on her remarriage.

Numbers cannot tell the whole story. The prevalence of life estates for widows can in no way be construed as a lack of concern for them. Many husbands endowed their wives far beyond the measure of dower. Jesse Brady of New Castle gave his wife whatever furniture she desired plus the use of one-half of all his property. Elijah Tompkins of Greenburgh gave his wife, Deb-

[70] Ibid., pp. 442–45.
[71] Ibid., pp. 440–42.

orah, the use of all of his property, real and personal, during her lifetime; the property was to go to an adult son and four married daughters in equal shares at Deborah's death or remarriage. He gave his three executors, one of whom was Deborah, complete discretion to sell or keep the farm, and instructed Deborah to run the farm if it were not sold. With a mature family, Tompkins' major concern was his wife.[72]

Provisions in lieu of dower ranged anywhere from Tompkins' generous allotment to arrangements that appeared to be considerably less than dower. In the latter case, the wife always had the option to elect dower over the terms of the will. Two wills, both crudely drawn and signed with an *X*, left all property to the wife outright.

As a general rule, the more extensive the assets and the more complex the will, the more likely was the widow's trust. A wealthy testator such as Dominick Lynch, whose assets consisted of New York City realty, gave his wife, Jane, an annuity of $3,000 per year. He stated that it was his intention and desire to provide this annuity for his wife during her life beyond the possibility of accident, and he gave her the choice of receiving her annuity from existing rent or from the invested proceeds of property sold.[73]

Wills often mirrored dower. Farmers who interpreted dower quite literally as the "widow's thirds," a term that appears frequently in 1825 wills, often spelled out personal versions of dower down to the specific rooms of the house to be set aside. Silas Constant gave his wife "the priviledge of one lower room and one chamber and priviledge in the kitchen for her personal accommodations," plus one cow and the use of the pasture and one-third of the fruit from his orchards. He also returned to his wife the property she brought to the marriage, including her furniture and notes due her that remained uncollected. Similarly Joshua Purdy gave his wife her choice of the best room of the house (another common bequest) plus her furniture, three cows, and all of her clothing.[74]

The problem with dower as well as the trust and life estate was

[72]Ibid., pp. 454–56, 423–25.
[73]Ibid., pp. 427–30.
[74]Ibid., pp. 415–19, 407–8.

that it precluded women from having clear title and direct control over property. Whatever advantages the widow enjoyed, they usually did not include the capital with which to become an entrepreneur because she rarely owned anything in her own name. Like all generalizations, this one has significant exceptions. Three widows in 1825 bequeathed realty, and one of them left a sizable estate. Catherine Thomas of Harrison left her son George 375 or 380 acres, including mills, in Harrison, and divided $8,000 plus 4,500 acres in Tioga County among nine other legatees. Catherine owned both the family homestead and the family business.[75]

The 1850 wills do not reveal a significant shift in patterns of testation. If a single change is evident, it is in the growth of stocks and New York City realty as assets. More complex wills involving larger assets produced larger life estates for daughters and widows. Of the 62 testators whose wills were probated in 1850, 13, or 21 percent of all testators, were women. Six were single and six were widows; only one was a currently married woman.

The incidence of trusts and life estates for women had not changed greatly since 1825. Discounting one charitable trust, 28 of 40 provisions for trusts or life estates were for adult females. Twenty-one were designed exclusively for widows, a statistic that reinforces the 1825 pattern of the widow's economic protection and lack of control (see Table 4).

The pattern of leaving realty to sons and cash or other items of personal property to daughters continued. Benjamin Reynolds of North Salem, for example, left his seventy-acre farm in North Salem to his son, stipulating that he pay each of three daughters $700 and two grandchildren $100. Bequests of land to sons contingent on their caring for a mother or paying her a fixed yearly sum were common. Benjamin Taylor of Yonkers left his farm to two sons, charging them to pay their mother $70 per year. One married daughter, Elizabeth, wife of Jesse Underhill, received $1,000, and another married daughter, Sarah, wife of Lawrence Underhill, received $1,000 in trust. Taylor obviously trusted one son-in-law far more than the other, as he made Jesse Underhill an executor and left his wife a direct

[75]Ibid., pp. 370–73.

Table 4. Number of trusts and life estates created by will for various categories of beneficiary, Westchester County, 1850

Beneficiary	Number
Parent	1
Children and grandchildren	7
Adult females (not testator's wife)	7
Testator's wife	21
Adult males	4

bequest; Lawrence Underhill must have been another matter.[76]

Inequality between sons and daughters in the 1850 wills remained proportionately the same. One-half of all the wills do not fit the category; one-fourth of the testators favored sons over daughters; one-fourth made a conscious effort to divide property equally among sons and daughters. Equal divisions were common in families of six or more children. When divisions were unequal, testators often conscientiously treated sons equally while slighting daughters. James White of Yorktown left his son Barton his homestead plus a $3,000 legacy, which he noted would "make him equal to my son William." Two married daughters received $1,000 each and one $700.[77]

In wills that involved larger and more complex assets, widows were handsomely cared for. Thomas Rumsey of Eastchester, after leaving his wife $1,000, a New York City leasehold, and all of his Erie Railroad stock in lieu of dower, ordered his executors to purchase a residence for a price not to exceed $8,000 or to pay her interest on that amount so that she could rent a place for herself and their unmarried children. A codicil indicated that Rumsey purchased a house for his wife. Rumsey went further than most testators, however, in removing responsibilities from his wife, and he used his common law right to appoint a guardian over his children. While he charged his children to "obey, honour and revere their mother and seek her comfort and happiness in all they do," he told his executors that should his wife remarry or should they at any time deem it appropriate, they were to remove her from the guardianship of the children and

[76] Ibid., 1850, Liber 2, bk. 32, 217–19, 312–15.
[77] Ibid., pp. 336–40.

substitute themselves.[78] Rumsey's will is unusual in this regard, but in recognition of their common law rights, many testators specified that their wives were to be guardians of their children so as to avoid misunderstanding.

Life estates to married daughters with the principal going to their children were prevalent in 1850. There is little evidence, however, that testators considered the sex of living grandchildren when they made bequests. One exception was James Purdy of Greenburgh, who willed his widowed daughter, Margaret Van Tassel, the use of his land and house and the yearly interest from $400. He ordered that after her death the land was to go to her son, Alexander, and the $400 was to be divided between her two daughters. Purdy's concern for his widowed daughter was evident in his order to his executors to draw on the principal of the $400 if they considered it necessary for his daughter's welfare.[79]

Purdy's will is interesting because he left other cash bequests to married daughters, the two largest of which were $800 each, yet he left his widow, Elizabeth, only $450, a cow, two featherbeds, and the interest from $1,000 in lieu of dower. Perhaps he assumed she would live with one of her daughters, but her dower was bound to exceed his bequest. In such a case, it is unlikely that the widow elected dower, especially if she were on good terms with her children. Purdy's will, however, supports a general tendency found by Lawrence Friedman in 1850 wills in Essex County, New Jersey, and which can be seen in Westchester wills in both 1825 and 1850: a tendency to favor children to the detriment of the widow.

The 1850 wills do have a few examples of sizable direct bequests to wives. George Halsted of Peekskill left his wife two houses and lots in lieu of dower, his forty-six-acre farm to two unmarried daughters, and a forty-acre farm to his son, George. In an effort to make all his children equal, he charged his son to pay each sister $500. Halsted not only had sufficient assets to make his wife and children independent, but obviously trusted his wife by making her one of three executors. William Ketchum of Bedford left his wife all his personal property plus his thirty-

[78]Ibid., pp. 346–54.
[79]Ibid., pp. 370–75.

six-acre farm and made her one of his two executors.[80] Most testators, however, continued to create life estates for their wives, and wealthy testators provided handsome annuities for widows in lieu of dower as long as they remained unmarried.

The two samplings together suggest that testators expected daughters to be taken care of by husbands. Although some wills created trusts for a married daughter's separate use, none reserved any powers to her. Many testators revealed affection and trust for sons-in-law by naming them as executors. In applicable situations, half the testators made an effort to have children share equally in their patrimony, although daughters in this category were more likely to receive cash bequests than realty. The greatest concern of most testators, after the care of young children, was the plight of unmarried daughters. This was the one circumstance in which the daughter was most likely to receive the use of realty such as the family farm or even an outright gift of realty.

Widows fared poorly in having control over their husbands' assets except when assets were so limited as to make survival a problem. When assets were substantial, widows had the use of property, but not the control of it. The number and types of wills made by female testators suggests that women—single, married, or widowed—had little to leave. Yet since each period reveals a few wills made by wealthy widows, widowhood seems to have offered a few women great economic independence while the rest were limited to lifetime annuities or less.

The most striking feature in these wills is not the paucity of bequests to women, but the types of the bequests. The tendency of fathers and husbands, especially the latter, to deprive women of economic autonomy suggests a confluence between testators' assumptions about the roles of women and common law assumptions. This tendency diminishes the likelihood of independent antenuptial bargains and raises doubts about the prevalence of the rich and powerful widow. One has only to look at Edward Pessen's list of the wealthiest persons in New York City to appreciate women's economic disadvantages. Women comprise approximately 3 percent of his lists for both 1828 and 1845.[81]

[80]Ibid., pp. 388–95, 517–21.

[81]Edward Pessen, "The Wealthiest New Yorkers of the Jacksonian Era: A New List," *New-York Historical Society Quarterly* 54 (1970):145–72.

An overview of the options available to women beyond those offered by the common law demonstrates that equity offered the widest options to a woman in advance of marriage. It was the antenuptial contract that held the greatest potential for a woman. As a theoretical equal in private law, a single woman could bargain with her fiancé for favorable terms in her marriage contract. At this stage she could exert the leverage of property she held or anticipated to transform marriage into a contract that bore little resemblance to the stipulations of the common law. She could even use her youth as an asset at the bargaining table. By applying the "will theory" to marriage contracts, New York chancellors undercut the legal fiction of marital unity and created an alternative to the baron-feme model of marriage. Equity's willingness to recognize diverse individual interests in the making of marriage contracts blunted nineteenth-century emphasis on marriage as a sacrosanct, monolithic institution. In this context, Mary Beard properly held out equity as a historically ignored corrective to the married woman's legal status.

Beard exaggerated, however, the power and scope of equity. First of all, the wife's ability to create a separate estate over which she exerted full control was ambiguous in both English and American equity; in New York it was seriously undermined by the Revised Statutes. Second, the potential wife was disadvantaged at the bargaining table by her alternative to the bargain, the common law rules governing marital property. In other words, any bargain she struck would ease the disadvantages of the standard marriage contract. Third, we can speculate that few women among the marrying population had the assets or the legal sophistication to forge much of a bargain.

To be sure, the chancery record does not constitute a representative picture of the participants in marriage settlements. Undoubtedly some less affluent women enjoyed separate estates. Do-it-yourself law manuals of the period include the forms for setting apart specific items and small amounts of cash. But an agreement for a featherbed and $100 created a separate estate of exactly that amount. To participate effectively in the marriage bargain, one needed the assets with which to bargain.

Working-class women were unlikely candidates for separate estates. Savings accounts, designed originally for the working class, provide the best available evidence of spare assets. Samples of depositors in three New York City savings banks list the occupations of numerous single women with small deposits. No accounts appear in the names of married women.[82] The newly emerging group of female wage earners employed as textile operatives, factory workers, domestics, dressmakers, teachers, and retail clerks tended to be single.[83] The prime legal issue for working women who were married already was the earnings they brought to marriage. Earnings were subsumed under their husbands' names until 1860.

Women who lived on small farms, the most typical mode of existence in the state throughout this period, and women who were marrying small-scale businessmen do appear in the available records as participants in antenuptial contracts and as beneficiaries of separate estates. Yet it is reasonable to assume that these special arrangements eluded most of the population. Families who struggled for subsistence or divided limited assets among numerous children could not create the patrimony that was the basis for the marriage bargain. Wills, moreover, suggest that despite the availability of testamentary mechanisms to free the wife from some of her common law disabilities, few women enjoyed patrimony either large enough or free enough from restraints to liberate themselves significantly from their common law disabilities. As Mary Ryan has noted, women tended to receive consumptive property, the use of houses and small cash bequests, rather than land or capital.[84]

Equity offered couples who had spare assets at marriage the opportunity to protect a portion of those assets from some of the risks of the marketplace. Some astute middle-class couples were bound to take advantage of this option. The separate estate, however, best served landed and mercantile elites, the same classes for whom the first exceptions to common law marital rules had been carved out in English equity. New York marital alliances among elites in the first half of the nineteenth century

[82] Third Annual Report of the Trustees of the Greenwich Savings Bank for the Year 1835, *NYSD*, March 1, 1836, vol. 2, no. 69; Annual Report of Bowery Savings Bank, *NYAD*, January 25, 1841, vol. 4, no. 99; Annual Report of the Bank for Savings in the City of New York for 1847, *NYSD*, February 12, 1848, vol. 3, no. 78.

[83] Daniel Scott Smith, "Family Limitation, Sexual Control, and Domestic Feminism in Victorian America," in *Clio's Consciousness Raised*, ed. Hartman and Banner, p. 120.

[84] Ryan, *Womanhood in America*, p. 103.

were similar to English marriage patterns and prevailed despite the popular Protestant ideal of marriage as a free choice based on mutual affection irrespective of social and economic status. Mercenary alliances were common throughout the period and increased in the 1840s. Marriage was simply an integral part of the acquisitive scramble in Jacksonian New York. For those who participated in a formal marriage bargain, the cash nexus of the husband-wife relationship was carefully spelled out.[85]

For most antebellum women, however, marriage, even without an antenuptial contract, was life's most promising material enterprise. Surely affection for one's mate and the desire to raise a family were important considerations in the decision to marry, but the alternative to marriage was far from promising. If the common law disabilities of married women were restrictive, the economic opportunities open to unmarried women were even more restrictive. Marriage was a partnership that promised support by the husband in return for the lifelong services of the wife. Deriding the American habit of fixing a price on everything, Thomas Low Nichols claimed that the American husband unconsciously valued his wife in the federal currency.[86] Despite the mawkishly sentimental rhetoric that surrounded the institution of marriage, it seems more likely that the American wife unconsciously valued her husband in the federal currency.

Aside from the limited inroads of equity, little else in the legal, economic, or social framework of the society supported the idea of a married woman's economic independence and initiative. Caught in a web of common law restrictions, limited expectations, and pseudo-deferential protection, New York wives were discouraged from the era's most promising business, which was business. Because of the law, the entrepreneurial wives who ran urban boardinghouses, managed farms, and headed businesses functioned as their husbands' agents. All the adjectives used to color the enterprise of the Jacksonian era—ambitious, indi-

[85]On marital alliances, see Douglas T. Miller, *Jacksonian Aristocracy: Class and Democracy in New York, 1830-1860* (New York, 1967), pp. 20-21, 173; Edward Pessen, "The Marital Theory and Practice of the Antebellum Urban Elite," *New York History* 55 (1974):389-410; Paul Goodman, "Ethics and Enterprise: The Values of a Boston Elite, 1800-1860," *American Quarterly* 18 (1966):437-51.

[86]Thomas Low Nichols, *Forty Years of American Life,* 2 vols. (London, 1864), 1:403-4.

vidualistic, energetic, and venturesome—had little to do with the main enterprise of its women. For them the chief business remained marriage, a partnership that entailed the surrender of their legal personalities.

Furthermore, in legitimating exceptions to the common law, the judiciary did not set out to alter gender roles by altering the basic rules of marriage. Chancellors did not anticipate an irresistible expansion of married women's rights. Rather they were responding to the requirements of the wealthy in a traditional way that was well-suited to the needs of commercial capitalism. They were on solid ground, drawing on English equity precedents and long-recognized marriage customs.[87] In the anxious climate of Jacksonian America, however, it was apparent to some reformers that the time-honored precedents of equity gave special advantages to a small segment of the population. Inevitably, the reform of the marital property system became the object of a vigorous and protracted public debate.

[87]On the long tradition of marital alliances, see Jo Ann McNamara and Suzanne Wemple, "The Power of Women through the Family in Medieval Europe: 500–1100," in *Clio's Consciousness Raised,* ed. Hartman and Banner, p. 114.

CHAPTER 4

A Confluence of Interests: The Background for Reform

> Nor have the Americans ever supposed that one consequence of democratic principles is the subversion of marital power, or the confusion of the natural authorities in families. They hold that every association must have a head in order to accomplish its object and that the natural head of the conjugal association is man.
>
> —Alexis de Tocqueville

It took the state of New York almost twenty-five years to pass a moderately comprehensive married women's statute. The battle, which began in 1836 in a judiciary committee of the state assembly and ended in 1860 with the Earnings Act, was one of the few legislative issues before the Civil War to inject the debate over the appropriate roles for women into the maelstrom of American politics. Therefore the outlines of the debate and the underlying motives for the legislation are historically significant. Nowhere was the confrontation between democratic principles and the patriarchal family more distinct or its resolution more ambiguous.

When one considers the dichotomies associated with transforming the marital property system, the difficulties inherent in statutory reform become apparent. On the one hand, the existing marital property system reflected an essentially feudal typology of deference and authority which was a troublesome anachronism by the 1830s. The husband and wife, according to the prescriptive literature of the period, were affectionate companions or partners who functioned in two equally important but sex-segregated worlds, one the public arena of politics and material production, the other the private sphere of domesticity and reproduction. Surely domestic relations law, the place where these two worlds conjoined, needed some updating if only to recognize the wife's new domestic autonomy. On the other hand, by the 1830s some women were supplying the need for labor in textile mills, serving as teachers in the expanding common school system, and even assuming public roles as reformers. Not all women were huddled at the hearth. To wipe out all that was paternalistic in the old legal relationship of baron and feme was to destroy the legal foundation of the wife's economic dependence, one source of her relegation to the domestic sphere.

But if the law itself was one genuine cause of women's economic dependence—as suggested here—and not merely a reflection of it, why were legislatures willing to alter it at all? Why were male legislators willing to ameliorate the legal disabilities of people who could neither reject nor reelect them at the polls? A few legislators were ardent supporters of women's rights, but they were hardly numerous enough to constitute a majority. The balance of support had to be found elsewhere.

Reform of the marital property system was the result of a shifting and tenuous network of support emanating from efforts to deal with three problems: the instability of the antebellum economy, the inequities of the legal system, and what contemporaries consistently called the woman question. Proponents of a married women's bill included those who favored more lenient debtor laws, those who advocated more legislative and less judicial control of the legal system, and those who wanted some improvement in the legal status of women.

Support cannot be located in a single political party. Even at the height of the second national party system in 1840, some support for a married women's statute can be found among both Whigs and Democrats. As national political parties fragmented in the years after 1840, elements of support came from some Whigs, Barnburner and Hunker Democrats, Antirenters, Free Soilers, the Liberty party, and eventually Republicans. Certain advocates followed certain political lines. Leaders of the codification movement in the 1830s tended to be Jacksonian Democrats. Women's rights advocates of the 1840s tended to follow the political permutations of antislavery.[1] Most supporters of a mar-

[1]For the political course of abolition, see Richard H. Sewall, *Ballots for Freedom: Antislavery Politics in the United States, 1837–1860* (New York, 1976).

ried women's property bill who remained active politically through the 1850s could be found in the Republican party by 1860.

Nothing illustrates the three strands of support better than Thomas Herttell's opening bid for a married women's property bill in the New York Legislature. In the spring of 1836, Herttell, a sixty-five-year-old Democratic assemblyman from New York City, introduced a resolution for the appointment of a committee to report on married women's property rights in the state. He introduced a bill in the 1837 session and supported it with an impassioned speech that was printed in pamphlet form and widely circulated as a women's rights tract. Herttell anticipated the themes that were explored over the next twenty-five years.[2]

First Herttell advanced a practical economic argument in his speech, one likely to receive sympathetic attention amidst the mounting bankruptcies of 1837. Herttell had long been an advocate of debtor relief. Underscoring a trend of boom and bust in the American economy, he pointed to husbands who had subjected their wives' property to the contemporary "hazards and vicissitudes of trade and speculation." Fusing the problems of the national economy, which were beyond individual control, with the husband's financial ineptitude and moral degeneracy, he drew a portrait of the improvident husband engaged in high-risk speculation, wasting his wife's patrimony on ill-chosen investments. Debunking one popular stereotype of feminine extravagance, Herttell drew on another of masculine intemperance. More often than not, he insisted, it was the husband who depleted the wife's resources.[3]

[2]There is no record of Herttell's resolution in the index of the 1836 Assembly journal. An Assembly committee did report on amending the powers and trusts provisions of the Revised Statutes. See *JNYA,* February 27, 1836, p. 446. Herttell and innumerable contemporaries, however, cite 1836 as the first date of the resolution. On his 1837 bill, see ibid., January 4, 1837, p. 35; March 2, 1837, p. 740; Thomas Herttell, *Argument in the House of Assembly of the State of New York in the Session of 1837 in Support of the Bill to Restore to Married Women "The Right of Property" as Guaranteed by the Constitution of This State* (New York, 1839); *HWS*, 1:38, 67. Herttell's pamphlet was financed by a bequest made by his wife, Barbara Amelia Herttell, in her will.

[3]On debtors, see Herttell, *Remarks on the Law of Imprisonment for Debt Showing Its Unconstitutionality and Its Demoralizing Influence on the Community* (New York, 1823). For his interest in temperance, see Herttell, *An Exposé of the Causes of Intemperate Drinking and the Means by Which It May Be Obviated* (New York, 1820). On the economy, see Herttell, *Argument in the House of Assembly,* p. 70.

The real villain in this scene was the common law. Because of the husband's overwhelming powers, the wife's property could be "sunk in trade,—wasted in wild speculation,—squandered in extravagant and stylish living,—lost at the gaming table, or spent in riot, drunkenness, and other homogeneous dissipation." Immobilized by their contractual incapacities, wives in straitened circumstances were prevented from entering suitable businesses or trades and were unable to support either their children or their improvident husbands. The common law, argued Herttell, not only endangered the family in times of economic hardship, but also created an exclusively male economy that shut women out of callings for which they were especially suited. One found men retailing pins and needles, in the millinery business, and even in midwifery, while wives were relegated to the single calling of servant to the husband. A change in marital property laws, he concluded, would open appropriate segments of the economy to women, reduce pauperism, and thereby save the public considerable expense.[4]

The second strand running through Herttell's argument was a plea for the thorough modernization of the legal system. Herttell considered the fictions, anachronisms, and complexities of the common law appropriate only to "the dark ages" of "human vassalage."[5] As an advocate of codification, a Francophile, and an admirer of continental community-property systems, Herttell pointed to the stability of marriage in France, where the law, he asserted, recognized the wife's separate financial interests. He placed special emphasis on the current ambiguities in the married woman's trust and the new limitations created by the revisions of 1828. Codrafters of his 1837 bill, it should be noted, were John Spencer, one of the 1828 revisers, and John Savage, former chief justice of the state Supreme Court. In pointing up the gaps created in 1828, Herttell was demonstrating the urgent need to complete the task the revisers had begun.

His objections to the 1828 Revised Statutes were twofold: the revisions failed to provide for a trust in personal property and stripped wives of any control. Because the statutes failed to deal

[4]Herttell, *Argument in the House Assembly*, pp. 58–59, 70.
[5]Ibid., p. 79.

with personal property, he asserted, money, bonds, and notes appeared to be excluded from the married woman's trust. By prohibiting trusts that gave considerable powers to the beneficiary, they made married women the dependents of trustees. Thus married women in a modern commercial society were relegated to being beneficiaries of caretaker trusts in realty. Furthermore, he argued, because the revisions were a reduction of what equity had formerly allowed to married women, they created great confusion within the legal profession.[6]

Herttell did not favor a return to a pre-1828 state of affairs, nor was he opposed to the general direction of the revisions; he simply wanted them to be more complete. Nevertheless, he was appealing to the more conservative members of the Legislature who favored the old married woman's trust by underscoring the problems of the revisions. So ambiguous had the law become, he claimed, that "a *trust* and *power created before marriage* . . . is seldom hazarded and never attempted by any well informed and discreet parent." Herttell attempted to garner legislative support by reducing the scope of his 1837 bill and concentrating on the gaps created by the 1828 revisions. He changed the title of his original bill from "An Act for the Protection and Preservation of the Rights and Property of Married Women . . ." to "An Act to Amend the Revised Statutes Relative to Uses, Trusts, and Powers. . . ."[7]

Emphasis on the vicissitudes of the economy and on the problems of the married woman's trust was a bid for support. The vital core of Herttell's argument, however, consisted in a radical appeal to the natural rights of women. Born in 1772, Herttell was a child of the American Revolution and thoroughly at home in its logic and rhetoric, which he applied with gusto. Appeals to natural rights, of course, were neither inherently conservative nor radical; they were rights that particular adherents believed one group or another in the society ought to have and then labeled as natural and God-given.[8] The right to hold property

[6]Ibid., pp. 12–14.

[7]Ibid., p. 22; *JNYA,* April 21, 1837, p. 961.

[8]Roscoe Pound, for example, contrasts natural rights in a society organized on the lines of kinship with natural rights in a society organized on the lines of competitive self-assertion. See *Introduction to the Philosophy of Law,* pp. 15–16.

and to enjoy its correlative political powers, for example, had been used to defend selective suffrage at the expense of the propertyless at the New York Constitutional Convention of 1821. Applied to antebellum wives, however, the natural right to hold property held radical implications.

Herttell argued that the common law deprived wives of their inalienable, natural right to property. Since wives held property before marriage, and marriage was itself an inalienable right, how could the state deprive a woman of rights she had held when she was single? "Married women," he proclaimed, "equally with males and unmarried females, possess the right of *life, liberty,* and *PROPERTY* and are equally entitled to be protected in all three." Any deprivation of the right of property was a violation of the principle of equal rights and due process, the very "objects of free government," and was therefore incompatible with the constitution of the state of New York and the Bill of Rights. The disfranchisement of women, he noted, was a similar violation of their civil liberties and a symptom of their total exclusion from the political process. Because women were compelled to obey laws made by men, they were deprived of property, excluded from voting, and stripped of full citizenship. Women, married and unmarried, he insisted, were entitled to vote and to hold property as citizens of the state and the nation.

Although Herttell cherished the concept of women's suffrage, he concentrated on the more immediate goal of improving the wife's legal status. The wife of the common law, he pointed out, was a species of property herself. In an analogy common among feminist-abolitionists, Herttell compared the legal status of a married woman to that of a slave. The wife of an "ill tempered and unprincipled husband," he maintained, "is constrained by law to be the servant and slave of [her] legal 'lord and master,' " and her condition "need not be envied by any decent negro-wench slave in Virginia or any other Christian country." Only her husband's inability to sell her separated her from unqualified slavery.

Herttell concluded with an exhortation for the spirit of innovation to subdue "superstitious mummery." With the soaring enthusiasm of the antebellum reformer, he urged fellow legislators to consider what the printing press had done for knowledge, steam power for transportation, and the doctrine of equal rights for the American Revolution. Was it not time to bring the women of New York into the modern age?[9]

Herttell's argument implicitly rejected the validity of women's separate sphere and suggested instead that such a notion was a form of economic and political exploitation. By insisting that the property rights of married women were natural, and by ignoring the distinctions between private, relative rights and natural, inalienable rights which such Enlightenment jurists as Blackstone had scrupulously maintained, he extended the whole concept of the rights of man to woman. He was challenging contemporary assumptions about implied distinctions of sex in the Constitution as well as in domestic relations law. Suffrage, however, was not imminent, and what probably sparked more immediate fear in the hearts of the legislators he addressed was his implicit extension of the ethos of competitive self-assertion to the family itself, including wives and daughters. Nevertheless, although these arguments had been voiced in the past, they acquired legitimacy in the hands of this respected legislator and jurist because they were attached to a specific legislative proposal. In this case the context was more important than the text. His bill never emerged from the Judiciary Committee, but the public debate had begun.

Almost simultaneously, beginning in June 1837, Sarah Grimké's *Letters on the Equality of the Sexes,* containing even harsher indictments of the common law status of married women, began to appear in the *New England Spectator.*[10] In New York, however, organized women's support for Herttell's bill appears to have been limited to one petition with six signatures collected by Ernestine Rose, and one other petition with meager support from Utica. Rose, a recently arrived Polish-Jewish immigrant who immediately became involved in Herttell's cause, later became one of the specialists on women's legal status for the women's movement. Reminiscing about the appalling lack of female support for Herttell's early bills, feminist leaders assessed

[9]Herttell, *Argument in the House of Assembly,* pp. 22, 23, 40, 44, 76.

[10]Fifteen in all, these letters were published as *Letters on the Equality of the Sexes and the Condition of Women* (Boston, 1838).

it as symptomatic of "the hopeless apathy and ignorance of the women as to their own rights."[11]

The assessment was not completely accurate. Women's support appeared in a more moderate form than Herttell's. It could be found, for example, in the impeccably respectable columns of *Godey's Lady's Book,* where Sarah Hale advocated passage of the 1837 bill in her "Editor's Table." Drawing on the analogy between slavery and marriage, Hale declared that the common law "degrades the woman to the condition of a slave and this degradation impairs her influence not only with her husband, but with her children." By stressing impairment of what *Godey's* celebrated as the innately superior moral influence of the wife, Hale was able to support married women's property rights in the name of woman's maternal, "self-sacrificing spirit."[12] Since *Godey's* shunned controversial issues as a matter of editorial policy, Hale's editorial suggests a broad awareness of and dissatisfaction with married women's disabilities.

The seeds of public and legislative acceptance of reform of the common law marital prototype had been taking root in the 1820s and 1830s. They were nourished by a pervasive sense of embarrassment over the common law, which smacked of feudal tenures and offended Romantic and democratic sensibilities. Caleb Cushing reflected this uneasiness in a *North American Review* article in which he claimed that "a spirit destitute of manliness and gallantry" permeated the law of husband and wife. Discussions of women and their property, however, drew attention to the disfranchisement of single women, a class of property owners to which married women would now be added. Cushing carefully outlined the limits reform should take by expressing his strong aversion to women's suffrage. "The constitution of Nature," he insisted, had settled the question of suffrage. He was not interested in plunging women into the political process or in subverting established gender roles. "It is not the institu-

[11] *HWS,* 1:38, 99; Yuri Suhl, *Ernestine L. Rose and the Battle for Human Rights* (New York, 1959), p. 55.

[12] "Editor's Table," *Godey's Lady's Book* 14 (May 1837):212–14. For Hale's support of a married woman's right to own a savings account in her own name, see *Godey's Lady's Book* 34 (May 1847):269. Barbara Berg documents similar support in the *Advocate of Moral Reform.* See *The Remembered Gate: Origins of American Feminism* (New York, 1978), p. 209.

tions of an Amazonian republic," he assured his readers, "that we seek to commend."[13]

Mounting pressure for improvement in the legal status of women in the 1830s was part of the woman question, a broad-based effort that simultaneously defined and questioned the place of women in Jacksonian America. The woman question was directly linked to the extension of suffrage. Legal inequities in the wife's status at common law loomed larger as men acquired new political rights and as the corresponding political status of women relative to men declined. Special awareness of the declining political status of white upper- and middle-class women intensified as a postrevolutionary egalitarian ideology replaced older hierarchical concepts of the colonial political order. With the abolition of property requirements for white male suffrage in most states—in 1826 in New York—support for reform of marital property laws was in some ways a compensatory effort to make up for the American woman's relative decline in political position.

Discussion of married women's property rights also coalesced with a shift in the economic position of antebellum women. To be sure, women's participation in household manufactures continued to be important, and some women benefited via their husbands from industrialization and commercial expansion, but generally the productive functions of women in the economy were diminishing. As Gerda Lerner has pointed out, with the gradual decrease in household manufactures and self-sufficient farms, employment opportunities for women increasingly were limited to low-status, low-pay work. As class distinctions hardened, the two extremes of Lerner's description, the genteel, dependent lady and the hard-working mill girl, became metaphors for the narrowing choices available to women.[14]

The shift in women's functions in the economy was reflected

[13]Caleb Cushing, "The Legal Condition of Women," *North American Review* 26 (April 1828):316–19. Other articles that advocated codification in this journal in the 1820s were C. S. Daveis, "Common Law Jurisdiction," 21 (July 1825):104–41; Henry D. Sedgwick, "Correspondence on the History of the Law," 23 (July 1826):197–201; W. H. Gardiner, "Revision of the Laws of New York," 24 (January 1827):194–200. See also Miller, *Life of the Mind*, p. 169, and Bloomfield, *American Lawyers*, p. 359.

[14]Lerner, "Lady and the Mill Girl."

in contemporary concerns about widowhood. In 1840, for example, the New York Legislature attempted to pass a bill to enlarge the widow's share in the real estate of men who died intestate.[15] The antebellum widow was viewed as an object of pity, an unsupported woman, and a potential drain on the resources of the community.[16] Some antebellum widows, of course, ran family farms and businesses, especially if they had worked at them while their husbands were living, but awareness of the economic hazards for women in an increasingly complex and specialized economy contributed to a demand for laws that would at least insulate the property a wife brought to marriage.

The woman question was there, emerging from time to time in national periodicals and public discourses. It was a source of tension and an object of scrutiny, but it was not yet a distinct catalyst for statutory reform. Not until the mid-1840s and after, when women organized and demanded improvement in their legal status in conjunction with demands for suffrage, was there any real woman-oriented pressure placed on the legislative process. Precipitous dips in the economy were another matter. The movement against imprisonment for debt and for homestead laws—laws that would exempt some portion of the debtor's assets from creditors—was integrally related to the drive for a married women's statute. It is worth noting that the two major statutes of 1848 and 1860 followed the depressions of 1839–43 and 1857. Married women's property laws, like laws easing bankruptcy, carried the possibility of saving some of the family's assets.

Because law increasingly was viewed as an instrument of economic policy, the profound economic changes taking place in New York were bound to be reflected in the legal system. Most New Yorkers remained farmers in the three decades before the Civil War; but there was a steady movement away from farming to industry and commerce. Farmers themselves became busi-

[15] *JNYA,* January 31, 1840, p. 256.

[16] Douglas, *Feminization of American Culture,* p. 57; W. Elliot Brownlee and Mary M. Brownlee, *Women in the American Economy: A Documentary History, 1675–1929* (New Haven, 1976), pp. 11–12, 17. The Brownlees cite the 1850s as the point at which employment opportunities for women were smallest; after the Civil War, the employment picture gradually improved.

nessmen, turning away from self-subsistence to cash crops. The completion of the Erie Canal, which made Buffalo the entrepôt of the Great Lakes and New York City the national center of shipping and auctioneering, precipitated an unprecedented boom in land speculation.[17] If New York's boom was great, so was its bust. Speculation in realty was rampant in the sparsely settled northern and western parts of the state as well as in New York and other cities. In an 1836 speech, Governor William L. Marcy noted that "vacant lands in and about our several cities and villages, have risen in many instances several hundred per-cent."[18] Unprecedented inflation between 1832 and 1837 and the panics of 1837 and 1839 resulted in financial disaster for the wage earner, whose wages failed to keep up with inflation, and for the over-extended speculator, who operated in an era marked by chronic shortage of capital. Insolvency became a common experience.

Understandably attitudes toward insolvency assumed new configurations. Although women's periodicals and temperance literature depicted the insolvent as morally degenerate and usually alcoholic, there was also a growing tendency to view insolvency as beyond a person's control. John Anthon expressed support of the enterprising bankrupt in a short guide for law students. The merchant in the economy, he explained, was exposed to "sudden and overwhelming reverses." Therefore laws to aid the insolvent were favored wherever commerce flourished so that the trader's "energies and enterprise may be again brought into action."[19]

As testimony to New York's speculative preeminence, over one-third of the indebtedness liquidated by the short-lived federal bankruptcy act of 1841 belonged to New Yorkers. *Hunt's Merchants' Magazine* estimated that $444 million was liquidated, of which $172 million came from the state of New York and

[17]George Rogers Taylor, *The Transportation Revolution, 1815–1860* (New York, 1951), pp. 32–37, 234–49, 338–45; David Ellis, *A Short History of New York* (Ithaca, N.Y., 1957), pp. 244–79; Douglas C. North, *The Economic Growth of the United States, 1790–1860* (New York, 1966), pp. 73–74, 169.

[18]*JNYA,* January 5, 1836, p. 22.

[19]John Anthon, *The Law Student, or Guides to the Study of the Law in Its Principles* (New York, 1850), p. 73.

$120 million from the Southern District (New York City) alone. Despite some abuses, *Hunt's* found that the law enabled "an army" of unfortunate but honest debtors to begin again.[20]

The federal courts applied the statute liberally on behalf of the wives of New York bankrupts. Emmeline Snow, who had inherited realty in Dutchess County before marriage, had sold it and taken a note for the proceeds, and had then had a new note issued in her husband's name at the time of her marriage; a judge in the Southern District decided that she was still the owner of the note, and thus placed it beyond the reach of her bankrupt husband's creditors. Obviously the decision was as advantageous to the husband as to the wife, but the court in its decision focused tenderly on the wife's legacy, even attaching sentimental significance to it. It was only natural, claimed the court, that "it should be cherished by her as a portion of her mother's estate without regard to the circumstances of her husband."[21]

The connections between married women's property rights and debtor-creditor laws become clearer on examination of legislative activity in 1840 and 1841. In response to the panic of 1837 and the subsequent depression, New York passed its own debtor-exemption laws prohibiting imprisonment for debt and exempting household furniture, clothing, foodstuffs, and the tools of one's trade. It also passed a statute giving interest to married women in lands sold under judgment.[22]

What is particularly revealing is the response of the 1841 Senate Juciciary Committee, which reported favorably on enlarging debtors' exemptions. In dealing with debtor-creditor relations, the committee focused on the plight of the bankrupt's wife. Here, as in Herttell's speech, the villian was the common law; it was the common law that was responsible for stripping the wife of her own property and then preventing her from acquiring more. The chairman of the committee pointed out that although

[20]An Act to Establish a Uniform System of Bankruptcy, August 19, 1841, 5 Stats. 440; "Laws Relative to Debtor and Creditor: New York," *Hunt's Merchants' Magazine* 4 (January 1841):74.

[21]"In the Matter of the Petition of George W. Snow and Emmeline, His Wife," *New York Legal Observer* 1 (February 1843):264–66. For a similar decision involving the wife's jewelry, see "In the Matter of Edward H. Ludlow, a Bankrupt," *New York Legal Observer* 1 (March 1843):322.

[22]*LNY, 1840,* chaps. 165, 177, 377 (an amendment to an 1831 law), 379.

the couple's dwelling was often purchased with money obtained by the wife's labor or from her "scanty endowment upon marriage," all was lost because of the husband's marital rights. The effects of this "fatal merging of her fortunes and those of her children in that of her husband" might be counteracted, the report suggested, by protecting household assets more liberally.[23]

The Senate report dramatizes how neatly the interests of debtors and married women meshed. The committee did not plead for expansion of the wife's powers; rather it urged the better insulation of family assets from creditors in order to protect the wife's domestic role just as it was. "Society is largely indebted," pointed out the committee, "to the quiet and unostentatious, yet powerful and pervading influence of virtuous wives and mothers in upholding the domestic relations, preserving the social order, and promoting the general prosperity."[24]

Similarly, labor literature of the period represented the working wife as being deprived of her special role in the social order as a result of her husband's wage slavery. Because men were poorly paid and deprived of free land—two favorite themes of the *Workingman's Advocate*—their wives were prevented from being "happy and independent mistresses of [their] own households" and forced instead into the labor market. Women, in other words, were the secondary victims of the economic dislocations of men.[25]

Much of the early support for a married women's statute focused on the economic dislocations of men; considerations of women were often secondary. Just as debtor exemption laws for

[23]"Report of the Committee on the Judiciary, on Several Petitions for a Law to Extend the Exemption of Personal Property from Sale on Execution or Distress for Rent," *NYSD,* April 22, 1841, vol. 3, no. 81, pp. 1–3.

[24]Ibid., pp. 3–4.

[25]"To the Working Women of New York," *Workingman's Advocate,* March 15, 1845, p. 2. Other articles in this journal that discuss working wives are "Female Labor," April 6, 1844, p. 2; "The Rights of Women," January 20, 1836, p. 2; and "View of Frances Wright D'Arusmont," March 8, 1845, p. 4. Wright found marriage laws an almost irrelevant object of reform, "as erroneous and as utterly worthless as all the rest of our legal system." Nevertheless, she was later represented by Timothy Walker, a leading Ohio advocate of married women's property rights, in a suit to recover her property from her former husband. See "Frances Wright D'Arusmont v. William Phiquepal D'Arusmont," *Western Law Journal* 8 (September 1851):548–62.

household items and tools eased the lot of farmers, artisans, and some wage earners and petty traders, so might a statute separating the wife's property from that of the husband have a similar effect. Furthermore, as the scale and complexity of the marketplace increased, and as the debtor-creditor relationship became more bureaucratic and less personalized, the legal formalization of that relationship was desirable for creditors as well as debtors. A married women's property statute could clarify and formalize debtor-creditor relations. Men defaulted and could not pay their debts. Putting them in prison or taking away their last stick of furniture was not a satisfactory solution. A statute could delineate precisely what was within the creditor's reach. Instead of the mass of conflicting equitable precedents that existed by the 1830s, a statute could apprise creditors of uniform rules governing marital property.[26]

Added to discussions of the woman question and the crises and dislocations caused by the economy was the third strand of support in the drive for a married women's property statute—the movement for codification and legal reform. The notion that legislatures should be the sole source of legal change and that law should be spelled out comprehensively in written form—what Gordon Wood has called a modern conception of statute law—emerged as a direct result of the Revolution. Committed to consent as the basis for law and fearful of the uncertainties of judicial discretion, Americans carried the promise of codification from the Revolution into the nineteenth century.[27] Antebellum reformers both in and out of the legal profession continued to raise the same basic questions about the relative functions of the legislature and the judiciary in the lawmaking process.

The movement for codification and legal reform dovetailed with the cause of married women's property rights in three specific ways. First, the literature for codification was an influential source of criticism of the common law. Second, the early attempt New York made to codify its statutes in 1828 created gaps in the married woman's trust, spurring further debate and legislation. Third, the campaign for legal reform in New York centered on the faulty administration of equity in the chancery courts and reflected strong disapproval of the principal legal tribunal re-

[26]Coleman, *Debtors and Creditors,* pp. 265–68.
[27]Wood, *Creation of the American Republic,* pp. 302–5.

sponsible for easing and adjudicating the disabilities the common law imposed on married women. Three New Yorkers were the leading lights of the codification movement. They were William Sampson (1764–1836), an Irishman transplanted to New York City and responsible for early agitation against the common law; Edward Livingston (also 1764–1836), a native New Yorker who moved to Louisiana and authored that state's code of civil procedure; and David Dudley Field (1805–94), who labored from the late 1830s through much of the century for a comprehensive New York code.[28]

The literature of codification, puncturing the pomp of English legal forms, was a veritable fountain of resentment against the feudal vestiges of the common law. Jurists who were ardent supporters of married women's property rights, such as Thomas Herttell and Ohioan Timothy Walker, tended to advocate some form of codification. Inasmuch as one goal of the codification movement was to discourage archaic fictions and complex and expensive legal forms, the legal fiction of marital unity and the devices used to circumvent it were logical objects of codifiers' attacks. In fact, one legal historian has argued that the codification movement was the primary cause of the married women's acts and contributed to the development of antebellum feminism.[29]

Not all proponents of codification, however, advocated the amelioration of married women's common law disabilities. Jeremy Bentham, for example, whose pure utilitarianism was the philosophical catalyst for the American codification movement, supported the principle of male legal dominion in marriage on the basis of the male's physical superiority. Man is stronger, he averred. "In his hands power sustains itself." Those who "from some vague notion of justice and generosity would bestow upon females an absolute equality," he warned, "would only spread a dangerous snare for them."[30]

Nevertheless, Bentham's irreverent critiques of Blackstone

[28] *DAB*, vol. 8, pt. 2, p. 321; vol. 6, pt. 1, pp. 309–12; vol. 3, pt. 2, pp. 360–62; Pound, *Formative Era*, p. 5.

[29] Rabkin, "Origins of Law Reform," pp. 751–53.

[30] Cited in Johnston, "Sex and Property," p. 1061. For Bentham's influence on New York codification, see Charles Stevenson, "Influence of Bentham and Humphreys on the New York Property Legislation of 1828," *American Journal of Legal History* (1957) 1:155–69; Maurice Lang, *Codification in the British Empire and America* (Amsterdam, 1924), pp. 31–34.

and the common law, to which he devoted much of his formidable ability, formed an important component in the drive for a married women's statute. Between 1811 and 1817 Bentham sent a series of letters variously addressed to President Madison, American governors, and the citizens of the United States, all deriding the common law and urging a complete code. "The next time you hear a lawyer trumpeting forth his *Common Law,* call upon him to produce a *Common Law,*" mocked Bentham in an 1817 letter to Americans. "Let him look for it 'till doomsday,—no such object will he find."[31]

Bentham's savage attacks on the common law were enthusiastically repeated by American codifiers. From the 1820s on, there was a strong conviction that the common law was wanting and inappropriate and that a new body of indigenous American law fashioned by legislators with the advice of skilled jurists was necessary. As an answer to those who celebrated the flexibility of the common law and feared the rigidity of statute law, David Dudley Field followed Bentham's line of reasoning, arguing that a flexible rule was not a rule at all. If laws needed change, asserted Field, then the Legislature was the proper judge of the time and manner of the change.[32]

Modernization became the favored word in regard to codification. William Sampson, who was personally responsible for much of the early agitation on behalf of codification in New York, reasoned that Americans had betrayed the imperatives of the Revolution by clinging to the old English common law. He lamented the fate of young law students who began their studies "with phrases strange to the ears of freedom," and paid "constrained devotion to ideas which their fathers have levelled in the dust."[33] Arguing in a similar vein, David Dudley Field proclaimed that the language of the common law was ponderous and redundant, while the language of American law ought to be

[31]"Jeremy Bentham to the Citizens of the United States, August, 1817," in *Codification of the Common Law: Letter of Jeremy Bentham and the Report of Judges Story, Metcalf and Others,* ed. David Dudley Field (New York, 1882), p. 4; Lang, *Codification,* p. 33.

[32]David Dudley Field, *Legal Reform: An Address to the Graduating Class of the Law School of the University of Albany* (Albany, N.Y., 1855), pp. 28–29.

[33]William Sampson, "An Anniversary Discourse Delivered before the Historical Society of New York on Saturday, December 6, 1823," in *The Legal Mind in America,* ed. Perry Miller (New York, 1962), p. 22.

simple and "undefiled." The common law, he insisted, was "an artificial system of procedure conceived in the midnight of the dark ages, established in those scholastic times when chancellors were ecclesiastics, and logic was taught by monks."[34]

By the 1830s, however, the codification movement was losing some of its ideological contours. Codification was becoming a complex technical problem for sophisticated professionals. At the same time, it moved toward a compromise between Bentham's unqualified rejection and Kent's staunch acceptance of the common law tradition. Kent's monumental *Commentaries,* the first volume of which was published in 1826, had served as a defense of the common law tradition against codifiers' attacks. But as the fiery radicalism of a William Sampson gave way to the polished professionalism of a David Dudley Field, the intensity of the 1820s battle gradually moderated. The dreaded word "codification" gave way to "revision," and even such judicial conservatives as Story and Kent admitted the need for some updating of the law.[35] Typical of the compromise effected was Theodore Sedgwick's assertion that codification was "a great superstructure" built on the stable foundations of the common law.[36]

By the 1840s, when the New York Legislature wrestled with some of the problems of legal reform, the report Arphaxed Loomis delivered for the Assembly Judiciary Committee marked the nature of the compromise already achieved. The Loomis committee urged revision of the common law while it simultaneously maintained the validity of common law principles. It advocated the cautious reshaping of existing materials. The purpose of legislation, Loomis said, was to restrict customary or common law usages "whenever they come in conflict with the interests of society," but also "to cherish all those time has nurtured, and which are found well adapted to the wants and conditions of men." The members of the committee, Loomis insisted, were too conscious of the "immense benefits derived from these usages,

[34]Field, *Legal Reform,* pp. 20, 23.

[35]Bloomfield, *American Lawyers,* pp. 86–87; Horwitz, *Transformation of American Law,* p. 257; Stevenson, "Influence of Bentham," p. 164.

[36]Theodore Sedgwick, "A Treatise on the Rules Which Govern the Interpretation and Application of Statutory and Constitutional Law," in *Legal Mind in America,* ed. Miller, pp. 297–306.

known as the common law, to seek to abrogate them, and they appreciate the difficulty of making the important changes which the present condition of society seems to demand, and of adapting them to existing laws."[37]

The moderating direction taken by the codification movement foreshadowed the extent to which American law would remain in large measure within the common law tradition, and by inference the extent to which the law of husband and wife would elude substantial change. Loomis, it should be noted, voted against the insertion of a married women's clause in the 1846 state constitution. Yet codification in New York, even in its more moderate form, generally created a climate favorable to the passage of the married women's statutes and spurred interest in existing statutes, especially the 1828 revisions.

The revisions were, in fact, the first steps in codification. New York had been collecting its statutes in various revisions since 1683, but these were updated collections of statute law and nothing more. Thus the revisions of 1789, 1801, and 1813 were merely compilations of existing law. In accordance with the provisions of the 1821 constitution, the Legislature of 1824 appointed three commissioners, Erastus Root, James Kent, and Benjamin F. Butler, to assemble once again a new compilation. Significantly, Kent declined to serve unless he were named the sole reviser, and John Duer was appointed by Governor Joseph C. Yates to replace him. Butler, a member of the Albany Regency, law partner to Martin Van Buren, and later Jackson's attorney general, and Duer, a Whig who later became a justice of the Superior Court, decided on a more complete revision, the object of which was to rearrange the law in a more "scientific" manner. They sent their plan to the Legislature and received approval in April 1825. Root wanted no part of codification, however, and he resigned. Henry Wheaton, who replaced him, resigned in 1827 to enter the Foreign Service and was replaced by John C. Spencer. Thus the final changes were made by Duer, Butler, and Spencer. The revision was accepted by the Legislature after a few amendments in December 1828.[38]

[37]"Report in Part of the Committee on the Judiciary in Relation to the Administration of Justice," *NYAD,* March 2, 1842, vol. 5, no. 81, p. 2.

[38]William Allen Butler, *The Revision of the Statutes of the State of New York and the Revisers: An Address Delivered before the Association of the Bar of the City of New York*

As the revisers themselves stated, their purpose was to "sweep away an immense mass of useless refinements and distinctions" and to relieve the law of real property of its "abstruseness and uncertainty." More important, they wanted to ensure that "means of alienation be rendered far more simple and less expensive," and that litigation be reduced.[39] In their sweep, however, they reconstructed the law of uses and trusts and created the ambiguities with which the chancery courts wrestled. Since John Spencer helped to draft Herttell's statute, it is possible that the revisers anticipated a married women's statute or that they inadvertently created a situation in which the full range of options established by the chancery courts was impaired temporarily.

Scrutiny of the New York chancery courts was the third facet of the movement toward legal reform that contributed support, at least indirectly, to a married women's act. Some bitterness toward the chancery court, with its separate procedures and ornate pleadings, existed anyway. Resentment only grew with chancery's inability to handle its ever-increasing load. In addition to inefficiency and delays, critics pinpointed an extraordinary concentration of power in the hands of the chancellor. It was not difficult to tar some jurisdictions with the brush of elitism. In the famous First District, Hones, Clarksons, Anthons, De Peysters, Beekmans, Livingstons, Kips, Lorillards, Stuyvesants, Van Cortlandts, and De Witts—names synonymous with New York's landed and commercial wealth—sued one another, settled with one another, represented one another, and in the case of the De Peysters, administered equity for one another. Such an array of substantial New York families among the participants and litigants of the court substantiated assertions that equity in general and the wife's separate estate in particular were designed to serve the rich and wellborn.

Charges of elitism and allusions to a conspiracy of wealth were common among the Jacksonians, but they were applied to the chancery courts of the state with some validity. Outrageously

(New York, 1889), pp. 5–9, 39–40. For one of the earliest attempts to improve the legal status of wives after the 1828 revisions, see the proposal that justices of the peace be enabled to "divest habitual drunkards" who temporarily abandoned their families of their property, in *NYAD,* February 23, 1830, vol. 3, no. 214.

[39] *RSSNY, 1836,* 3:584.

high court costs, unwieldy procedures, and unrelenting delays were becoming a serious public concern. The inefficiency of chancery occupied New York politicians from the 1830s until the demise of the court in 1847. In an 1837 speech, Governor Marcy referred to protracted delays and increased business in that jurisdiction and urged a multiplication of chancellors.[40] In 1840 Governor William H. Seward urged an abridgment of the power and patronage of the chancellor by dividing his jurisdiction among three chancellors in order to ameliorate "vexatious delay and intolerable expense." Forms of pleading, said Seward, were "prolix, dilatory, and evasive," and the public might be better served by simpler forms in the common law courts.[41] "That serious complaints have for several years existed in respect to the extended powers of the Court of Chancery" there can be no doubt, said the Judiciary Committee.[42] An average suit in chancery, asserted one writer, cost 15 to 20 percent of the sum recovered and lasted five years.[43]

This criticism suggests not only that chancery was diminishing as a viable appellate court, but also that the legal status of wives, who automatically came within its jurisdiction as legal incompetents, was bound to be an integral concern of those who sought to remedy the inequities of the common law. Furthermore, since to some extent the public clamor was an attack on the bar, the movement for legal reform and for married women's property rights was led by members of the bar. While many attorneys responded as a professional elite who were attempting to hold the line against the illiterate mob, others spearheaded reform as a pragmatic response, a professional commitment, or both.[44] It

[40]"Governor's Address," *JNYA,* January 3, 1837, pp. 11–12.

[41]"Governor's Address," *JNYA,* January 7, 1840, p. 17.

[42]"Further Report of the Committee on the Judiciary," *NYAD,* March 2, 1842, vol. 5, no. 1, pp. 1–2.

[43]"Constitutional Reform," *USMDR* 13 (December 1843):570.

[44]For a typical defense of the lawyer against the mob, see James Jackson, "Law and Lawyers: Is the Profession of the Advocate Consistent with Perfect Integrity?," *Knickerbrocker Magazine* 18 (November 1846):378–83. For attacks on lawyers, see "Bar Associations," *New Yorker* 5 (September 1838):99; "The Abuses of the Law Courts," *USMDR* 21 (October 1847):305–11; and "The Legerdemain of Lawcraft," *USMDR* 23 (August 1848):134–48. For a retrospective view underscoring the high costs of recourse to the chancery courts, see John Worth Edmonds, "Law Reform," *Western Law Journal* 6 (October 1848); on the concentration of power in chancery, see "New Constitution of New York," *Western Law Journal* 4 (May 1847):374.

behooved members of the bar to do all in their power to improve their public image by assuming leadership of the movement for legal reform and to direct the course of that reform.

Like most state legislatures, New York's had its share of attorneys. In 1846, for example, over one-fourth of assemblymen listed themselves officially as attorneys.[45] Lawyer-legislators worked to defend their profession with considerable elan while they simultaneously came to terms with its deficiencies.[46] It was to lawyer-legislators, most of whom were familiar with the technicalities of the married woman's legal status, that the task of reform went. Reform-minded lawyers, aware of the ambiguities of the Revised Statutes, formed a crucial core of support for a married women's statute. It was just such a group from the New York City bar that petitioned the Legislature in 1847 for comprehensive legal reform. Among the petitioners were the staunchest supporters of married women's property rights: Elisha Hurlbut, an active and articulate feminist; Robert Morris, former mayor of the city, who had supported a married women's clause in the constitution of 1846; Theodore Sedgwick, Jr., a prominent Barnburner Democrat, brother of Catherine Maria Sedgwick, and columnist for William Leggett's *New York Evening Post;* and David Dudley Field, an active proponent of a married women's statute and the guiding force behind the New York codification movement.[47]

By the 1840s, however, the thrust of codification was procedural rather than substantive. Lawyer-reformers did not bring fresh ideas to the marital equation, but only new ways of implementing what was at hand. Unlike Thomas Herttell, they did not hold a vision of constitutional equality between the sexes. They drew on the model with which they were familiar, the separate

[45]"Statistical List," *NYAD,* April 11, 1846, vol. 6, no. 205.

[46]A committee on lawyers' fees admitted that many clients had been fleeced by less than honest members of the profession, but it also opposed the setting of fees, arguing that every man was free to select his own lawyer ("Report of the Select Committee on Lawyers' Fees and Costs in Courts of Law," *NYAD,* April 15, 1845, vol. 6, no. 227, p. 3).

[47]"Memorial of Members of the Bar of the City of New York Relative to Legal Reform," *NYAD,* February 9, 1847, vol. 2, no. 48. Theodore Sedgwick, Jr. (b. 1811), joined his uncle's firm of Henry and Robert Sedgwick in 1834. David Dudley Field also worked for this firm of legal reformers and later became a partner. See Arthur Schlesinger, Jr., *The Age of Jackson* (Boston, 1945), pp. 187–89.

estate carved out by equity. The statute they promoted consisted in allowing a married woman to own a separate estate in the property she brought to marriage or inherited afterward without the special device of a trust or antenuptial agreement. While it destroyed the power of the chancellors, it did not alter the marital prototype.

David Dudley Field encapsulated the procedural emphasis of the legal reform movement. In an 1842 letter to an assembly judiciary committee, he noted that one might file a bill in chancery that day and not be sure the case would be ended in 1852; nor was it possible to have any idea about the costs. This situation, he pointed out, was not the fault of lawyers. Lawyers, he insisted defensively, were not overpaid for their services; they were simply asked to perform a great many services because of the inefficiency of the legal system. True reform, he argued, necessitated the streamlining of a legal system that was "unreasonably arbitrary, dilatory, and expensive," and such reform, he insisted, was increasingly supported by lawyers themselves. "Justice," said Field in a trenchant pamphlet in 1847, "is entangled in a net of forms."[48]

Clearly, by the 1840s the New York Legislature was prepared to untangle those forms that enveloped the law of husband and wife. The panics of 1837 and 1839 and the ensuing depression generated concern to protect a portion of the family's assets. The married woman's trust was riddled with legal ambiguities and in popular disrepute, and the administration of equity was under public attack and legislative scrutiny.

Yet despite the mildness of anticipated reforms and the plausibility of arguments set forth, resistance to a married women's statute remained stiff. It flourished in the judiciary committees of the state legislature and reflected, in part, a reluctance to extend what were clearly the redistributive advantages of the married woman's separate estate to a new group. A married women's statute was a legislatively authorized redistribution of those advantages as opposed to the narrower judicial redistribu-

[48]David Dudley Field, "Appendix to the Committee on the Judiciary in Relation to the More Simple and Speedy Administration of Justice," *NYAD*, March 2, 1842, vol. 5, no. 94, pp. 25, 27, 30–31; "What Shall Be Done with the Practice of the Court?" in *Speeches, Arguments, and Miscellaneous Papers of David Dudley Field*, ed. A. P. Sprague, 3 vols. (New York, 1884), 1:228.

tion that had taken place in equity. Such a statute would scarcely touch the urban working classes, crowded into tenements, virtually propertyless, and living an economically marginal existence, but it was bound to reach people of the middling sort whose wives brought something in the way of a dowry. As Edward Pessen noted, the very wealthiest segment of the economy not only weathered depressions well, but often managed to take advantage of them.[49] For the very wealthy, whose interests were represented by a segment of the bar and the judiciary, even the newly narrowed and ambiguous equitable estate was preferable to a general statute that created advantages for potential new wealth.

A far broader-based resistance, however, came from the fear of a sexual revolution set off by changes in the laws of marriage. Many contemporaries viewed a married women's statute as a Pandora's box; once opened, they claimed, it would throw relations between the sexes into total chaos. Keeping the lid on was essential. Along with a few radical feminists, the resisters were, in fact, the only group aware of the ideologically radical potential of the movement for married women's property rights. In some ways they evinced great respect for the vast body of politically invisible and economically dependent women who might reach for a great deal more than male legal reformers were offering. Equity, as a legal concept, and equality, as a political concept, were two completely different ideas. It was equity that legislators offered; it was equality that women subsequently demanded.

[49]Edward Pessen, *Riches, Class, and Power before the Civil War* (Lexington, Mass., 1973), pp. 130–48.

CHAPTER 5

For Good or for Evil: The 1848 Statute

> The bill giving to married women the separate control of their own property—a measure of great public moment, for good or for evil, passed the House yesterday, precisely in the shape which it had passed the Senate, and requires only the Executive approval to become law.
>
> —*Albany Argus,* April 7, 1848

The debate over the first major married women's statute in New York did not take place on the floor of the Assembly or Senate. Unlike clashes over banks, canals, and rent, all of which dramatized the factionalism of New York politics, clashes over the legal status of married women were relegated to the private recesses of successive judiciary committees. Only at the Constitutional Convention of 1846 did debate erupt into the open. Between 1840 and 1848 a number of bills introduced by highly competent legislators failed to emerge from judiciary committees to the voting stage. Occasional reports from those committees intimated that there was little point in wasting the Legislature's time on a bill that had no chance of passage.

It is quite possible, however, that the judiciary committees refused to risk passage of a statute to which they were opposed. In any case, they refused to put bills they received to the test despite considerable pressure. Pressure in the 1840s came not only from lawyers dissatisfied with the confused status of the married woman's equitable estate, but also from feminists engaged in petitioning campaigns. The drive for a statute was distinguished during this time by the active support and agitation of three New York women: Ernestine Rose, a pioneer in delineating a feminist position on married women's property rights; Paulina Wright Davis, who led petitioning campaigns in the 1840s in the western part of the state; and Elizabeth Cady

Stanton, the guiding force of the nineteenth-century movement. These three women addressed judiciary committees during this period, and there is evidence that Stanton already was using her extensive political connections and exerting her formidable political skills on behalf of a statute.[1] All this activity took place before 1848.

Furthermore, a national trend toward married women's statutes was under way. Mississippi passed a married women's statute in 1839, Maine in 1844, and Massachusetts in 1845. A married women's clause appeared in the Texas Constitution in 1845, and a similar clause was in the proposed Wisconsin Constitution of 1847, but was rejected by voters.[2] These statutory provisions were limited in scope and the constitutional clauses were vague in intent. Nevertheless, they suggest that the legal status of married women was a lively national issue.

Legislation in New York moved forward in areas least likely to permit a major realignment of powers between husband and wife. As part of its commitment to new enterprise, for example, in 1840 the New York Legislature passed a married women's insurance act that enabled a wife to own life insurance on her husband and to receive its benefits free from the claims of his creditors.[3] This statute marked the emergence of life insurance as an important business as well as legislators' awareness of the widow's plight in an increasingly complex economy.[4] Business journals greeted the statute with enthusiasm and found no threat in it to the institution of marriage.[5] Five years later, the Legislature passed a statute enabling a wife to own her own patent. Although this was the only law of its kind in the nation, it was scarcely a broad, meaningful commitment by the state of New York to married women's property rights.[6]

[1]Elizabeth Cady Stanton, *Eighty Years and More: Reminiscences, 1815–1897* (1898: reprinted New York, 1971), p. 150; *HWS,* 1:38; Stanton to Elizabeth Smith, February 15, 1843, in Stanton-Blatch Letters, 2:8; Suhl, *Ernestine L. Rose,* pp. 58–59.

[2]Goebel, *Cases and Materials,* pp. 554–55.

[3]*LNY, 1840,* chap. 80.

[4]For the development of actuarial tables and a system of selling policies in the state, see Ellis, *Short History,* p. 264.

[5]See, for example, "Insurance on Lives for the Benefit of Married Women," *Hunt's Merchants' Magazine* 2 (June 1840):534.

[6]*LNY, 1845,* chap. 11; Warbasse, "Changing Legal Rights," p. 222.

Meanwhile agitation for more thorough reform continued under the leadership of Thomas Herttell. Back in the Assembly in 1840 after a two-year hiatus, Herttell introduced "an act for the more effectual protection of the rights of property of married women." This bill, like those of 1836 and 1837, failed to emerge from the Judiciary Committee. This was Herttell's last year in the Legislature, but from 1841 until 1848, the year before his death, Herttell continued to lead petitioning campaigns for legislation. In 1841 legislative leadership of the drive for a statute passed to John L. O'Sullivan, New York City assemblyman and editor of the *United States Magazine and Democratic Review.* Between 1841 and 1848, eight major bills for a married women's statute were introduced in the Legislature, four in 1846 and 1847 alone.[7] None emerged from committee to the voting stage.

Though the debate was muted in the Legislature, it emerged in national periodicals. The cause was taken up for a time by the *United States Magazine and Democratic Review,* the unofficial journal for the Democratic party. An 1839 article insisted that marriage laws were unjust because they imposed too much power on one side and too much dependence on the other. Affirming the special role of women in the society, the writer argued that an improvement in the legal status of wives would be helpful in "elevating and purifying the matrimonial relation."[8]

Although writers in national periodicals rarely approached the earlier radical sweep of Thomas Herttell or Sarah Grimké, they did indeed grow bolder in the 1840s. In 1844 the same Democratic journal printed an indignant protest by an anonymous woman who focused on men's usurpation of tangible political power as the source of married women's legal difficulties. "It is one of those monstrous things to be accounted for," she remonstrated, "that even at this period of the world 'free Christian enlightened women', if married, have no more power over their property and earnings than slave women." Why, she asked, do such laws prevail? Because men made them to keep women in economic dependence, she answered.[9]

[7] *JNYA,* 1840, pp. 910, 1049, 1086; 1841, p. 75; 1843, p. 305; 1844 pp. 172, 367; 1846, pp. 501, 1212; 1847, pp. 47, 284; Warbasse, "Changing Legal Rights," p. 222; Suhl, *Ernestine L. Rose,* p. 55.

[8] "American Women," *USMDR* 6 (August 1839):137.

[9] "The Legal Wrongs of Women," ibid. 14 (May 1844):478.

There can be no question that a challenge to the common law status of married women was in progress. It may even account, in part, for the intensity with which popular writers outlined sex-role prescriptions in the antebellum period. The burden of proof in the debate over property rights, however, was on the reformer. A vast body of legal literature supported the status quo in marriage. Religious literature, from Genesis and St. Paul to nineteenth-century sermons, advocated wifely deference and dependence. So pervasive was the idea of the wife's inferiority and so entrenched as a habit of thought that it served as a contemporary metaphor for conservative views of the organic body politic, a function it had served for centuries of Western culture.

James Fenimore Cooper used it in precisely this way. Disillusioned with nineteenth-century egalitarianism, Cooper selected the common law status of wives as the perfect paradigm for the naturally hierarchical structure of all human relationships. He used the common law marriage contract to demonstrate the validity of the domination, representation, and protection of the naturally inferior by the naturally superior. Equality of rights, said Cooper in *The American Democrat* in 1836, can never be absolute. Employing the old argument of virtual representation that had been used by Loyalists against Patriots in the American Revolution, Cooper pointed out that women were denied political rights "because their interests are so closely identified with those of their male relatives. That is why the wife cannot sue and be sued, and why the husband is responsible for legal claims made over the wife." Cooper then alluded to St. Paul to underscore religious support for the obligation of deference imposed upon wives.[10]

Cooper's faith in the propriety of the marriage relationship at common law, his reliance on its immutability, and his assumption of its natural harmony dramatically attest to the wall of resistance that reformers invariably encountered. The questioning of woman's place in the marriage equation was not new, but with its linkage to the drive for statutory reform the discussion took on a new intensity, an even sharper exhortatory, didactic quality. A bevy of guidebooks and marriage manuals supported the principle of wifely subservience with a piety more resolute

[10]James Fenimore Cooper, *The American Democrat* (New York, 1969), pp. 37–38.

than that found in comparable late-eighteenth-century and early-nineteenth-century materials, which were at least occasionally relieved by lighthearted banter.[11]

William Alcott, one of the most popular manual writers of the day, defined matrimony for women as an act of submission and concession, best symbolized by the wife's assumption of her husband's name. The more cheerful and voluntary the submission, he predicted, the better the marriage.[12] Wifely submission, moreover, frequently carried elements of compensation in the form of spiritual superiority. "The province of our sex, though subordinate, is one of peculiar privilege," reasoned Lydia Sigourney, one of the most successful female writers of the period. Submission, she argued, led to piety. Since women were unable to protect themselves, they placed their trust in heaven; they leaned "on the Divine arm."[13] Leaning directly on the Divine arm was less than flattering to men—in fact, it ignored men—and it did not seem to do much for women as far as their legal status was concerned. But although in some ways emphasis on women's proximity to heaven and on their righteous superiority diverted them from their earthly problems even as it consoled them, in other ways it underscored the gap between their legal position and their social position.

Samples from this large body of prescriptive literature, which historians have explored so imaginatively, are presented here only to underscore the agonizing conflict involved in attempts to change the law of husband and wife. Clearly, any change in marital-property laws entailed the traditional dilemma of reconciling stability and change in its most extreme form. For many Americans, marriage represented the last stronghold of social

[11]See, for example, American versions of Lord Chesterfield's famous manual, which proclaimed that every "good fellow" was "the dupe of a woman" one way or another (*The American Chesterfield, or Way to Wealth* [Philadelphia, 1828], p. 203). For a pioneering survey of this material, see Arthur Schlesinger, Sr., *Learning How to Behave* (New York, 1947).

[12]William Alcott, *The Young Wife, or Duties of Woman in the Marriage* (Boston, 1837). pp. 29–30.

[13]Lydia H. Sigourney, *Letters to Young Ladies,* 5th ed. (New York, 1837), p. 91. On assumptions about women's moral superiority, see Carl N. Degler, *At Odds: Women and the Family in America from the Revolution to the Present* (New York, 1980), pp. 30–32. For a sensitive analysis of antebellum attempts to reconcile women's moral superiority with their political inferiority, see Sklar, *Catherine Beecher,* pp. 155–56.

control, order, and stability. To free the wife legally and economically might further fragment what was already perceived as an atomized society.

Although most legislators were resolutely committed to serving the legal needs of an expanding market economy, they were disturbed by its social consequences. They were concerned about eroding the sexual division of labor. If the wife were liberated from her common law restrictions, she might very well enter the commercial arena as a wage earner or, even worse, an entrepreneur, becoming in a sense her husband's competitor. Why should legislators or delegates to a constitutional convention endanger such a well-ordered, time-honored socioeconomic structure? Were there no limits to the concept of equality? Were they to encourage a knifelike individualism to invade and divide the family itself, the remaining haven in a brutally competitive society?

Male authors of advice books revealed a particularly deep fear of and revulsion toward the idea that women might assume any position of status or power. T. S. Arthur, one of the leading writers of homiletic fiction in the mid-nineteenth century, advised young women that there was something "so absurd and revolting in taking woman out of her present sphere, and her present high and holy uses," and placing her instead "side by side with man in the world's rough arena," or more precisely "in contest with him for honor and fame and wealth," that he would not waste his time in serious argument against it. Arthur, of course, expended considerable time in such argument. His attack, moreover, was not on mill operatives or seamstresses or domestics, the women who constituted an important portion of the marginal, low-paid labor force. It was on "intellectual ladies" who aimed for men's jobs "on the bench, at the bar, in the pulpit," and even "in the dissecting room, or hospital with the operator's knife in . . . hand."[14]

Arguments of this sort often threatened that if women pushed too far, men would withdraw their protection and leave them to struggle on their own. Protection and financial support were the underpinnings of the wife's common law status. One popular

[14]T. S. Arthur, *Advice to Young Ladies on Their Duties* (Boston, 1847), pp. 126, 134.

advice manual for women admonished, "You were not made to wrestle with the rough forces of nature. You were not made for war, nor commerce, nor agriculture." Passive acceptance of this basic truth was crucial. "Recognize your dependence gladly and gracefully" or you will lose the protection of men.[15] Another popular argument projected chaos from any change in sex roles. If women abandoned the home for "political life, speculation, and debate," warned a Universalist preacher, "there would be a dying out of nature, a dropping away of that mysterious, inexpressible love, that unseen magnetism which refines the elements of social life and binds them together."[16]

Perhaps nobody expressed the fear of female competition with a bolder metaphorical leap than the writer for *Hunt's Merchants' Magazine* who proclaimed that "Adam was created and placed in the Garden of Eden for business purposes" and would have been better off if he had followed God's original plan.[17] Eve, by extension, had drawn Adam away from God's pure commercial design. The female temptress was the flaw in the almost Edenic perfection of the garden of nineteenth-century commerce.

In the light of these arguments against change in women's roles, the middle-of-the-road support for a married women's statute which was necessary for its passage stressed the spiritual improvements to be achieved rather than any economic or political victories for women. Until the antebellum women's movement was fully under way, few proponents of reform overtly voiced the idea that marriage, the institution in which Americans seemed to place their most abiding values, was a dubious bargain. a social and economic arrangement in which women gave up legal autonomy in return for support. Nor could they agree with Blackstone that the main purpose of marriage was to guarantee the legitimacy of children as the conduits for family wealth. They argued, instead, that they were interested in preserving and buffering the special nonmaterial qualities in marriage against the gaudy materialism of the age. Marriage, in-

[15]Timothy Titcomb, *Letters to Young People,* 21st ed. (New York, 1861), p. 55.

[16] Edwin Hubbell Chapin, *Duties of Young Women* (Boston, 1856), pp. 160–62.

[17]Matthew Smith, "The Elements of Business Success," *Hunt's Merchants' Magazine* 31 (1854):56, cited in Irvin G. Wylie, *The Self-Made Man in America: The Myth of Rags to Riches* (New York, 1954), p. 61.

sisted almost all proponents and opponents of reform, was ideally a spiritual union for spiritual purposes. Opponents of legal change translated this position into an assertion that a separation of economic interests would foster spiritual and emotional discord. Proponents of change argued that legal reform would free women from the mercenary aspects of marriage and thereby restore marriage to its true spiritual functions. The purpose of marriage, argued Harriet Martineau, a staunch advocate of marital property reform, was "to protect the sanctity of the love of one man for one woman."[18]

Demand for reform on the grounds of constitutional or natural rights occupied a narrow place at the radical end of the spectrum of support. Such magazines as *Godey's* labored carefully to separate their support of married women's property rights from a broader demand for women's rights. "When a married woman talks excessively of women's rights," warned an 1839 article, "then you can guess that woman is less than conscientious about performing her wifely duties."[19]

The differences between radical and moderate support were delineated with remarkable clarity in a series of 1843 articles written by John Neal and Eliza Farnham in Neal's contentious *Brother Jonathan.* Neal argued that inequitable laws in marriage were a direct result of the inability of women to participate in the lawmaking process. Farnham replied that women in reality were not political agents and needed no political powers. Neal insisted that women were the servants of men, tied to their servitude by economic dependence; Farnham replied that it was men who were the servants of women, "chained to a desk like bond slaves."[20] They drew on two contemporary female stereotypes, the drudge and the butterfly. He depicted the wife as legally enslaved by the power-hungry husband; she dipicted the husband as financially enslaved by his luxury-loving wife. He ar-

[18]Harriet Martineau, "Marriage," *Harbinger* 4 (December 1846):25. For a discussion of companionate marriage and the place of the family in the nineteenth century, see Christopher Lasch, *Haven in a Heartless World: The Family Besieged* (New York, 1977), pp. 6–8, 168–69.

[19]"A Chapter of Inferences," *Godey's Lady's Book* 18 (January 1839):33.

[20]"Rights of Women: The Substance of a Lecture Delivered by John Neal at the Tabernacle," *Brother Jonathan* 5 (June 1843):183–85; Eliza Farnham, "Rights of Women: Reply to Mr. Neal's Lecture," ibid., pp. 236–38.

gued that the interests of men and women were politically disparate: she argued that they were confluent.

What is important about the Neal-Farnham debate, however, is Farnham's willingness to support married women's property legislation. Her support at this stage, like Sarah Hale's, marked the basic recognition on the part of moderates of the need for property rights. Neal, as editor, took the last word in the debate, arguing that the current common law status of wives was a perfect example of how politically antithetical the interests of men and women were.[21]

Although the drive for a married women's statute was well under way by the 1840s, the literature of the era reveals profound tensions underlying the passage of such a statute. Some sort of reform was necessary; new economic structures impelled a certain amount of legal change. The life insurance business, for example, could not have grown and flourished under the old common law terms of marriage. But the assertion that the interests of men and women were politically antithetical was menacing. To give wives more tangible power might erode the separation of the public arena of work and politics from the private sphere of domesticity and reproduction. The sexual division of labor was a critical ingredient of industrial capitalism. In a harshly competitive society, cooperative attributes became the province of women. As Ann Douglas has pointed out, the antebellum lady had two jobs: saint and consumer.[22]

Reports from judiciary committees of the Assembly, the only available barometer of legislative attitudes before 1848, reveal many of the same underlying tensions. In 1842 John L. O'Sullivan, representing the Assembly Judiciary Committee in a report on the petitioning campaign for a married women's bill, said the committee unanimously supported a bill, but saw no possibility of its passage that year. The committee, he said, favored "a more liberal extension of the rights of married women," as the petitioners did, but "how far it might be proper to go," he admitted, "must of course be a subject of much diversity of individual opinion." In a statement of general principle, the committee exhorted New York legislators "to engraft at least partially upon

[21]Farnham, "Rights of Women," ibid. (July 1843), pp. 266–68; Neal, "Letter to Mrs. T. J. Farnham," ibid., pp. 304–9.

[22]Douglas, *Feminization of American Culture,* p. 60.

the hard and stubborn trunk of the common law the more liberal principle" applied with respect to married women's property on the European continent.[23]

Although the committee urged that the materials of the civil law be used as a source for changes in the common law, its report was vague and ambivalent. Even as the report supported some kind of reform, it projected caution. Even as committee members acknowledged that the current state of statute and common law in New York was oppressive to many women, they raised the specter of chaos as a result of precipitous reform: "In a change so important and delicate in what may be regarded as the very fundamental institution of society, as it is certainly the most sacred and precious, no degree of caution can be too great to guard against rash derangement of whatever may be good in the existing settled order of things."[24]

The ambiguities of the 1842 report undoubtedly stem from divisions among the members as well as some ambivalence in individual legislators. Only two other Judiciary Committee reports appear among the official legislative documents before 1848 to give us some clues about prospects for a married women's statute. They remain the only available evidence of the spectrum of legislative attitudes.

The report of the 1844 Assembly Judiciary Committee is of particular interest because it spoke directly to the natural rights principles on which feminist petitioners for a married women's statute increasingly relied. In the application of natural rights the committee found menacing new possibilities unfolding, and urged, instead, a more limited and practical approach. Such petitions, they noted, failed even to mention the married woman's trust, that safe and long-used device for easing the rigidities of the common law. This was the area in which the law needed clarification. The committee urged the bridging of some of the gaps created by the Revised Statutes with "an Act in Relation to Uses and Trusts."[25]

[23]"Report of the Judiciary Committee on the Petitions to Extend and Protect the Rights of the Property of Married Women," *NYAD,* April 12, 1842, vol. 7, no. 189.

[24]Ibid.

[25]"Report of the Committee on the Judiciary on Petitions Asking the Passage of a Law for the Protection of Married Women," *NYAD,* February 26, 1844, vol. 3, no. 96, pp. 10–11.

In its appeal to common sense and in its plea for reduced goals in statute law, the 1844 report was characteristic of much anticodification literature. Defending the general outlines of the common law on the grounds of historicism, as Kent and Story had done, the 1844 committee reserved its harshest criticism for the mystique of codification. They compared centuries of accepted usage with a few years of agitation; they weighed the mass of detailed legal precedents against the extravagant rhetoric of codification. They were not insensitive to popular hostility to the feudal vestiges of the husband-wife relationship at common law. The concept of an inviolable marital unity, they admitted, was dubious in principle, but they insisted that with the help of equity, it worked in fact. "As a general rule, it is safe to say," they reasoned, "that the body of the people suffer less by a law, wrong perhaps in principle, working no great actual wrong in practice, which is permanent and well understood." Real evil came from the attempts of reformers to remedy small problems with grandiose solutions.[26]

This practical approach, however, gave way to the old dialectic of virtue and corruption. The intense antagonism of this committee to codification and to the Napoleonic Code was symbolized in its vision of French women and French morals. Separate property in France, they declared, had led to infidelity in the marriage bed, a high rate of divorce, and increased female criminality. This assertion was a step beyond the one taken by Blackstone, who had underscored boldly the ties between economic independence and sexual infidelity, but who had not gone so far as to link economic independence with female criminality. The members of the committee voiced their fervent hope that Louisiana might avoid the French experience by virtue of the influence of its common law neighbors and settlers, and thus escape the turning of marriage from "its high and holy purposes" into an affair of "convenience and sensuality."[27]

In contrast to the O'Sullivan committee of 1842, which had acknowledged serious problems with the law as it was, the 1844 judiciary committee found the complaints of petitioners exaggerated if not unfounded. One group of petitioners, for exam-

[26]Ibid., p. 2.
[27]Ibid., pp. 9–10.

ple, had argued that the common law diminished the woman's self-respect and encouraged a "spirit of meanness and duplicity" in marriage. The committee failed to see any such spirit in English or American marriages, but found the inference that respect for wives was in any way related to the property they controlled exceedingly degrading to American womanhood.

More important, to neutralize the natural rights arguments to which petitioners appealed, the committee advanced its own natural rights arguments, thereby inadvertently demonstrating how natural rights served a multitude of causes. All persons, asserted their report, surrendered some rights after the formation of government, just as husbands and wives did after marriage. In all relationships, someone had to yield and become "the lesser star in the constellation." The marriage contract at common law, "based on the immutable laws of nature and the welfare of society," was in complete correspondence with the laws of nature.[28]

Finally, the committeemen resorted to religion, affirming wifely subservience in language that was closer to canon law than common law. "It has been ascertained to be necessary," they declared, "that man and wife should have but one interest, one feeling, one existence, that they should be as one, and become for all civil purposes 'one flesh.' "[29]

By the 1840s the lines of the debate over a married women's statute were well established and national stereotypes were very much a part of it. There was a tendency to exaggerate the wife's powers in French law and to ignore the extent to which she came under her husband's tutelage. Francophobes found that the wife's separate property encouraged loose morals and marital discord, and was the natural by-product of an inferior culture or "race." Conversely, the common law, they believed, encouraged fidelity, legitimacy, and stability, and was the natural by-product of a superior "Anglo-Saxon race."[30] Anglophobes pointed with pride to the success of French marriages, to the economically liberated condition of French women, and to their wider partici-

[28]Ibid., pp. 5–6.

[29]Ibid., p. 5.

[30]For an argument on behalf of the superiority of Anglo-American sexual mores, see "The Anglo-Saxon Race," *North American Review* 73 (July 1851):145–46.

pation in all aspects of French life. They found American wives, by contrast, passive, servile, and completely dependent.[31] Both sides made impassioned religious appeals, one to the one-flesh doctrine, the other to true Christian equality in marriage. The one-flesh doctrine, used throughout the nineteenth century, was becoming in many ways a desperate retrogressive effort in the light of the growing impetus for reform and the sharp distinctions between the husband and wife recognized in equity. Equitable remedies, however, were in disarray.

In addition to professional confusion about the current state of established equity precedents, there was the problem of public knowledge and access to equity. Probably the safest and most popular argument made on behalf of reform was a democratic one, not on behalf of women relative to men, but on behalf of ordinaries relative to elites. The Judiciary Committee of the Assembly made this argument quite effectively in 1846. This committee insisted, as had its 1844 counterpart, that it was satisfied with the general principles established in equity relative to a married woman's separate estate, but it suggested not only that there was considerable professional confusion about those principles because of the Revised Statutes, but also that the vast majority of people were ignorant of equity altogether. The committee was drawing attention to the fact that for most couples the crude outline of the common law was the law they knew and was therefore the law that prevailed over their marriages. Consequently, reported the committee, the rights of married women at common law "are among the remnants of feudal law that linger among us, but little ameliorated by the progress of the age." The liberal sway of equity precedents, if they "were more generally understood by the public, is amply sufficient to protect a married woman," they argued; therefore, if those principles were embodied in a statute, as a matter of public education, the problem would be solved.[32]

[31]August Carlier defended the moral superiority of French marriage law and took strenuous exception to Alexis de Tocqueville's tranquil picture of American marriages. Marriage laws in America, insisted Carlier, were designed "to increase the population, without regard to moral considerations or the future of the family." See Carlier's *Marriage in the United States* (1867; reprinted New York, 1972), p. 43.

[32]"Report of the Committee on the Judiciary in Relation to Divorce and the Separate Property of Married Women," *NYAD*, May 9, 1846, vol. 6, no. 219, pp. 1–2.

Avoiding the controversy between Francophiles and Anglophiles, between codifiers and the common lawyers, between feminists and antifeminists, this committee supported statutory reform on the old legal grounds of historicism and on the newer political grounds of democratization. A society that recognized historic equity precedents for some but failed to make them known or available to all violated the most basic democratic principle—equality (of men) before the law.

Making the law more available through improved administration and greater simplification became a goal of the Constitutional Convention of 1846. One hundred and twenty-eight delegates met to confront the state's legal institutions. As Marvin Meyers has shown, they pursued the quest for democratization of the law with a fairly high degree of consensus on certain issues. They voted, for example, to ensure the responsibility of judges to voters through their direct election. No longer, insisted Meyers, could politicians treat democracy like "a black box with a loud tick." At the convention of 1821, such Federalist-intellectuals as James Kent and such patroons as Stephen Van Rensselaer argued for selective suffrage against Democrats such as Martin Van Buren and Erastus Root; but by 1846 most Whigs and Democrats had slipped into agreement on the general direction legal reform should take.[33]

Dominated by antirenters and supported by Whigs, the convention abolished all feudal tenures and restricted agricultural leases to twelve years.[34] Most legal reform, however, was administrative and procedural. Forty-five of the delegates were lawyers. The subject of court procedures and costs studded discussions of legal reform in the early stages of the convention. Delegates moved to eliminate what they believed were the abuses of chancery by voting 89 to 6 to abolish the office of chancellor and its numerous suboffices, and to place the future administration of equity within the jurisdiction of the common law courts.[35]

[33]For popular election of judges and reorganization of the courts, see *Constitution of the State of New York, 1846,* art. 6, in *NYSD,* January 8, 1848, vol. 1, no. 6; Meyers, *Jacksonian Persuasion: Politics and Belief* (Stanford, 1957), pp. 235–37.

[34]*Constitution of the State of New York, 1846,* art. 1, secs. 12–14.

[35]Equity jurisdiction was to be placed in the Supreme Court and divided into eight individual districts, with four judges in each district. The highest appellate court, the Court of Appeals, was to be made up of four judges elected by voters and four elected by justices of the Supreme Court. See *Journal of the Convention of the State of New York Begun and Held at the Capital in the City of Albany, on the First*

This vote was a rough index of public hostility to the way equity had been administered in the chancery courts.

The convention's actions on married women's property rights, however, were quite extraordinary. The delegates of the 1846 convention voted to insert a married women's clause into the state constitution. Then three days later they rescinded it. However great the consensus on some issues, on the issue of married women's property rights the convention was almost equally divided. The fact that the division cut across party lines made the accompanying debates no less bitter. Nevertheless, here at the convention in the fall of 1846, New York politicians squarely confronted the legal status of married women for the first time, and a large number of them for a variety of reasons found it wanting.

The proposal of Ira Harris, on which the delegates first debated and voted favorably, came ironically from a committee on the rights of man. Yet its emergence from this committee and its inclusion in this section of the constitution implied that the use of "man" in this case was generic, an application Thomas Herttell had urged with respect to the United States Constitution. If a liberal married women's clause had been included in the constitution, it would have marked New York's recognition that at least some rights of woman, like the rights of man, were guaranteed as a fundamental assumption of the government, a self-evident principle. Although the practical results may not have differed significantly, a constitutional guarantee of rights is theoretically quite different from a statute that remedies old laws by extending them to more persons. The Harris proposal was fairly limited, however, and envisioned a registration of the wife's property. The proposal written by this Albany County Whig, who was elected with antirent support, illustrates the financial advantages implicit in insulating the wife's property. It read as follows:

> All property of the wife, owned by her at the time of her marriage, and that acquired by her afterwards by gift, devise

Day of June, 1846 (Albany, 1846), 2:859–60; *Constitution, 1846,* art. 6, secs. 2–4; William Prentice, "Historical Sketch of the Courts of New York," NYHS address, January 18, 1870, pp. 55–58, typescript, NYHS.

> or descent, or otherwise than from her husband, shall be her separate property. Laws shall be passed providing for the registry of the wife's separate property, and more clearly defining the rights of the wife thereto as well as to property held by her with her husband.[36]

Harris' was not the only proposal. Ansel Bascom, a Seneca County Whig and feminist who later attended the women's rights convention at Seneca Falls, desentimentalized marriage, taking the rare position that marriage was a contract, the details of which concerned only the contracting parties. Bascom was especially interested in obliterating the husband's responsibility for the debts accumulated by the wife before marriage and proposed the following skeletal resolution: "The contract of marriage shall not be held to vest in either of the contracting parties the property of the other or to create a liability upon either to discharge the debts or obligations of the other."[37]

George Simmons, an Essex County Whig, wanted a clause on the wife's equity to a settlement from her own property and from her potential dower to be written into the constitution. Simmons' proposal read: "The Legislature shall provide by law for a competent livelihood to be secured to married women and to her [sic] infant children out of the property owned by her, and out of the use of one-third of her husband's real property owned during coverture."[38]

Questions of constitutionality arose. Solomon Townshend, a New York City merchant who was worried about negating the obligation of contracts, nervously suggested that the Harris proposal include words to rule out the possibility of ex post facto laws that would impair such obligations. Questions arose about the extent of public support. George Patterson, a Chautauqua Whig, reminded the delegates that the issue of married women's property rights had been before the Legislature for a decade, and if there had been genuine public demand for it, it would

[36] *Journal of the Convention,* 2:1264–65.

[37] For Bascom's ties to the feminist movement, see Dexter C. Bloomer, *Life and Writings of Amelia Bloomer* (New York, 1895), p. 30; on his proposal, see William G. Bishop and William H. Attree, *Report of the Debates and Proceedings of the Convention for the Revision of the Constitution of the State of New York* (Albany, 1846), p. 1039.

[38] Bishop and Attree, *Report of the Debates,* pp. 1041–42.

have been translated into a statute by that time. Patterson neglected to mention that the issue had never come before the entire Legislature.[39]

Charles O'Conor, a prominent New York City lawyer and a Hunker Democrat who had opposed the merger of law and equity, led the opposition to the Harris clause. O'Conor pleaded for delay, warning delegates that such a proposal, which "would tend greatly to impair domestic harmony," required far more deliberate consideration. Arphaxed Loomis, a Herkimer County Barnburner, John T. Harrison, a Richmond Whig, and Horatio Stow, an Erie Whig, joined O'Conor in demanding more time and in questioning the propriety of placing such a provision in the constitution.[40]

Conrad Swackhamer, a Barnburner mechanic from Kings County, made the major speech on behalf of the Harris proposal. Though his arguments had already become familiar, they were distinguished by the passion with which Swackhamer advanced them. The issue of married women's property rights was for him a matter of right versus wrong, good against evil, light over darkness. He launched a vitriolic attack on the motives of the opposition. Male greed, he insisted, and male licentiousness motivated those who supported the existing legal arrangements in marriage. By giving the husband legal and economic autonomy in marriage and withholding it from the wife, opponents were encouraging a double standard of sexual behavior.

Working to neutralize familiar predictions of chaos and traditional appeals to religious precedents, Swackhamer labeled such arguments "a subterfuge resorted to by the enemies of this measure," a move in which "the spirit of darkness" assumed "the garb of light." As for the Bible, it had been grossly misinterpreted. The one-flesh doctrine never indicated male dominance; it was a doctrine of equality and justice. "But man for sordid and mercenary motives, had supplanted the ordinance of God by substituting conditions as derogatory to the character of woman as it was degrading to his own."[41]

[39] Ibid.

[40] Ibid., pp. 1038, 1042.

[41] Ibid., pp. 1039–41. For another version of the debate, see Sherman Croswell and Richard Sutton, *Debates and Proceedings in the New York State Convention for the Revision of the Constitution by S. Croswell and R. Sutton, Reporters for the Argus* (Albany, 1846).

Swackhamer pursued the woman question to its larger ramifications, touching on limited job and educational opportunities for women, and on the issue of taxation without representation. But while he argued that females were "mentally, and morally equal to males," he carefully avoided any suggestion of women as economic competitors. The main purpose of the Harris proposal, said Swackhamer, was not to build up separate interests between man and wife, but to protect the wife against the "fortune-hunting villain who married the money and not the woman, and who estimated domestic happiness and female virtue by the amount of property secured." Swackhamer addressed the issue of married women's property rights with the same compassionate spirit that he had displayed in discussing the poverty of urban laborers and mechanics. Worried about any national underclass and wary of elites, Swackhamer spoke with the voice of the antebellum reformer. On the other hand, even as he depicted women as a powerless, manipulated underclass, he assured delegates that they would not enter the political and economic mainstream of American life.

In any case, Swackhamer and Harris had the votes, a situation O'Conor may very well have suspected, for his opposition on the day of the first vote was brief and limited to an attempt at delay. Thus on October 2, 1846, the delegates to the New York Constitutional Convention voted 58 to 44 to place the Harris proposal in the constitution of the state. New York apparently had taken a giant step in the cause for married women's property rights. The *Evening Post,* a New York Barnburner paper, asserted that no longer would marriage "work a complete civil annihilation of woman." They claimed the clause was "a great and important change" for which the delegates deserved the thanks of the community.[42]

Three days later, on October 5, O'Conor reopened the debate with a counterattack that was almost a perfect prototype for support of the status quo in marriage. He focused on the complexity and fragility of marriage as a social institution and on the crude draftsmanship of the constitution makers. Delegates, said O'Conor, had not reflected sufficiently on the enormity of their

[42]Bishop and Attree, *Report of the Debates,* p. 1042; *New York Evening Post,* October 6, 1846, p. 2. For descriptions of the factional affiliations of state newspapers, see Herbert B. Donovan, *The Barnburners* (New York, 1925), pp. 124–26.

decision, but would surely change their minds on more deliberate speculation. If any single thing should remain untouched by the hand of the reformer, it was the sacred institution of marriage. The indivisible union of husband and wife, he continued, had its roots in the Bible, in English ancestry, and had survived a transatlantic crossing and a revolution. Now it was about to be destroyed in one thoughtless blow that might produce change in all phases of domestic life.[43]

O'Conor claimed that marriage was a bargain, but it was a bargain quite different from any other, made by nature and governed by laws of "Divine origin." Control and custody of the wife, he argued, "is the price which female wants and weakness must pay for their protection." He warned against the dangers of female competition, raising the specter of the wife-competitor, the Amazon in the marketplace. A wife with a separate estate, he insisted, "might be a sole trader; she might rival her husband in trade or become the partner of his rival." With rare consistenty and as a defense against egalitarian arguments, O'Conor even attacked the married woman's trust and marriage settlement. It was a precedent, he said, quoting Judge Jonas Platt, that grew up "in the hot-bed of wealth and luxury," a device that was used only by a handful of Americans, and one that should not be levied upon all classes. In freeing women from dependence on their husbands, it prevented them from "enjoying their dependence."[44]

Finally O'Conor attacked the proponents of the Harris clause with as much savagery as he had received from them three days earlier, and with even greater imagination. Drawing on the ever-popular Garden of Eden image, he claimed that the proposition for this reform came in a "deceitful form," like "the serpent's tale to the first woman," and that "it tended—if it did not seek—to degrade her."[45]

Robert Morris, Democrat and former mayor of New York, focused on the weakness in O'Conor's attack on equity precedents. He asked why the provision that any wealthy and prudent man made for his daughters should not be available to all the

[43]Bishop and Attree, *Report of the Debates,* pp. 1056, 1059–60. Ira Harris responded that American women occupied their "proper rank" with the help of Christianity, but despite the common law.

[44]Ibid., p. 1057–58.

[45]Ibid., p. 1057.

citizens of the state, and he urged that the original vote remain. Another delegate expressed fear that the Harris clause might put the state "under the curse of the married relation as it existed under the civil law."[46]

Now it was O'Conor that had the votes, and it is likely he reopened the debate only when he knew he had a good chance of getting the Harris proposal rescinded. Five delegates who had supported the Harris proposal switched to O'Conor's side, and a new group of delegates was present. This time the Harris proposal was defeated by a vote of 59 to 50. Only Alvah Worden explained his shift, asserting that the Harris proposal went too far and he favored something less radical. A few feeble final attempts were made for a married women's clause. One delegate tried to include a provision in the constitution under a section on realty which would have exempted the profits of the wife's realty from the husband's debts. Another proposed to exempt $600 from debts in case of the husband's bankruptcy in order to support the wife and children. Both were defeated.[47]

It seemed to many that a golden opportunity had been lost. There was resentment at the overturn of the original vote, a perception that victory had been achieved and then somehow snatched away. The *Albany Argus*, a Hunker paper, regretted the defeat. New York feminists pointed out that the 1846 convention was the appropriate place for reform to begin, a place where "one would naturally think that a chance ray of justice might have fallen aslant the wrongs of woman." Yet despite the final defeat, the convention had crystallized the issues, placed them in the political arena, and engendered some expectation that passage of a married women's act was merely a question of time. The issue was no longer relegated to a single assemblyman, to the back pages of prestigious literary reviews and technical law journals. The *Evening Post* pointed out that "the subject is fortunately left within the power of the legislature, which will soon obey the voice of public opinion."[48]

[46]Ibid., p. 1059.

[47]Ibid., pp. 1060, 1064.

[48]*Albany Argus*, October 6, 1846, p. 1; see also "The New York Constitutional Convention," *USMDR* 19 (November 1846):347, for an article lamenting the delegates' failure "to secure to females the right to hold, transfer or devise property as fully as before marriage"; *HWS*, 1:63; *New York Evening Post*, October 7, 1846, p. 2.

Furthermore, to all the male discussions, temperate and intemperate, rational and religious, moral and political, there was now added the inchoate anger of American women, dramatized and exploited by a small group of articulate feminists. New York feminists began to expose that sense of deprivation and alienation which ran as an undercurrent in the writings of their more moderate sisters. The feminists' sense of being grossly wronged, and even worse, ignored, coalesced around the single reform with a realistic chance for success—a married women's statute.

The women of Genesee and Wyoming counties, petitioning the New York Legislature in 1848, stated with revolutionary gusto, "Your Declaration of Independence declares, that governments derive their just powers from the consent of the governed." If "your declaration" was an exclusively male declaration, they were preparing the foundation for a female one. "And as women have never consented to, been represented in, or recognized by this government," they continued, "it is evident that in justice no allegiance can be claimed for them." These women were asserting that the failure of the Legislature to pass a married women's statute was evidence of their lack of representation. "Our numerous and yearly petitions for this most desirable object having been disregarded, we now ask your *august* body," they said with some sarcasm, "to abolish all laws which hold married women more accountable for their acts than *infants, idiots,* and *lunatics.*"[49]

The path for passage of the 1848 statute was already cleared by the time the Legislature received the petition. None of the opponents at the 1846 convention sat in the predominantly Whig legislature of 1848. A bill was introduced in January by John Fine of St. Lawrence County, who wrote it and undertook the leadership of its passage in the Senate with the help of George Geddes of Onondaga. Robert G. Campbell managed its leadership in the Assembly. After twelve years of controversy it sailed through the Assembly by a vote of 93 to 9 and the Senate by a vote of 28 to 1 and was signed into law on April 8.[50]

[49]"Petition of Forty-four Ladies of Genesee and Wyoming, Praying for the Repeal of Certain Laws to the Legislature of the State of New York," *NYAD,* March 15, 1848, vol. 5, no. 129. See also "Syracuse Petition," *JNYS,* February 23, 1848, p. 214.

[50]Progress of the bill may be followed from notice of introduction to passage in *JNYS,* 1848, pp. 37, 47, 157, 214, 242, 250, 314, 352, 354, 420, 432, 442, 541; and *JNYA,* 1848, pp. 37, 181, 966–67, 1025, 1032, 1129–31.

The long and acrimonious debate, which had dragged on for more than a decade, had doubtless become familiar to legislators. Spurred by debtor-creditor problems, the drive for codification, and the burgeoning intensity of the woman question, support finally coalesced to create a favorable environment for passage of the statute. The close contest at the constitutional convention confirmed that a measure of public support existed. Recalling the progress of the 1848 bill, George Geddes pointed out that it received unlooked-for support. He stressed confusion over the married woman's separate estate as the most important source of support. Judge John Fine, he claimed, the author of the bill and a widower, had endeavored for years to keep his wife's property separate from his own, but was dissatisfied with existing legal options. Geddes himself had an elaborate will drawn up by his old preceptor, former vice-chancellor Lewis Sanford, in which he had created a trust for his daughter. Yet neither he nor Sanford, he claimed, was completely satisfied with the trust. Geddes' retrospective view of the 1848 statute, however, was confused. On the one hand, he insisted that after 1848 he was able to tear up his old will, so secure was his daughter under the new law. On the other hand, he admitted that statutory revisions of marital property laws had been less than satisfactory.[51]

Problems in the Fine bill were immediately apparent to some members of the Assembly. They came not so much from what the statute said as from what it neglected to say. It failed, for example, to spell out contractual or legal powers for the wife. David Collins tried to amend the bill to give wives contractual powers over their real and personal property, to give them the legal capacity to sue and be sued, and to make married women responsible after marriage for debts contracted before marriage. Collins also advocated permitting wives to serve on juries and to hold judicial offices if they held property, a suggestion that was of course totally unacceptable to the Legislature. Yet Collins pointed to the necessity for women whose property was affected by law to be part of the adjudication process. So inadequate did Collins find the Fine bill that he voted against it. As evidence of perennial interest in the fate of the debtor, another assemblyman advocated an amendment exempting $10,000 of a married

[51]Geddes to Matilda Joslyn Gage, November 25, 1880, in *HWS*, 1:65.

woman's property from the reach of the husband's creditors, an amendment totally unnecessary if the Fine statute were completely effective in creating a wife's separate estate.[52]

Section 1 of the 1848 statute stated that the real and personal property of any woman who married after the bill became law would continue as her sole and separate property as if she were single. This property, moreover, was not to be subject to her husband's debts. Section 2 repeated the same provisions for women who were already married, a clause of dubious constitutionality which was destined for defeat by the judiciary. Section 3 enabled a married woman to receive by gift, grant, or devise real and personal property free from her husband's disposal and from his creditors. Section 4 recognized the ongoing validity of antenuptial agreements.[53]

The model for the legislation was equity; the statute followed the major precedents established in English and American equity. Not only was this a difficult technical task at best, because the most efficient devices creating a separate estate delineated the extent of the wife's property, but it also limited the focus to the area of inherited property. Thus the statute failed to encompass two large classes of wives: those who ran family farms, boardinghouses, and retail stores and participated in household manufactures, and those who earned wages from labor outside of the house.

Geddes offered one clue about legislative intent. "We meant to strike a hard blow," he said, "and if possible shake the old system of laws to their foundations, and leave it to other times and wiser councils to perfect a new system."[54] His statement suggests that details were intentionally left to be ironed out by the courts and future legislatures, and that legislators were fully aware of gaps. In fact, the filling in of these gaps impelled a series of minor statutes during the decade.

Just as the 1828 Revised Statutes had raised questions about the married woman's separate estate in equity, so the 1848 statute that was passed to remedy some of those problems raised new questions. Practical efforts to clarify the ambiguities in the

[52] *JNYA,* April 6, 1848, pp. 1129-30.
[53] *LNY, 1848,* chap. 200.
[54] *HWS,* 1:65.

1848 statute began almost immediately. Although the 1848 statute enabled a married woman to own real and personal property as a legal rather than an equitable estate, and to hold it "to her sole and separate use, as if she were a single female," it failed to give her any contractual powers. This omission constituted a highly undesirable impediment to the flow of commerce, ostensibly leaving the wife with property that neither she nor her husband could sell or invest. An 1849 statute amended this section to allow the wife "to convey and devise real and personal property . . . as if she were unmarried." Then, in recognition of older practices, the Legislature aimed a blow at the married woman's trust. Not only did the trust continue as a viable vehicle for creating married women's estates, but the 1848 statute did not affect those trusts that were already created. A new provision of the 1849 statute, however, enabled a married woman who was the beneficiary of a trust to petition a justice of the Supreme Court for personal control of her property. After she had submitted a request in writing to her trustee and after the court had examined "the capacity of such married woman to manage and control" her property, it was within the discretion of the court to order the trustee to convey all or a part of the trust to the woman.[55]

The limitations of the statutes of 1848 and 1849 reflected the limitations of earlier equitable exceptions to the common law. The Legislature focused on property acquired by gift or inheritance, as the chancery courts had done. The 1849 amendment undoubtedly improved the wife's post-1828 status, but it took the wife's contractual capacities no further than the earlier precedents of equity. Even the blow at the married woman's trust contained the assumption that the capacity of a woman to manage her property was questionable and needed to be evaluated by the courts.

In some areas of law, economic developments spawned more innovations than self-conscious attempts at legal reforms. Savings banks provide an example. Total deposits in U.S. savings institutions were more than six times as great in 1850 as they had been in 1835, and tripled again by 1860. The bulk of this growth took place in New York and Massachusetts. Designed originally

[55] *LNY, 1849,* chap. 375, secs. 3 and 4.

to encourage habits of thrift in the poor, savings banks by 1850 included depositors of substance. The Legislature passed a statute in 1850 that protected the deposits of married women in savings banks in the state. Any female depositor who was married was permitted unilaterally to withdraw her deposits. This act actually was designed, as the statute declared, "for the protection of savings banks . . . receiving deposits from married women," so that the wife's receipt might constitute a legal discharge of the bank's responsibilities.[56] Yet in unequivocally preventing the husband from suing the bank for his wife's deposits, the act gave the wife control of her own savings. For the woman who worked before marriage and saved a small nest egg (a relatively common pattern among mid-nineteenth-century female wage earners) and for the woman who brought a cash legacy to her marriage (a fairly common type of bequest to females in nineteenth-century wills), this act held tangible economic advantages. By placing the wife's deposits out of the reach of the husband's creditors while actually making them available for the couple's mutual needs, the statute held economic advantages for the husband as well.

Statutes of this type were passed to eliminate the gray areas of earlier legislation. Under a strict common law interpretation, the wife's cash or stock—all her personal property—would have belonged to the husband outright. But if the wife's contractual powers were unambiguously delineated in the 1849 act, then the savings statute should have been superfluous. This, evidently, was not the case. A wife's name on a bank account was insufficient evidence of her separate ownership and control until the 1850 statute.

In addition to savings, the increasing importance of personal property in the form of stock produced further legislation. With little fanfare, in 1851 the Legislature stipulated that a married woman who owned stock could vote in person or by proxy for corporate officers.[57] As a result of this act, a father could bequeath stock to his daughter and remain confident that she would be able to vote it. This act at least made all stockholders in a corporation equal regardless of sex or marital status.

[56]Taylor, *Transportation Revolution,* pp. 321–22; *LNY, 1850*, chap. 91, sec. 1.
[57]*LNY, 1851*, chap. 321.

The wife's procedural disabilities were also improved in this period by the New York Code of Civil Procedure, known as the Field Code. When an action concerned a wife's separate property or when it was between her and her husband, she could sue alone, but in all other situations in which she was a party to a suit, she had to be joined by her husband. An 1851 amendment added that when her husband could not be joined with her, she must prosecute or defend by her "next friend."[58]

The primary goal of these early statutes was to clarify and codify the legal relationship between the married couple and the commercial world by transforming the separate equitable estate into a legal one. The statutes were the logical result of the procedural and jurisdictional merger of law and equity. Nevertheless, greater economic autonomy for some wives was certainly one outcome. Until the Earnings Act of 1860, however, no statute was aimed specifically at a fundamental readjustment of the husband-wife relationship.

Clearly, the 1848 statute was crudely drafted and limited in scope, and it necessitated numerous amendments. But in some ways it was the Pandora's box that its opponents had feared. It invited further scrutiny of the marriage equation, which in turn cleared the way for the Earnings Act. So mixed were the signals emanating from its passage that the usually outspoken *Albany Argus* acclaimed its momentous importance but was unable to ascertain whether it was for "good or evil." But to the women who went on to demand greater rights that summer of 1848 at Seneca Falls, it was unquestionably good. It was "the death-blow to the old Blackstone code for married women in this country." It was the inspiration for organized and sustained political agitation. From the passage of this statute in the spring of 1848, they envisioned a steady advance to nothing less than "their complete equality."[59]

[58]On legislative amendments to the Field Code, see *LNY, 1848,* chap. 379, pt. 2, chap. 4, tit. 3, sec. 94; *LNY, 1849,* chap. 438, pt. 2, chap. 4, tit. 3, sec. 114; "The Code of Procedure of the State of New York as Amended by the Legislature," July 10, 1851, pt. 2, chap. 3, tit. 3, sec. 114, in *LNY, 1851,* Appendix.
[59]*HWS,* 1:64.

CHAPTER 6

A Bridge between Spheres: The Women's Rights Movement and the Earnings Act of 1860

> Woman is a slave, from the cradle to the grave. Father, guardian, husband—master still. One conveys her, like a piece of property, over to the other.
>
> —Ernestine Rose

Between 1848 and 1860, the drive for married women's property rights in New York assumed new contours. What distinguished this stage of the drive was the presence of an active, organized women's rights movement. Feminist criticism of domestic relations laws proliferated and began to exhibit recognizable configurations. Crippled by the lack of the vote and acting on the periphery of state politics, a small but articulate group of women was able to generate a significant amount of publicity. Personal ties to political reform networks provided these women with some political leverage as well.

Antebellum feminists systematically exposed the patriarchal core of coverture, and in so doing constructed a bridge between spheres. In demanding greater legal autonomy for the wife in the domestic sphere, they increasingly challenged male economic and political power in the public sphere. By refusing to separate law from politics, and by stressing the inherently political nature of law, they contributed to the fuller integration of women into political thought. At the end of the antebellum period, even the staunchest supporters of the status quo in marriage were compelled to consider the political status of women, if only to justify their conservatism effectively. The drive for married women's property rights extended the individualistic, egalitarian premises of the Revolution to the women of the nation, not only in their capacity as wives and mothers but also as independent citizens of the state.

As Linda Kerber brilliantly demonstrated, the Revolution's political legacy to American women was encapsulated in the ideal of Republican Motherhood. The concept of female citizenship was fused with the concept of motherhood when the nurturing of the next generation of male citizens was designated as the woman's primary civic role. The ideal was limited, she suggests, a measure of the conservatism of the Revolution, and it conveniently masked the political powerlessness of women. Thus the subsequent political history of American women might be viewed as the effort to accomplish what the Revolution had failed to do.[1]

The antebellum feminist drive for married women's property rights comprised a significant stage in that enduring effort. Between the 1820s and the Civil War, the language of Republican Motherhood became heightened and sentimentalized. Technological improvements in printing and increases in literacy ensured the broad dissemination and easy vulgarization of Republican Motherhood, an ideal that gradually congealed into the cult of domesticity. The ideal antebellum woman—the True Woman, as she was called—was more elevated, more spiritual, more moral, more ethereal, and even more remote from the centers of politics than her republican mother or grandmother. Her power was in the home, in the guidance and nurture of her family. Yet the chasm between this popular ideal and the legal typology of the family was becoming too broad to be sustained. As the first married women's statutes promoted debate over coverture, the gulf between the True Woman and the feme covert was exposed. As soon as legislatures began to make modest improvements in the legal status of married women, some women demanded greater improvements. Radical feminists asserted that the very absence of those improvements demonstrated that it was no longer possible to relegate the political values of women exclusively to the domestic sphere.

Many female reformers, as Ellen DuBois has noted, wanted

[1]Kerber, *Women of the Republic,* pp. 11–12.

only to modify women's subordinate status within the domestic sphere.[2] Surely this was true of such women as Sarah Hale. But the radical edge of antebellum feminism cut directly into the political sphere in order to eradicate women's subordinate status. Thus feminists exposed the real inseparability of those public and private worlds. The drive for married women's property rights provided them with a perfect bridge, permitting the cautious to remain on the domestic side, the intrepid to invade the political side, and some to move gradually from one to the other. Organizing for an improvement in the legal status of wives was an important precursor of the independent, post–Civil War suffragism DuBois has described. Demands for suffrage, made in this earlier period in conjunction with demands for married women's property rights, demonstrated that the more women penetrated the political world, the more likely were they to effect improvements in the domestic world. There can be no doubt that New York feminists exerted tangible political pressure on the Legislature and were influential in the passage of the Earnings Act of 1860.

Not only did this 1860 act include female wage earners and businesswomen for the first time, but in touching the sensitive area of child custody, it blunted fundamental common law assumptions about the husband's dominant role in the family. This statute, moreover, gave married women full legal visibility by allowing them to bring actions in their own names for damages or personal injury. It permitted a wife to own property acquired by "trade, business, labor, or services" and to be a joint guardian of her children with her husband, and it equalized intestate succession in realty by reducing the husband's share.[3]

One could argue that the Earnings Act, like former acts, marked the pragmatic legislative recognition of a new economic development—the presence of substantial numbers of female wage earners in the economy. However, married women did not constitute a significant portion of females in the labor force. According to Daniel Scott Smith, throughout the nineteenth

[2]DuBois, *Feminism and Suffrage,* pp. 16–17.

[3]*LNY, 1860,* chap. 90. A wife still needed her husband's written permission to sell her realty, but he needed her permission to sell his realty, too. If she could show that his refusal was unreasonable, the court could authorize her sale. See secs. 4–6.

century, 95 percent of the white women in America did not work outside of their homes while they were married. Whatever the limitations of this evidence—the omission of black women and certain types of work as well as the differences bound to exist in an area as industrial as New York—it is unlikely that married female wage earners were sufficiently numerous or influential to generate legislative pressure. We know, however, that some working-class women supported a married women's statute as well as every other demand put forth by middle-class advocates of women's rights.[4] But measures that included earnings as separate property, reduced the husband's rights in cases of intestacy, or improved the wife's status as a guardian of her children cannot be linked, as life insurance can, to legislative recognition of new economic developments. Rather they have to be seen as more woman-oriented goals.

To some extent, of course, the direction of the statutes followed a certain internal logic. Once a married woman had a separate legal estate, it was reasonable that she be able to control it. If she were to control it effectively, she had to become a legal entity, capable of suing and being sued. Once she acquired these new legal capacities, it was ludicrous to regard her as a minor incapable of being the guardian of her own children. But it was precisely this step-by-step accumulation of the wife's legal and economic powers that challenged the patriarchal family. For years American jurists and legislators had fought off this trend by sustaining the dichotomy between the married woman's status in equity and at common law. The first married women's acts, which established legal estates, made it impossible to sustain this dichotomy, and by the late 1850s, American feminists were creating additional pressures. Every provision of the 1860 statute, it should be noted, was a specific goal of the women's movement. The New York Earnings Act, in other words, was the significant legislative realization of demands by women for women.

The married women's acts and the women's movement interacted in a cause-and-effect relationship. Initiated to meet legal and commercial needs, the earliest acts stimulated public

[4]Smith, "Family Limitation," p. 120; Philip S. Foner, *Women and the American Labor Movement: From Colonial Times to the Eve of World War I* (New York, 1979), pp. 69–70.

awareness of married women's common law disabilities and encouraged the development of the women's movement. Given an issue around which to cohere, the women's movement pressed legislatures to respond at least minimally to their increasingly radical demands, including the demand for suffrage.

The first of these propositions—the effect of the early acts on the women's movement—has been supported in *History of Woman Suffrage,* compiled by Elizabeth Cady Stanton and her colleagues in the movement. Among the three major influences on their movement, feminists named the ideology of abolition, the work of pioneering feminists, and an awareness of married women's legal disabilities, which was sparked by the first married women's acts. They claimed that the debate over the statutes, "heralded by the press with comments grave and gay, became the topic of general interest around many fashionable dinner-tables, and at many humble firesides." Discussion touched on all phases of the question "involving the relations of the sexes, and gradually widening to all human interests—political, religious, civil and social." As opposition became vigilant, "woman herself seemed equally vigilant in her efforts to step outside the prescribed limits." In retrospect they viewed married women's property rights as inseparable from the entire movement for suffrage, and as "a legitimate outgrowth of American ideas—a component part of the history of our republic."[5]

Because of the 1848 act, moreover, New York held a distinctive place in the annals of the women's movement. Feminists celebrated that statute and singled out New York as the "first State to emancipate wives from the slavery of the old common law of England and to secure to them equal property rights." Then, following this "death-blow to the old Blackstone code for married women," they explained, "legislation has been slowly but steadily advancing toward their complete equality."[6]

Feminists' failure to cite other statutes or liberal equity precedents cannot be construed as gross ignorance. Elizabeth Cady Stanton was both the daughter and the wife of a lawyer. Her preoccupation with women's legal status is legendary, dating

[5] *HWS,* 1:51–52.

[6] Ibid. pp. 63–64. By the summer of 1848, twelve northern and seven southern states had passed some legislation on married women's property rights. See Warbasse, "Changing Legal Rights," p. 272.

back to an incident in her childhood when she tore from her father's lawbooks pages that referred to laws discriminating against married women.[7] As early as 1843 she was consulting with prominent New York jurists about the legal status of married women in the state.[8] Amelia Bloomer, whose temperance and women's rights journal followed the activities of the New York Legislature with considerable precision, was also an attorney's wife. Ernestine Rose, who consistently mastered those details important to her campaigns, had refused at the age of sixteen to let her father sign away her inheritance in an impending marriage contract, and went into a Polish court to defend her claim—successfully.[9] Susan B. Anthony frequently relied on sophisticated legal advice, and on one occasion read a speech to the Legislature prepared by a New York jurist.[10] Caroline Dall, a New Englander who wrote on married women's property rights in the late 1850s, managed to assemble a fairly comprehensive national picture of the legal status of married women.[11] The leaders of the movement used the issue of married women's property rights, however, as a convenient ideological focus.

Married women's property rights provided an organizational focus as well. In New York the legal status of married women was the issue for which Ernestine Rose, Paulina Wright, and Elizabeth Cady Stanton first organized and engaged in political agitation. Other women in other states followed similar patterns, lobbying for a married women's statute while they simultaneously laid the foundations for local feminist organizations. This was true of Jane Swisshelm in Pennsylvania, Mary Upton Ferrin in Massachusetts, Clarina Howard Nichols in Vermont and Kansas, and Frances Gage, Hannah Tracy Cutler, and Elizabeth Jones in Ohio.[12] Feminists noted the political significance of

[7]Stanton, *Eighty Years and More,* pp. 31–33.

[8]Stanton to Elizabeth Oakes Smith, February 17, 1843 in Stanton-Blatch Letters, 2:8. For evidence of additional advice in an 1854 speech, see Stanton to Susan B. Anthony, December 1, 1853, in ibid., 2:54–55.

[9]*HWS,* 1:96.

[10]Anthony's speech on women's rights petitions to a New York Assembly committee on March 3, 1854, was written by Judge William Hay of Rochester. See *HWS,* 1:607.

[11]See Caroline Dall, *Woman's Rights under the Law* (Boston, 1861).

[12]Keith Melder, *Beginnings of Sisterhood: The American Woman's Rights Movement, 1800–1850* (New York, 1977), p. 144; *NAW,* 1:224, 2:2–6, 625–27; *HWS,* 1:171–200, 208, 212–15.

these fledgling organizations in an 1852 convention at Syracuse, where they stated that "the way for the movement was prepared by petitions from women and men of several different states asking for a recognition by the State of [married women's] civil rights."[13]

The timing of the 1848 statute in relation to the official beginning of the women's movement reflects the influence of the statutes on the women's movement. The historic meeting at Seneca Falls took place on July 19 and 20, a few months after the married women's statute of April 7, an event that all delegates construed as a victory for the cause of women's rights. In fact, Ansel Bascom, a delegate at the New York Constitutional Convention of 1846 and a state assemblyman, delivered an address at Seneca Falls on the 1848 statute.[14] Yet at that convention in the midst of the burned-over district, an area Whitney Cross labeled the "psychic highway" connecting New England visionaries with the West, the question of married women's property rights was an urgent one.[15] In the Declaration of Sentiments, the long list of allegations against man, New York feminists insisted, "He has made her, if married, in the eye of the law, civilly dead. He has taken from her all right in property even to the wages she earns."[16]

Feminists have been accused by Mary Beard, among others, of not being careful students of jurisprudence, and of literally advertising Blackstone's metaphor of civil death "throughout the Western world."[17] But it was not precisely the law that interested them. It was not the complexities of New York equity or the minutiae of slowly changing statutes that was their primary concern. They underscored the legal fiction of marital unity as symbolic of women's political, economic, and social subservience. Any equation in which one plus one equaled one by virtue of the

[13] *The Proceedings of the Woman's Rights Convention Held at Syracuse, September 8th, 9th, and 10th, 1852* (Syracuse, 1852), p. 1.

[14] *HWS*, 1:69. See also the report of Mary Bull (Bascom's daughter, who attended the convention with him), in " 'Woman's Rights and Other Reforms in Seneca Falls': A Contemporary View," ed. Robert Riegel, *New York History* 46 (1965):49.

[15] Whitney Cross, *The Burned-Over District: The Social and Intellectual History of Enthusiastic Religion in Western New York, 1800–1850* (Ithaca, 1982), pp. 3–6.

[16] *HWS*, 1:70.

[17] Beard, *Woman as Force in History*, p. 125. For similar criticism, see Robert Riegel, *American Feminists* (Lawrence, Kans., 1963), p. 187.

woman's invisibility was a vivid symbol of male dominion in a cultural as well as a legal context. They set out to exploit the sexual politics resonating from the metaphor of the wife submerged in the husband as dynamically as possible, and continued to do so for the balance of the nineteenth century.

Feminists' challenges to the common law depicted marital unity in its harshest and most unremitting form, and as Mary Beard insisted, perpetuated an image that was legally imprecise and historically inaccurate. A richly suggestive and readily available metaphor, the legal fiction of marital unity was a convenient vehicle for the women's rights movement. It became the pivot on which antebellum feminism turned. Feminists wanted publicity and an opportunity to place their demands before the public as persuasively as possible, and the property rights of married women provided them with an appropriate issue. As successful propagandists they embraced and synthesized the concerns and experiences of a wide audience.[18] By linking property rights to more radical goals, they created a public forum for themselves. There was no danger of the woman question's dying for lack of press, asserted Stanton in a buoyant letter to George Cooper in the fall of 1848.[19]

Feminists, however, were more concerned with the woman question and all of its ramifications than with whether or not a wife could contract without her husband's permission. They extended discussion of married women's property rights to larger and more explosive issues. The questions they raised involved the roles women were to play in the entire society. The solutions they proposed required the full participation of women, married or single, in the nation's social, political, and economic life—what was tantamount to a revolution in gender roles. Ernestine Rose expressed the larger goals of the movement when she demanded of men, "Stand aside; give us space to grow. Our title-deed to life, and to all that belongs to it, to make it useful and happy, is as clear as yours."[20]

[18]For an analysis of propaganda and political symbols, see Murray Edelman, *The Symbolic Uses of Politics* (Urbana, Ill., 1976), p. 124.

[19]Stanton to Cooper, September 14, 1848, in Stanton-Blatch Letters, 2:18–19. Cooper was the editor of the *National Reformer* of Rochester, which published the letter. It may be found also in *HWS,* 1:806.

[20]*Proceedings of the Seventh National Woman's Rights Convention Held in New York City at the Broadway Tabernacle, Tuesday and Wednesday, November 25th and 26th, 1856* (New York, n.d.), p. 76.

The emotive rhetoric with which American feminists invested the doctrine of marital unity reflected the propagandistic functions they gave it. To the extent that the old legal fiction served their larger purposes, they used it. Participants for the first time in organized political protest against their legal status, they quickly learned to exploit legal symbols, attacking those that demeaned them and embracing those that carried potential advantages. So, too, they learned to welcome political support from any source. As Stanton once put it, in the cause of women's rights, "if the Devil steps forward ready to help, I shall say good fellow come!"[21]

Intellectual rigor and logical consistency were not requisite for their immediate goals. In legal theory, moreover, they were self-educated, and the limited range of their legal sources was an indication of their exclusion from the upper levels of professional education. Thus even as they deplored Blackstone's classic formulation of common law marriage principles, making it the object of their most vitriolic rhetoric, they reverently cited his analysis of natural rights, selectively quoting passages from the *Commentaries* that they found relevant and appealing. One Seneca Falls resolution drawn directly from Blackstone stated, "This law of Nature being coeval with mankind and dictated by God himself, is of course superior in obligation to any other." Laws in conflict "with the true and substantial happiness of women," it concluded, were "contrary to the great precept of nature" and therefore invalid.[22]

Despite intellectual inconsistencies, nineteenth-century American feminists were extraordinarily effective in exposing what they perceived to be the intolerable contradictions in their society. These were contradictions that Alexis de Tocqueville noted and dismissed when he insisted that Americans never supposed "that one consequence of democratic principles [was] the subversion of marital power."[23] They were not convinced. Fully aware of how former arguments for natural authority in

[21]Stanton to Studwell (probably E. A. Studwell of Buffalo), November 30, 1867, typescript in Elizabeth Cady Stanton Papers, Vassar College. Stanton was defending her association with George Francis Train, a Copperhead and a racist.

[22]*HWS,* 1:71–72.

[23]Alexis de Tocqueville, *Democracy in America,* trans. Henry Reeve, 2 vols. (New York, 1889), 2:221–24.

governments had fallen before the onslaught of natural rights, they fervently believed their evocation of natural rights would bring similar results in relations between the sexes. Abolition encouraged the application of natural rights to distinctions of sex as well as race. Gerrit Smith, Stanton's cousin and one of the state's leading abolitionists, stated in a handbill distributed in his congressional district "that political rights are not conventional, but natural—inhering in all persons, the black as well as the white, the female as well as the male."[24] Frederick Douglass, who had attended the Seneca Falls convention and was one of the movement's staunchest and most eloquent supporters, put the case for women's natural rights as succinctly as possible. "Our doctrine is," he said, "that right is of no sex."[25]

Surely the basic ideas they generated were not new. Attacks on coverture were commonplace in the first half of the nineteenth century, and even the causal relationship between coverture and the disfranchisement of women had been fully explored long before 1848. The organized political context in which they disseminated these ideas, however, was new. Yet their natural rights arguments were so comfortably familiar that they sometimes obscured the radical uses to which they were being put. Stanton was characteristically perceptive about the ideological position of the women's movement in relation to the American mainstream. "[I]nasmuch as we are inmates of the old house," she pointed out, "we must patch it a little to make life endurable; but let us begin today to dig the foundations of the new." Stanton urged women to drop reform work in those male-dominated institutions that sapped their energies and gave them no power, and advised separatism as an alternative. "Let us have a separate purse, separate schools, and a new code of laws for our special benefit."[26]

Antebellum feminists did not create the new and separate foundations Stanton envisioned, but they did transform older

[24] "To the Voters of the Counties of Oswego and Madison, 5 November 1852, Peterboro, New York," handbill in Smith Family Papers, New York Public Library.

[25] *North Star,* July 28, 1848, cited in *HWS,* 1:75. For another example of male abolitionist support based on a natural rights approach, see the speech of William Lloyd Garrison, *Proceedings . . . Woman's Rights . . . Syracuse,* p. 20.

[26] "Address of E. C. Stanton, Evening Session, Women's Temperance Convention, State of New York, 20 April 1852," *Lily* 4 (May 1852):40.

Enlightenment materials. And always at the heart of this transformation was their attack on the legal fiction of marital unity. At a series of women's rights conventions between 1848 and 1860, and in speeches, pamphlets, magazines, and newspaper pieces, they gradually integrated their assault on the common law status of married women into a bold argument for change. Charges made a decade earlier by Sarah Grimké and Thomas Herttell were renewed. They repeated the same demands in every tract, supported them with letters and personal testimony, and spelled them out in petitions to state legislatures until the outlines of their argument became sharp, familiar, and predictable. Applying an eclectic mixture of English libertarianism and American Romanticism to the legal status of married women, they managed to forge the lines of an economic, domestic, and political feminist theory. Indeed, the development of these three facets of feminism remains a historically significant legacy of the married women's property acts and deserves closer analysis.[27]

The economic feminism they evolved in conjunction with demands for married women's property rights had considerable popular appeal. At the more conservative end of the ideological spectrum, economic feminism was invariably allied to temperance and stressed the inability of the wife to protect herself financially against the extravagances of her alcoholic spouse. Not only did this position permeate feminist and temperance literature, but it could be found in almost all the popular women's literature of the period.[28] Nowhere, however, did the feminist implications of the standard temperance tale appear with greater regularity than in Amelia Bloomer's *Lily*. Attacked by some temperance advocates for her increasingly strident

[27]This analysis of the literature of the women's movement is drawn from printed proceedings of local and national women's rights conventions, published books, periodicals, pamphlets, petitions, and handbills from the Alma Lutz Collection at Vassar College, and from the special collections of the New York Public Library and the New York State Library at Albany. Some of this material is reprinted in *HWS*. The pamphlet literature reveals that certain speeches were widely reprinted. As early as 1853 a number of speeches and articles were assembled into ten pamphlets for sale or distribution. Authors included Samuel J. May, Paulina Wright Davis, Abby Kelley Foster, Harriet Taylor Mill, Elizabeth Oakes Smith, Clarina Howard Nichols, Matilda Joslyn Gage, Angelina Grimké Weld, Elizabeth Cady Stanton, and Ernestine Rose. For a description of this collection of tracts, see *Una* 2 (May 1853):64.

[28]Douglas, *Feminization of American Culture*, pp. 68–69.

support of women's rights, Bloomer persistently argued for the inseparability of the two goals. "That woman has rights," she averred, "we think that none will deny; that she has been cruelly wronged by the law-sanctioned liquor traffic, must be admitted by all."[29] Noting the banking law of 1850, Bloomer announced triumphantly that a married woman in the state could now draw her own savings out and no one else, "not even her liege lord, be he drunk or sober, wise or foolish, sane or insane," could stop her.[30] Bloomer's original focus, like that of Susan B. Anthony, had been temperance, and she frequently delivered women's rights lectures at temperance meetings. Underscoring Bloomer's predilection for lumping the evils of the rumshop with married women's legal disabilities, the *New York Times* pointed out that although an 1853 temperance meeting that she attended in New York City was convened "nominally to promote the cause of Temperance," it propagated "all the wild extravagances of Woman's Rights."[31]

The *Lily* reprinted stories by such established favorites as Sarah Hale, Lydia Sigourney, and T. S. Arthur, as well as by Jane Swisshelm and other feminists. This type of fiction often carried feminist legal and economic implications that Bloomer was delighted to spell out in her nonfiction columns. In the typical temperance tale, the husband squandered all the couple's resources. Usually, even as creditors clamored at the door of his home, he indulged "in the wine cup to drown his care."[32] Legally incapacitated, the wife could not stop him from dissipating the little that remained, nor could she earn money and keep it out of his reach. Because of the legal merger of their persons, her finances and her future were hopelessly tied to his alcoholism.

Such maudlin tales rationalized the middle-class woman's role of moral preceptor. The wife was unable to exert her own morally superior efforts over the husband because of her legal disabilities. Nevertheless, such tales reflected a real legal prob-

[29] *Lily*, April 1853, cited in Dexter C. Bloomer, *Life and Writings of Amelia Bloomer* (New York, 1895), pp. 97–98. See also the flyer announcing the dual goals of temperance and woman's rights for the *Lily*'s fourth volume, January 1852, in NYHS.

[30] "Legislative Doings," *Lily* 2 (May 1850):38.

[31] "Temperance and Woman's Rights," *New York Times*, February 8, 1853, p. 3.

[32] "The Governess," *Lily* 1 (May 1849):33.

lem to which at least one specialized manual addressed itself. In *Every Woman Her Own Lawyer,* the author urged the wife who was the victim of her husband's intemperance to have him declared incompetent and to have his assets placed under the control of a committee.[33] Alcoholism was more than a convenient subject for maudlin fiction; it was a pressing social and legislative concern. New York, which experimented briefly with limited temperance legislation and then rescinded it, never reached the goal of temperance advocates, a prohibition law.[34] One clue to the impact of alcoholism appears in New York legislative documents. An official report issued by the state mental asylum suggests that intemperance and loss of property were the two major contributors to mental breakdown, exceeded in importance only by a condition the overseers termed "religious anxiety."[35]

In the 1850s, however, as they failed to gain full acceptance in the New York temperance movement, New York feminists began to concentrate on women's rights. Among the most famous rebukes that alienated them was the refusal of a Syracuse temperance convention in 1852 to seat Amelia Bloomer and Susan B. Anthony as delegates.[36] At a meeting of the Woman's State Temperance Society in June 1853, Stanton pointed out, "We have been obliged to preach women's rights, because many instead of listening to what we had to say on temperance, have questioned the right of a woman to speak on any subject."[37] By 1854 Stanton maintained in an address to the New York Legislature that the "wives of 50,000 drunkards" in the state had registered their complaints through the petitioning campaigns of the women's rights movement.[38]

Clearly, feminists relied heavily on the woman-as-victim theme, a motif that meshed neatly with the Victorian tendency to allot women compensatory virtues and indirect control in the

[33]George Bishop, *Every Woman Her Own Lawyer* (New York, 1858), pp. 211–12.

[34]An 1845 local-option act made 80 percent of the state dry within a year. The law was repealed in 1847. An 1855 prohibition act was declared invalid by the Court of Appeals. See Ellis, *Short History of New York,* pp. 309–10.

[35]"Interpretations of Causes for Incarceration in State Lunatic Asylum," *NYSD,* 1847, vol. 1, no. 3.

[36]*HWS,* 1:485–86.

[37]Ibid., p. 495.

[38]Stanton, *Address to the Legislature of New York Adopted by the State Woman's Rights Convention Held at Albany . . . February 14 and 15, 1854* (Albany, 1854), p. 17.

place of economic and political power.[39] Yet instead of celebrating women's suffering and self-abnegation, they demanded economic power. Instead of accepting the exaggerated deference and sanctification accorded to women, they demanded justice, and they demanded it in the form of property rights, a term so fundamental to the political and legal foundations of the country that no American then or now would have any difficulty apprehending its appeal. Most of their contemporaries could agree that the possession of property brought material pleasure and psychological well-being to its owner, and that its protection was one of the principal objects of government. "A proper self-esteem," said Elisha Hurlbut, a leading New York advocate of women's rights, "oftentimes depends on this possession."[40] Feminists consistently appealed to this indigenous respect for the sanctity and benefits of property and transmuted the woman-as-victim theme into a drive for female autonomy and dignity.

Their demands for the right of a wife to control her earnings exposed the fallacies of the common law rationale of protection. Low pay and limited job opportunities for female wage earners, married or single, were consistent topics at women's rights conventions and were invariably connected to the common law assertion that women were protected by men. Feminists asked how one could reconcile the legal ideal that professed to insulate women from the hardships of the marketplace with the economic reality that forced women to work for less than subsistence wages. Caustically citing Blackstone, they explained that this situation existed because "so great a favorite is the female sex in the laws of England."[41]

Fittingly enough, in an age of enterprise they demanded the right to be entrepreneurs and to control earnings from business and investments. "We re-claim also our right of merchandize

[39]For fine descriptions of the compensation theory from different perspectives, see Douglas, *Feminization of American Culture,* pp. 10–11; Sklar, *Catherine Beecher,* p. 113.

[40]Elisha Hurlbut, *Essays on Human Rights and Their Political Guarantees* (New York, 1850), p. 168. See also Samuel J. May, *The Rights and Conditions of Women: A Sermon Preached in Syracuse, November, 1845,* Woman's Rights Tracts, no. 1 (1853), p. 12.

[41]*Proceedings of the Woman's Rights Convention Held at Akron, Ohio, May 28 and 29, 1851* (reprinted New York, 1973), pp. 17, 27–31.

and its profits," announced Paulina Wright Davis at a New York convention.[42] Ernestine Rose spoke of a friend in the boarding-house business who could not rent premises without her husband's signature. The landlord insisted that the husband could claim her earnings and refuse to pay the rent on the grounds that the contract was made without his permission.[43] Every "true woman," asserted Elizabeth Oakes Smith in a fresh twist to that seductive and familiar phrase, has a right to financial independence.[44]

Another constant demand was for improved provisions of dower and intestate succession. Feminists had their share of stories about the husband who squandered his wife's legacy—or even worse, her earnings—and left her with little in the way of her widow's thirds. Wendell Phillips told of an heiress who brought $50,000 to her marriage and was widowed within a year. "In his remarkably generous and manly will," the husband "left her the use of her own money as long as she remained his widow."[45] At the death of a husband, asserted Matilda Joslyn Gage, the wife "is left a queen or a beggar, as the option of her lord dictates."[46]

Attacks on dower, like attacks on coverture, undermined the principle of male protection that underlay the husband-wife relationship in law. Common law jurisprudence presented dower as a generous gift by the law to the wife, an example of the special place women held within its precepts. Phillips' story of the heiress took the protective, chivalric stance attributed to the husband and the common law and made a complete mockery of it. Feminists attacked the common law principle of protection with devastating effectiveness and acerbic humor. Frances Gage amused one women's rights convention by creating a will with reversed gender roles. In her will the testatrix left her son the family carriage and horses and eighty acres of wild land in Iowa. She left her daughter a 160-acre farm with all of its stock and

[42] *Proceedings of the Woman's Rights Convention Held at the Broadway Tabernacle in the City of New York on Tuesday and Wednesday, September 6th and 7th, 1853* (New York, 1853), p. 29.

[43] Ibid., p. 48.

[44] Elizabeth Oakes Smith, *Woman and Her Needs* (New York, 1850), p. 42.

[45] *The Speech of Wendell Phillips* [*and Abby Kelley Foster*] *to the Convention in Worcester, October 1851*, Woman's Rights Tracts, no. 2 (1853), p. 8.

[46] *Proceedings . . . Woman's Rights . . . Syracuse,* pp. 43–44.

equipment and the farmhouse. To her husband she gave her Bible, $100, forty acres of wild land in Illinois, and the use of their bed and house for as long as he should remain her widower. Recommending her husband to the care of her daughter, she also made the daughter sole executrix.[47] Gage's will, which brought roars of laughter, made four important points: first, that married women's legal disabilities encouraged fathers to leave daughters only tokens of wealth and status instead of property of genuine value; second, that dower or provisions in lieu of dower were often inadequate to support the widow; third, that the husband's bequest to the wife was frequently dependent on her fidelity to him beyond the grave; and fourth, that widows were often placed in a position of complete dependence on their sons.

Tales about the unfairness of dower accompanied by practical advice appeared regularly in Amelia Bloomer's *Lily.* In "Love, Property, and Principle," for example, a widow who has lost the farm she purchased to her husband's brother is compelled to go to work. She meets a suitor who proposes to "protect" and "elevate" her for the rest of her life, a gentleman who flawlessly meets contemporary requirements of the ideal husband. This widow, however, explores the covert exploitation inherent in the wife's protection and elevation. Having learned her lesson in her first marriage, she demands an antenuptial agreement. "Never again," she declares, "will I give up *all* for love, while I am subjected to laws that have no higher mission than to oppress the weak and protect the strong." The message is clear. Protection and elevation are inadequate compensation for economic dependence and possible impoverishment. The heroine advises every woman "to look well to her own property lest she find herself a beggar."[48]

Women's rights advocates argued that the young girl's financial vulnerability put her in a poor bargaining position in the marriage market. By contrasting the theoretical legal equality of the contracting parties with their customary financial inequality, they raised questions about the economic underpinnings of the institution of marriage. Because men and women rarely ap-

[47] *Proceedings . . . Woman's Rights . . . Broadway Tabernacle, 1853*, pp. 63–64.

[48] "Love, Property, and Principle by Belinda Budget," *Lily* 6 (January 1854):1–3.

proached marriage as economic equals, ran their argument, testaments to legal equality were specious. Since most women married for support, marriage could be construed as a form of legalized prostitution. Some, moveover, married because of social pressure. Real financial independence for single women might free them from being driven into marriage by fear of the "snubbings, shrugs, dependence, and solitude" that characterized the spinster's life.[49] Better economic opportunities for women and improved property rights for married women would discourage young girls from marrying older men and from seeking in marriage what they should be able to enjoy from their own efforts.

Allusions to age disparities in marriage had some statistical validity in New York. An official report of marriages in the state in 1847 noted that of the 11,437 marriages recorded, persons under the age of twenty numbered 325 men and 3,013 women. Numbers of men and women who married between the ages of twenty and twenty-five were almost exactly equal. But in the twenty-five-to-thirty range. there were 2,956 men and only 1,386 women.[50] Of special concern to feminists were those women under twenty, who accouted for almost one-third of all the marriages in the state and who had little or no experience in earning a living.

The marriage contract, they insisted, was economically disadvantageous for the wife. Once married, most women became "partners in toil, not in profits."[51] As for those who apparently married well, sudden reverses in the economy or the sudden death of the husband might leave them unprepared for sheer financial survival. "The day may come," warned Lucy Stone, "when the hand that provides the luxuries in which you roll, shall be cold in the grave."[52] Economic independence, on the other hand, would bring confidence, self-esteem, and genuine security to its possessor. "To be more dependent upon a husband's bounty," said Stanton in one of her most widely circulated

[49]Smith, *Woman and Her Needs,* p. 43.

[50]"Report of the Secretary of State of the Number of Births, Marriages, and Deaths, for the Year of 1847," *NYSD,* April 12, 1848, vol. 3, no. 73, Table 3. The age disparity between men and women at marriage was far greater in such urban areas as New York County than in rural counties of the state.

[51]Paulina Wright Davis, "Woman's Rights," unpublished manuscript, ca. 1852, in Alma Lutz Collection, Vassar College, p. 21.

[52]*Proceedings . . . Woman's Rights . . . Broadway Tabernacle, 1853,* p. 92.

lectures, "is as galling to a proud woman as to be a pensioner on an unwilling father or brother."[53]

The movement's quest for economic power was persistent and unmuted. Participants expanded the specific demand for married women's property rights to more general demands for women's full participation in the entire life of the society. These demands stood in direct defiance of the contemporary belief that women were compensated for their legal disabilities by their domestic powers. In working out their campaign for married women's property rights, feminists questioned not only the economic underpinnings of marriage, but also the power of women relative to men in the domestic sphere. In fact, it was in probing the legal restrictions on women in the domestic sphere that they shattered the compensation theory and created domestic feminism, the second major ideological strand they evolved in the drive for married women's property rights.

Here again, as in their demands for property rights, they exploited the gap between the cult of domesticity and the common law marital prototype. Just as they had ignored equitable precedents in their demands for property rights, they ignored the extent to which judicial precedents were refashioning family law. When separations and divorces were granted, especially after the 1840s, custody of children often went to the mother.[54] Nevertheless, until the Earnings Act, the New York husband retained his right to appoint a guardian other than the mother in his will. Although husbands rarely exercised that right, the option remained available to them.

In guardianship antebellum feminists had a particularly effective issue. Guardianship went to the nub of the common law assumption that the children of the marriage, along with the property and person of the wife, came under the husband's control.[55] Because the husband was the guardian of the wife, he was responsible for selecting the place of domicile. He was responsible for his wife's behavior and entitled to chastise her for

[53]Stanton, "Our Young Girls," *Lily* 5 (March 1853). A typescript of a later version of this lecture, which refers to the Thirteenth Amendment, is at Vassar College.

[54]On custody, see Zainaldin, "Emergence of a Modern American Family Law," pp. 1038–89.

[55]For a comprehensive study of changes in the entire typology of family law, see Grossberg, "Law and the Family."

aberrant behavior just as if she were a child. How could a culture that had elevated mother to the status of a saint relegate her to the legal status of a child? Few areas of coverture were more directly at odds with the cult of domesticity than the father's common law right of guardianship. The campaign for the wife's guardianship rights was, in part, a sincere effort to obliterate the husband's right to appoint by will a guardian other than the mother. Feminists' larger purpose, however, was to exploit the husband's guardianship rights as the quintessential symbol of the patriarchal family, in which all property and persons, including the children, were controlled by the husband.

This facet of the campaign relied on a comparison of the biologically unquestionable parenthood of the mother and the less reliable claim to parenthood of the father. Yet to declare their biological claims in this way would have created doubts about the sexual fidelity of women in marriage. Instead, feminists celebrated the sanctity of motherhood, drawing freely on the cult of domesticity. The common law, they protested, violated the sanctity of motherhood. The child a mother bore "in agony, has nurtured with her own life, and watched over with such love as only a mother can know" could be taken from her by a clause in her husband's will.[56] Thus even as they battled for the right of women to participate freely in the marketplace, they simultaneously argued that the care of children was woman's own special function. In at least one case, direct action followed theoretical discourse. Susan B. Anthony became embroiled in an interstate confrontation over legal guardianship when she abducted and sheltered the wife and child of a Massachusetts legislator in order to keep the child from her father's custody.[57] The child subsequently was abducted from a New York Sunday school by the father, and the incident achieved national notoriety.

Arguments for the moral superiority of women often accompanied feminist demands for female guardianship. Antoinette Brown cited the case of the husband who gave the custody of two older sons to relatives. The eldest, she concluded, became a "drunkard" like his father and the second son was imprisoned

[56]Davis, "Woman's Rights," p. 23.
[57]Dorr, *Susan B. Anthony*, pp. 137–40; *HWS*, 1:469.

for robbery because they had no female hand to guide them. All the courage and moral resources a mother might have brought to the situation were denied these boys, she reasoned, because of the wife's lack of guardianship rights.[58]

Although assertions of women's moral superiority flourished in feminist guardianship arguments, the major thrust of these arguments was to draw attention to the wife's childlike status at common law despite her vaunted superiority. Protests against the wife's legal status in marriage were incorporated in private marriage contracts published by couples who consciously refashioned the rules of the husband-wife relationship. One of the earliest and best known of such contracts was made in New York by Robert Dale Owen and Mary Jane Robinson in 1832. "Of the unjust right which in virtue of this ceremony an iniquitous law tacitly gives me over the person and property of another," stated Owen, "I can not legally, but I can morally divest myself." Owen, son of the founder of the Utopian community of New Harmony, a collaborator of Frances Wright, and later an agitator for liberalized divorce laws in Indiana, registered his indignation at the "barbarous relics of a feudal, despotic" legal system.[59]

Similarly Henry Blackwell and Lucy Stone protested in their marriage contract against laws that gave to the husband "the custody of the wife's person" and "the exclusive control and guardianship of their children."[60] Stone, moreover, refused to follow the custom of assuming her husband's surname because she viewed such a practice as symbolic of the wife's legal obliteration after marriage. In a speech in 1858 to the Shirt Sewers' and Seamstresses' Union in New York City, she called marriage a partnership with one partner because the husband could put his finger on the famous passage in Blackstone. And as if this were not demeaning enough, proclaimed Stone, the wife's loss of identity "follows her all the way down to her very grave, and on her tombstone insults her memory by writing there that she is the relict of somebody—a piece of the man she was merged in."[61]

[58] *Proceedings . . . Woman's Rights . . . Broadway Tabernacle, 1853*, pp. 94–95.

[59] *HWS*, 1:294–95.

[60] Ibid., p. 261.

[61] "Lucy Stone on the Right of Woman to Elective Franchise," *New York Times*, April 23, 1858, p. 5.

Aaron M. Powell, New York feminist and friend of both Anthony and Stanton, and J. Anna Rice, who married themselves without a minister or public official in Ghent, New York, on April 15, 1861, recorded their "united protest against the inequality and injustice" of marriage laws "which assign to the wife a position of legal inferiority." That this contract was made after New York passed one of its most liberal married women's acts only demonstrates the formulaic quality embodied in such protests. "The marriage contract," the couple stated, "is framed in ignorance, inequality, and injustice," and makes one party "civilly dead and legally buried. The individuality of the wife is merged in the husband."[62]

Feminists' attacks on the concept of the woman as an extension of the man's volition generated more subversive lines of thought. They knew they warred "directly with the thought so deeply rooted and so hoary, that Woman is only an appendage, and not an integral part in the fabric of human society."[63] Discussions of the wife's lack of autonomy in marriage were especially jarring when they led to the conclusion that women were the victims of a male political conspiracy. Marriage laws, Sarah Grimké had earlier suggested in her *Letters on the Equality of the Sexes,* were enacted "to destroy [women's] independence and crush her individuality."[64] The wife's legal invisibility became synonymous with her destruction as a separate individual, a classic example of the tyranny of the male sex over the female sex.

This more hostile tack was often softened by assurances that better laws and economic advantages for women would enhance the sanctity of marriage and make it more than "a household arrangement for thrift and economy."[65] Financial independence in the next generation of daughters along with better domestic relations laws could prevent them from "marrying the purse instead of the man."[66] Bolder arguments, however, stressed the

[62]"Married," *New York Daily Tribune,* April 20, 1861, p. 7.

[63]Lucy Stone, Paulina Wright Davis, and William Henry Channing, "Woman's Rights Convention," *Lily* 3 (September 1851):67. This was a call for the upcoming convention in Worcester, Massachusetts.

[64]Grimké, *Letters on the Equality of the Sexes,* p. 74.

[65]Elizabeth Oakes Smith, *The Sanctity of Marriage,* Woman's Rights Tracts, no. 5 (1853), p. 22.

[66]*Speech of Wendell Phillips . . . at Worcester,* p. 22.

exploitation of women by men. Reporting on the common law at an Akron convention, Maria L. Giddings pointed out, "It is in the married state that woman labors under the greatest legal disabilities. At the moment of marriage, the law disrobes woman of her name. In the language of commentators her legal existence is suspended during coveture [sic]." Jurists argued, she continued, that the purpose was to make the marriage indissoluble, when in fact the law divested the wife of rights, lest she oppose her husband.[67] Men, in short, arrogated power to themselves by manipulating the law.

One group assembled in Rutland, Vermont, in 1858 and, led by Julia Branch, whom the *New York Times* called an advocate of free love, proposed the following resolution: "That the slavery and degradation of women proceeds from the institution of marriage; that by the marriage contract she loses control of her name, her person, her property, her labor, her affections, her children, and her freedom."[68] Ernestine Rose, who attended the Rutland convention, was compelled to defend herself in a letter to the editor against charges of being an advocate of free love. All she wanted, she insisted, was equality in the marriage relationship.[69]

In addition to being labeled advocates of free love, feminists were frequently denounced as "infidels"—especially Rose, who was the movement's only prominent Jew and an atheist to boot. Most feminists attempted new biblical interpretations to accompany their new legal demands. Grimké admonished women that their obligation was directly to Christ as their ruler, and not to their husbands. Women who feared to sign an abolitionist petition because of their husbands' disapproval surrendered moral responsibility to them, and chose their husbands over Christ.[70] Antoinette Brown and Lucretia Mott also tried to reshape the biblical interpretations that traditionally accompanied arguments for the wife's inferior legal position. Rose, who deplored religious analyses, pointed out that Indiana delegates had relied on religious arguments to defeat a married women's clause at

[67]*Proceedings . . . Woman's Rights . . . Akron,* pp. 12–13.
[68]"A Spicy Time on Free Love," *New York Times,* June 29, 1858, p. 1.
[69]Letter to the Editor, *New York Times,* July 2, 1858, p. 5.
[70]Grimké, *Letters on the Equality of the Sexes,* pp. 86–87.

their constitutional convention.[71] Caroline Dall was able to bridge these two positions with a broad Unitarian approach that asserted, "You should make woman in the eye of the law what she has always been in the eye of God—a responsible human being. . . . "[72]

The demands for equality, responsibility, and dignity that emerged from the debate over the common law status of married women left a rich legacy to feminist theory, but the realization of those demands was neither tangible nor imminent. Protests were often vague and elusive. Economic and domestic issues created a cogent challenge to long-accepted assumptions about the institution of marriage and they widened the scope of the woman question, but they did not create political pressure. This was supplied by feminist demands for suffrage. Most contemporaries envisaged suffrage as the most menacing of all feminist goals. The demand for suffrage was essential to the development of an independent and politically self-conscious women's movement and was related at least tangentially to the passage of the married women's acts.

Feminists argued that the very existence of married women's legal disabilities was evidence that the interests of women were not represented in all-male legislatures elected by all-male voters. Ernestine Rose, for example, was convinced that only women who acted in the political arena would be able to protect themselves. When woman becomes politically equal to man, she predicted, "then she will not be obliged to marry for a home and a protector."[73] Legal and political invisibility were manifestations of the same problem; a woman was invisible in marriage and "a cipher in the nation."[74] Representation and consent, the principles over which Americans had separated from England and created a revolution, were applied to the interests of women as opposed to those of men.

An 1849 memorial to the Ohio Constitutional Convention demanded immediate correction of married women's legal dis-

[71] *Proceedings . . . Woman's Rights . . . Syracuse,* pp. 67–68.

[72] Caroline Dall, *The College, the Market, and the Courts: A Woman's Relations to Education, Labor, and Law* (Boston, 1867), p. 307.

[73] Letter to the Editor, *New York Times,* July 2, 1858, p. 5.

[74] Grimké, *Letters on the Equality of the Sexes,* p. 74.

abilities. "Not being represented in those bodies from which emanate the laws to which they are obliged to submit," the petitioners found themselves "protected neither in person nor in property."[75] In an article titled "Why Must Women Vote?" Stanton boldly declared that man cannot legislate for woman. "Our statute books and all past experience force this truth upon us. His laws made for our special benefit have been without exception unjust, cruel and aggressive."[76] It was a familiar argument; it had been elaborately worked out in the 1770s and was even more convincing by the middle of the nineteenth century, after the extension of male suffrage.

Arguments for representation and consent, however, held the same dilemma for the women who employed them as they had for eighteenth-century patriots. How were women to justify their demand for suffrage in such states as New York, which were beginning to grant them what they wanted in the form of married women's laws? One solution was to concentrate on those women who held property and were taxed without being represented. Lucy Stone urged all female property holders to refuse to pay taxes. "Resist," she urged; "let the case be tried in the courts; by your own lawyers; base your cause on the admitted, self-evident truth, that 'taxation and representation are inseparable.' "[77]

Another solution was to view the statutes as nothing more than temporary gifts rather than inalienable rights, and therefore a poor substitute. Ernestine Rose was one of the foremost advocates of this position: "The ballot-box is the focus of all other rights; it is the pivot upon which all others hang; the legal rights are embraced in it, for if once possessed of the right to the ballot-box, to self-representation, she [woman] will see to it that the laws shall be just, and protect her person and her property as well as that of the man."[78] Rose designated any favorable statutes that were passed as forms of charity that might be taken away as casually as they were given. Furthermore, even legal and political rights, she believed, were meaningless abstractions without a

[75] *HWS,* 1:105.
[76] Stanton, "Why Must Women Vote?," *Lily* 2 (May 1850):3.
[77] *Proceedings . . . Woman's Rights . . . Syracuse,* p. 34.
[78] *Proceedings . . . Woman's Rights . . . Broadway Tabernacle . . . 1856,* p. 74.

female bar and judiciary. The time is coming, she promised, "when we shall be our own lawyers and our own judges" and "our own jury too."[79]

At the core of the suffrage argument was the notion that the interests of men and women were not the same. Radical advocates of women's rights could agree with Antoinette Brown that men cannot represent women, that "they differ in their natures and relations. The law is wholly masculine."[80] Feminists were fully aware of how subversive an idea this was, especially in the context of nineteenth-century assertions about the protection of women. "Do we fully understand," queried Elizabeth Oakes Smith, "that we aim at nothing less that an entire subversion of the existing order of society, a dissolution of the whole existing social compact . . . ?"[81]

Feminists' reliance on the political sources of the American Revolution encouraged a contempt for traditional authority and was an integral part of their onslaught against the patriarchal family. The Declaration of Independence, the model for their Declaration of Sentiments at Seneca Falls, fostered analogies between the politics of colonialism and the politics of sex. The full promise of revolution, they suggested, was thwarted because America continued to permit an aristocracy of sex. The tyrants were men, "the lords of creation"—a common phrase in feminist rhetoric—who exerted unlimited power over women.

If there were no historic precedents for female equality per se, there was a vibrant revolutionary tradition on which they could draw. It did not matter, asserted Elizabeth Oakes Smith, that ancient precedents for equality between the sexes were absent because Americans were "not such sticklers for time-honoured usages."[82] Stanton, who was familiar with the works of Thomas Paine, reiterated this theme in her 1854 speech to the New York Legislature, in which she demanded better domestic-relations laws. "The tyrant Custom," she declared, "has been summoned before the bar of Common Sense."[83] Harriet Taylor Mill, En-

[79] *Proceedings . . . Woman's Rights . . . Broadway Tabernacle . . . 1853*, p. 48.
[80] *Proceedings . . . Woman's Rights . . . Syracuse*, p. 20.
[81] Ibid., p. 16.
[82] "Lecture at the Hope Chapel," *New York Times*, October 23, 1852, p. 1.
[83] "So at the present writing Tom Paine and Fanny Wright lie on my table!" See Stanton to Elizabeth Smith Miller, September 20, 1855, in Stanton-Blatch Letters, 2:61; Stanton, *Address to the Legislature of New York . . . 1854*, p. 3.

glish feminist and perceptive observer of the American movement, considered it outrageous that Americans guaranteed inalienable rights to only "a moiety," or one-half of their citizens. It was only fitting, she pointed out, that abolitionists and feminists should form "the first collective protest" against "an aristocracy of color" and "an aristocracy of sex."[84]

In her 1854 speech to the Legislature, Stanton managed to give the same theme an ethnocentric twist. Demanding full recognition of women as citizens of the Empire State, she insisted that women were still "classed with idiots, lunatics, and negroes.... Yes, gentlemen," she continued, "in republican America in the nineteenth century, we, the daughters of the revolutionary heroes of '76, demand ... a new code of laws." Like Mill, Stanton underscored the existence of an aristocracy of sex, but implied that it violated a more genuine aristocracy by placing "the ignorant and vulgar above the educated and refined—the alien and the ditch-digger above the authors and poets of the day—an aristocracy that would raise the sons above the mothers that bore them."[85]

Stanton was particularly effective in tying her demand for married women's property rights to demands for the ballot and more. In the balance of her speech, she outlined the remaining disabilities of married women in New York, insisting on the wife's right to guardianship, to her earnings, to equal laws of intestacy, and to sue and be sued—all requests that were granted by the Legislature six years later, in 1860. She managed simultaneously to project the inevitability of suffrage onto those rights that were not yet acquired. "The right to property will of necessity, compel us in due time to the exercise of our right to the elective franchise, and then naturally follows the right to hold office." She assured those who considered her approach atypical that the demands did not come "from a few sour, disappointed old maids and childless women." "The mass of women," she said, "speak through us."[86]

All three elements of the feminist challenge—economic,

[84] "*Enfranchisement of Women" by Mrs. John Stuart Mill, Reprinted from Westminster and Foreign Quarterly Review for July 1851*, Woman's Rights Tracts, no. 10 (1853), p. 4.

[85] Stanton, *Address to the Legislature of New York . . . 1854*, pp. 3–5.

[86] Ibid., pp. 11, 17.

domestic, and political—worked to undermine the husband-wife relationship at common law. Effective opposition to the legal fiction of marital unity required that wives be be removed from the common law subsystem of private, relative rights, which mandated inferior legal status to wives by its very organization, and placed instead in the national mainstream of fundamental, inalienable rights. Liberal-feminist opposition to the common law applied the political rhetoric of natural rights to the private relationship of husband and wife. This application reversed the traditional pattern of using the family as a model for the authoritarian state, and used the democratic state as a model for the family. Only by merging the public and domestic spheres, which English and American jurists had so carefully segregated, could they carry natural rights doctrines to nonsexist conclusions.

In retrospect it seems as if the most radical elements of the women's campaign occurred in the areas of economic and domestic feminism. But to their contemporaries, it was suffrage that loomed as the greatest revolution. In the mid-nineteenth-century political context, women's suffrage was the clear and inviolable validation of equality between the sexes that state legislators were not prepared to give. Statutes that gave greater equality in domestic relations were more ambiguous. Their impress depended on future adjudication and on the way the public would use them. Precipitous readjustments in the institution of marriage would certainly be tempered by the persistence of older customs and social values. Nevertheless, by exploiting the legal fiction of marital unity as the symbol of their harshest deprivations, and by merging their demand for improvements in marriage laws with larger political demands, New York feminists subjected the woman question to full debate and influenced the Legislature to meet the least menacing items on their long list of demands.

From 1848 through the 1850s, New York feminists, especially Stanton, Anthony, and Rose, concentrated on lobbying in Albany. The campaign for married women's property rights in New York was a strategic part of their drive for suffrage. There can be little doubt that some of the impetus for that drive came from the earlier married women's acts. Stanton, as usual, was forthright about earlier influences. Chiding her cousin Gerrit Smith in 1856 for his lack of faith in the women's movement, she expressed confidence because New York had already elevated "*a femme covert* into a living, breathing woman—a wife into a property holder, who can make contracts, buy and sell." She was convinced that "in due time these property holders must be represented in the government."[87] Amelia Bloomer noted that the 1848–49 statutes in New York were "but a forecast of the enlightened sentiment of the people of New York," and that they would "pave the way to greater privileges."[88]

The antebellum drive for women's suffrage anticipated the post–Civil War dispute over the Fourteenth and Fifteenth amendments. With hindsight the drive seems premature and unrealistic. Yet the sixty years it took to pass a constitutional amendment for suffrage may not accurately reflect the power of the earlier drive. By the end of the 1850s, no discussion of the woman question took place without a discussion of suffrage. By that time, it was no longer considered totally outlandish that American women one day would vote.

Feminists were cognizant that some supporters who favored married women's property rights were opposed to women's suffrage. Lobbying efforts centered on petitions, drafted each year at women's rights conventions and then carried throughout the state. Potential signers usually had a choice of a petition requesting better domestic relations laws and another demanding suffrage and full legal and political equality for women. One early sample, presented to the New York Legislature in 1851, merged these two demands, but later campaigns often separated them in order to win as wide support for marital property reform as possible.[89] Women's rights conventions sometimes attempted to unify all petitioning campaigns. William Henry Channing urged an 1853 group to include six specific items in all legislative petitions, but since one of the six was divorce for drunkenness, an even more controversial issue, and women's suffrage, they were not uniformly adopted.[90]

Petitioning in New York began as early as 1836 on behalf of

[87]Stanton to Gerrit Smith, January 3, 1856, in Stanton-Blatch Letters, 2:63–64.

[88]*Lily*, March 1850, cited in Bloomer, *Life and Writings of Amelia Bloomer*, pp. 57–58.

[89]This petition, reprinted in *Lily* 3 (February 1851):14, stated that "taxation without representation is tyranny."

[90]*Proceedings of the National Women's Rights Convention Held at Cleveland, Ohio, on Wednesday, Thursday, and Friday, October 5th,6th, and 7th, 1853* (Cleveland, 1854), p. 70.

Thomas Herttell's bill, and approached a sophisticated level of organization in 1853 at a state women's rights convention in Rochester. The purpose of this convention was to prepare to bring the legal and civil disabilities of New York women to the attention of legislators at the beginning of the next legislative session; it would meet again in Albany at the opening of the session. All petitions were funneled through Anthony and were to be in her hands by February 1854. Announcements were made in reform papers with instructions for collecting signatures.[91]

Between December 1853 and February 1854, Anthony collected a total of 10,000 signatures on two petitions, one for suffrage, the other for married women's property rights.[92] In 1954 the campaign moved into high gear. The year was distinguished by improved organization and increased political awareness. Activity in that year was strengthened by Anthony's abandonment of the temperance movement and clearly showed the full concentration of her skills and energies on women's rights in New York. Meeting in Albany in February of that year, New York feminists established a lobbying pattern that continued through 1861. Yearly assaults were made on the Legislature. In the *History of Woman Suffrage,* the participants carefully recorded the impressions of the 1854 convention reported in the Albany press. The *Albany Transcript,* they noted, called the 1854 convention "the first Convention of women designed to influence political action." Whatever the outcome, it continued, "it is well to make a note of the *first effort* to influence the Legislature."[93]

Eighteen-fifty-four was the year in which Stanton, Rose, and Anthony appeared before the Joint Judiciary Committee of the Legislature to deposit their 10,000 signatures as well as to address the committee and several hearings in both houses. It was not the first appearance of Stanton and Rose, but it was the first time a woman—Stanton in this case—had made a major speech

[91]Signatures on petitions presented by the state women's rights movement to the New York Legislature numbered 6,000 in the previous campaign for the opening of the 1853 session. This statistic was mentioned in an 1854 appeal to the women of New York. See *HWS,* 1:857; "Woman's Rights Circulate Petitions," *Frederick Douglass' Paper,* December 25, 1853, cited in *Frederick Douglass on Women's Rights,* ed. Philip S. Foner (Westport, Conn., 1976), pp. 65–67.

[92]Stanton, *Address to the Legislature of New York . . . 1854,* Appendix.

[93]*HWS,* 1:606.

to the New York Legislature and received all of its attendant publicity. Planning was meticulous. With the support of Thurlow Weed's *Albany Evening Journal,* publicity preceded as well as followed Stanton's appearance. Henry Cady, Stanton's father, who was unsympathetic to his daughter's activities, still researched a few points of law for her and put the finishing touches on the speech. Stanton's speech, given first on the evening of February 15 at the Albany women's rights convention, was printed and distributed to every legislator on February 20, and 20,000 copies were subsequently "scattered like snow-flakes over the state."[94]

Anthony, who had already started on next year's petitioning campaign, interrupted her activities on March 3 to address a special committee created by the Assembly to deal with the mass of petitions. Reading a speech prepared by Judge William Hay of Rochester, she advocated joint ownership of all marital property with equal rights of survivorship. On the same day Rose spoke to the committee and demanded seriousness from the legislators, stressing the historic opportunity they had to alter the status of American women by improving the status of New York women. "These are not the demands of the moment or the few," she warned the legislators in characteristically prescient fashion; "they are the demands of the age; of the second half of the nineteenth century."[95]

From 1854 until the Civil War the state was canvassed yearly. Anthony became general agent, directing county captains in arranging local conventions and petitioning campaigns. Between Christmas Day of 1854 and May of 1855, she personally visited fifty-four of the sixty counties of the state. She began this campaign with $50 of seed money, a loan from Wendell Phillips, and returned in May with a $76 surplus.[96] Through meticulous bookkeeping and with unflagging energy, she managed to collect enough at each local meeting to pay for the next one, but she was seriously impeded by lack of funds.

Finances improved considerably near the end of the decade. In 1858 Phillips informed Anthony that he was turning over

[94]Stanton, *Eighty Years and More,* pp. 187–89; *HWS,* 1:595.

[95]*Albany Argus,* March 4, 1854, cited in *HWS,* 1:607.

[96]Eleanor Flexner, *A Century of Struggle: The Woman's Rights Movement in the United States* (1959, 1968; reprinted New York, 1971), p. 87.

$5,000 from an anonymous donor to her campaign for women's rights in New York. Phillips and the donor, who was Francis Jackson of Boston, were convinced that the best way to spend the money was on lobbying for a liberal married women's statute in New York, a measure they considered nationally significant. This sum, although small even by nineteenth-century lobbying standards, undoubtedly made a considerable difference to Anthony. Anthony, traveling in the summer of 1859 to New York's finest watering spots—Saratoga Springs, Ballston Spa, Sharon Springs, Lake George—increasingly directed her drive at wealthy and politically influential supporters. An appeal addressed "To the Women of the Empire State" in the summer of 1859 noted that former campaigns had been crippled by lack of funds, but because of bequests in the past year, agents would reach every corner of the state.[97]

The legislative response to the mountain of petitions ran the gamut from ridicule to respect. The petition, Stanton herself pointed out, was the only way for "disenfranchised classes" to be heard.[98] Actually it was an effective instrument of agitation and a wellspring of publicity. Assemblyman Jonathan Burnet of Essex greeted the 1854 barrage by claiming that these women "do not appear to be satisfied with having unsexed themselves, but they desire to unsex every female in the land, and to set the whole community ablaze with unhallowed fire." Assemblyman Daniel P. Wood of Onondaga, who presented the petition on behalf of the women and requested the formation of a select committee, insisted that the sheer number of signatures demanded a dignified response from the Legislature.[99]

The exchange between Wood and Burnet revealed a familiar obstacle in the way of attempts to get a bill before the entire Legislature. Burnet, as chairman of the Assembly Judiciary Committee, the body to which almost all of the petitions and bills for married women's property rights were channeled, could bury the bill. In addition to legislative support, proponents of a

[97]Dorr, *Susan B. Anthony,* pp. 128–29; *HWS,* 1:676. Jackson was a Garrisonian abolitionist. For the schisms in abolition, see Sewall, *Ballots for Freedom,* pp. 30–32.

[98]Stanton, *Eighty Years and More,* p. 192.

[99]*Albany Evening Journal,* February 20, 1854, cited in *HWS,* 1:613; *HWS,* 1:614–15.

married women's bill needed a friend ot two on the judiciary committees. Wood asserted that if the Assembly failed to deal with these petitions separately, they would go to the Judiciary Committee and "there will be no danger that anyone will be fired up by it, for it will then be sure to sleep the sleep of death." The Assembly voted to refer the 1854 petitions to a select committee created especially for the purpose of reviewing women's rights, as did the Senate, so that the 1854 demands received a full hearing.[100]

The 1854 select committee of the Assembly was not a great improvement. Its report insisted that "jest and ridicule never yet effectively put down either truth or error," and that "many thoughts which today are laughed at as wild vagaries are tomorrow recorded as developed principles, or embodied in experimental facts." Promising to treat the subject seriously, however, was as far as it would go. "A higher power than that from which emanates legislative enactments," it proclaimed, "has given forth the mandate that man and woman *shall not* be [equal]." The husband, it advised in familiar terms, was the sovereign head of the family. As for arguments about taxation and representation, it relied on the old British assurance of virtual representation. An assemblyman or senator represented his whole district, voters and nonvoters, men and women. Marriage, it insisted, was not, as Stanton claimed, merely a civil contract, but one that was "more binding" and with "more solemn specialties." This committee did recommend better guardianship laws as well as laws to enable a wife to collect her own earnings if her husband was unable to support her.[101] In the following year, after another petitioning blitz, a similar committee—now called "a select committee on petitions for woman's right of suffrage," and listing among its members Henry Stanton, Elizabeth Cady Stanton's husband—recommended a moderate change in descent in real estate.[102]

In 1856 petitions were again placed in the hands of a judiciary committee, which produced an official report ridiculing the en-

[100]*HWS,* 1:614–15.
[101]*NYAD,* March 27, 1854, vol. 4, no. 129, pp. 1–4. The report of this committee was forwarded by "Senex" (Assemblyman Anson Bingham) to *Lily,* which printed it in April 1854.
[102]*NYAD,* April 6, 1855, vol. 5, no. 129.

tire women's movement. Samuel A. Foote, who delivered the report, took a bantering tone. Foote assured the Assembly that the "ladies" who demanded equality between the sexes had "the choicest tidbits at the table," the "best seats in cars, carriages, and sleighs," and "the warmest place in winter and the coolest place in summer." Their dresses, he said, cost three times as much and took up three times as much space as male attire. It was the men, claimed Foote, who were oppressed. Finally noting that in several instances husbands and wives signed the same petition, the report recommended that those couples request a law authorizing a clothing switch "so that the husband may wear the petty-coats, and the wife the breeches, and thus indicate to their neighbors and the public the true relation in which they stand to each other."[103]

New York feminists were stung by the tone of the report. William Hay attempted to comfort Anthony in a letter in which he called Foote "an old fogey" who had "disgraced the assembly chamber." He assured Anthony that the cause could not be wiped out by "contemptuous silence, vulgar abuse, or conservative scorn." Women's suffrage, he said, had been discussed "incidentally" several times in the Assembly and the Senate in the past week. Subsequent petitions for women's rights, he pointed out, would be presented to a committee of claims instead of the Judiciary Committee, where they were bound to be ridiculed or buried.[104]

Petitioning continued, as did piecemeal legislation. In 1858 the Legislature updated the married woman's insurance law.[105] In 1859 a married women's earnings act was introduced and passed the Assembly by a vote of 102 to 2 but failed to reach the voting stage in the Senate.[106] In 1860 once again New York feminists gathered in Albany in February, and their position was stronger than ever before. The Republican Legislature included innumerable allies. Support had been demonstrated by the vote of the Assembly in 1859, and this time they had friends on both judiciary committees. Early in February Anson Bingham, who had written on behalf of married women's property rights in a

[103]*NYAD,* March 14, 1856, vol. 4, no. 147.
[104]Hay to Anthony, March 20 and 21, 1856, in *HWS,* 1:631.
[105]*LNY, 1858,* chap. 187.
[106]*JNYA,* April 8, 1859, p. 1137.

number of reform journals under the name "Senex" and who was chairman of the Assembly Judiciary Committee, advised Stanton and Anthony to polish their best speeches for the Legislature. Further support came from Andrew J. Colvin, a member of the Senate Judiciary Committee. Anthony, in constant contact with Colvin, persuaded him to replace the 1859 bill, which she considered merely an extension of the 1848–49 acts, with a more complete bill. On February 18, 1860, in another widely reprinted speech, Elizabeth Cady Stanton addressed a joint session of the Legislature and appealed for suffrage and improved married women's property rights. The passage of the Earnings Act, however, was already ensured. On February 27 it passed the Senate 18 to 3, and on March 15 it passed the Assembly 95 to 5. It was signed into law on March 20.[107]

The battle for a liberal married women's property bill took place in the press as well as the Legislature. No sources provide a better index of the extent to which New York feminists moved public opinion than newspapers and periodicals. One trend seems clear: there was support for improved rights to begin with. Also, the more consistent the demands for women's suffrage, the wider the acceptance of married women's property rights. The feminists' appeal for abstract justice made in combination with specific demands for property rights filled the periodicals of the 1850s. Friend or foe, any editor interested in news opened his columns to them. The message became familiar to everyone. In an 1852 letter to the editor of the *New York Times,* for example, Elizabeth Oakes Smith proclaimed that women had no independent existence and were "in fact, just what the law regards [them] as, 'idiots' or poetically 'innocents.' "[108]

Antifeminists responses included references to women's economic inadequacies as well as appeals to a higher law of nature that validated male sovereignty. One editorial likened the women's rights advocate to the French valet who wanted every servant to be more than equal to his master until he realized there would be nobody to pay his wages.[109] The *United States Magazine and Democratic Review,* formerly the champion of married wom-

[107] *HWS,* 1:678–85: *JNYS,* 1860, p. 458; *JNYA,* 1860, p. 663; *LNY, 1860,* chap. 90.

[108] "Woman's Rights," *New York Times,* October 19, 1852, p. 2.

[109] *New York Times,* November 25, 1856, p. 4.

en's property rights, but now estranged from that distinctly abolitionist cause, insisted that man had the "subtle intellect" to compel woman to minister to his needs. As part of the law of nature, some had the "means of obtaining assistance and support from others, either by exciting fear, exerting force, or inspiring affection."[110] Some antifeminist responses were defensive. Citing the feminist predilection for the rhetoric of the American Revolution, *Putnam's* was shocked that women believed they were "tyrannized by law, society, and their husbands."[111]

Increasingly, however, opposition tended to focus on women's political participation and suffrage. The *New York Times,* whose editorial policy between 1852, the year it began, and 1860 can be conveniently traced because of the existence of an editor's index, showed precisely this trend. Gradually the paper supported bills for married women's property rights and saved its scorn for suffrage. An 1859 editorial objected strenuously to a proposal in the New York Senate to amend the state constitution by including women's suffrage.[112] The paper supported the 1860 Earnings Bill, but it insisted it could not see what else Mrs. Lucy Stone might want without waging "war upon human nature itself and the ordinances of high heaven."[113] "Leo," a *Times* correspondent in Albany in February 1860, reported favorably on Stanton's speech. Protesting that he "never cherished a profound admiration for the female philanthropists who have preached woman's rights—her right to vote and to be voted for," he described Stanton as making her plea "forcibly" and with "the feeling of a true woman." Leo found the Earnings Act the "most sweeping innovation ever made upon any established usage." Who will say, he asked, "it is not time the world moved somewhat in that direction?"[114] The *Brooklyn Daily Eagle* printed the bill on its

[110]"Female Influence in the Affairs of State—Politics Not Woman's Sphere," *USMDR* 43 (April 1859):175. See in the same journal "Bloomer Rights," 29 (September 1851):216; "Dr. Dewey on Woman's Rights," 30 (February 1852):180; "Human Nature in Chunks: Chunk No. 1—Woman's Rights," 34 (November 1854):434.

[111]"Men's Rights," *Putnam's Monthly Magazine* 7 (February 1856):208–13.

[112]*New York Times,* March 10, 1859, p. 4.

[113]"Female Emancipation," *New York Times,* February 10, 1860, p. 4.

[114]*New York Times,* March 21, 1860, p. 5.

front page and suggested it gave women "the privileges on which the right to vote is based." Women's suffrage, it predicted, was only a matter of time.[115]

The *North American Review* chose to assess the act as the logical result of economic exigencies. Comparing New York's domestic relations laws with those of England and the Continent, it insisted that "the more constant and violent fluctuations in property and business" created "the need of further legal protection to the fortunes of married women."[116] A married women's property bill also seemed to be a reform that might take the steam out of the women's movement and put a stop to radical ideas about constitutional equality for the female sex. "Sex," declared an 1860 *Times* editorial, "is a distinction of which the Constitution may take notice with quite as much justice as age, color, or place of birth."[117]

Sex, however, was a constitutional distinction that Stanton, Anthony, and Rose were determined to obliterate, and they started with the constitution of New York. Attacks on the New York Legislature diminished not because of the Earnings Act, but because of the Civil War. In November 1860, as New York women prepared to make their annual trek to Albany, their new petitions demanded the ballot, trial by a jury of their peers, and an equal right to the joint earnings of the marriage partnership.

Married women's property rights had become, of course, their justification for suffrage. In her appeal to the women of the state, Stanton asked how a woman who could hold a legal right to her own earnings could fail to carry the cause of women's rights forward. Her message reflected the rising expectations that had characterized the 1850s. The petition Stanton exhorted the women of New York to sign assumed that full political equality for women was possible and was the prerequisite for a larger social equality between the sexes. It read as follows: "We, the undersigned citizens . . . , respectfully ask that the word

[115] *Brooklyn Daily Eagle,* March 20, 1860, p. 1.

[116] "The Law of Divorce," *North American Review* 90 (April 1860):414–28. Four years later this journal, in a retrospective article on married women's property laws, saw the New York Earnings Act as politically significant for women. See "The Property Rights of Married Women," ibid. 99 (July 1864):43–64.

[117] "Impracticable Rights," *New York Times,* February 6, 1860, p. 3.

'Male' shall be stricken from our State Constitution, that henceforth our Representatives may legislate for humanity and not for privileged classes."[118]

The legacy of the antebellum drive for married women's property rights was larger than the passage of the New York Earnings Act. It was the bridge that feminists constructed between the proverbial female sphere and male sphere. To the extent that feminists justified women's penetration of the male sphere on the basis of women's special place in the female sphere, the direction of their movement remained ambiguous. Yet even as they drew on the sentimental language of the cult of domesticity, they fashioned a challenge to the typology of the patriarchal family.

Focus on the legal fiction of marital unity, the "myth" that Mary Beard disparaged in her discussion of the women's movement, was a testimony to early feminists' appreciation of its power and resonance. Marital unity, with the wife's concomitant legal invisibility, was a myth in the sense of an exaggeration, an imprecise depiction of the legal status of married women; it was also a myth in the larger sense of a powerful collective belief that had informed centuries of Western political theory and jurisprudence. It provided a convenient way of thinking about women as eternally subordinate. As Susan Moller Okin has pointed out, political theorists were consistently able to deprive women of political personhood by relegating them to the domestic sphere and then assuming the necessity of a male-headed unity and harmony to prevail in the domestic sphere. Thus even egalitarian theorists envisaged equality in the form of male-headed households that were equal to one another. Single women, she notes, did not escape; they were viewed as women who ought to marry, deviations from the norm.[119] Concentration on greater equality within the household, therefore, was a critical first step toward demands for women's political rights.

As feminists demanded greater equality within the household, along with their more conservative sisters, they also concentrated on one source of sexual inequality—laws that legitimated

[118] *Appeal to the Women of New York* (November 1860), p. 4.

[119] Susan Moller Okin, *Women in Western Political Thought* (Princeton, N.J., 1979), pp. 144–46, 250–52, 272–73.

and exploited existing inequalities. This strategy enabled them to take the next step, to demand political rights for women not only in their capacities as wives and mothers, but as citizens of the state. The contribution was not in the originality of their ideas, but in the systematic, coherent, and pragmatic way in which they disseminated them. By demanding more of what legislators were already giving, married women's property rights, they created a public forum for developing and refining their more radical demands.

CHAPTER 7

The Critical Test: The Courts

> Wealth, in a commercial age, is made up largely of promises. An important part of everyone's substance consists of advantages which others have promised to provide for or to render to him; of demands to have the advantages promised, which he may assert not against the world at large but against particular individuals.
>
> —Roscoe Pound

Antebellum feminists and many of their contemporaries viewed the married women's acts as a legal and social revolution. The critical test, however, took place in the courts, where judges clearly demonstrated the weakness of the statutes relative to the strength of the common law. For this reason, the married women's acts cannot be construed as a revolution. They failed to obliterate the historic barriers the common law had thrown around married women. Failure stemmed from the sheer inability of piecemeal, remedial legislation to reconstruct comprehensively the vast body of domestic relations law which was an intrinsic part of the Anglo-American legal tradition. Failure came also from the readiness of the judiciary to interpret the intent and spirit of the legislation as conservatively as possible.

Mid-century judicial resistance to the legislation was part of a larger trend. Morton Horwitz has attributed this trend to a once aggresively procommercial judiciary eager to consolidate the gains it had already achieved. Earlier in the century, the judiciary had consciously redistributed wealth to the advantage of merchants and entrepreneurs at the expense of workers, farmers, and consumers. Mid-century judicial hostility to new legislation emanated from a fear that legislatures would continue the redistribution in a more egalitarian way. New statutes on private property were a threat to judicial power and interests. The judiciary responded by presenting the law as a science, the details of which were to be deduced from certain inexorable rules. Thus judges moved, explains Horwitz, from "instrumentalism" to "formalism" in order to freeze benefits that already had accrued to commercial interests. In New York the shift from instrumentalism to formalism was particularly striking and was borne out by a dramatic increase in the judicial review of legislation during the 1840s and 1850s.[1]

The married women's acts of 1848–49 were distinctly an extension of the redistribution that had been favored earlier in equity. The Earnings Act of 1860, moreover, legitimated the presence of women in the marketplace. The legislative innovations were bound to be resented by a judiciary eager to preserve the status quo. Some members of the judiciary, of course, were exceptions. At the appellate levels, the New York judiciary included Elisha Hurlbut, women's right advocate, and Ira Harris, author of the major married woman's clause at the constitutional convention of 1846. Nevertheless, the general outlines of Horwitz's thesis illuminate the dismal fate of the married women's property acts in the New York courts. The judges' resort to formalism gave common law rules the appearance of being inexorable. With respect to the married women's statutes, judges invoked the old common law fiction of marital unity as the foundation for all of Anglo-American domestic relations law. Statutes were merely small inroads on the broad path of the common law's incontrovertible logic.

The narrow judicial construction in the New York courts is significant because the statutes embodied two national legislative patterns. In one, seen in the New York acts of 1848 and 1849, wives were accorded some powers in the ownership and management of property they brought to marriage or inherited afterward; in the other, seen in the New York acts of 1860 and 1862, they were given extensive powers over their property and over their earnings from commerce and labor. Adjudication in the New York courts, then, reflects early judicial responses to both patterns in a single state. A number of legal scholars have

[1]Horwitz, *Transformation of American Law,* pp. 253–66.

suggested that adjudication of the nineteenth-century married women's statutes was similarly restrictive in other states.[2]

Restrictive judicial interpretations did not abrogate completely the symbolic or concrete role of the New York statutes. Symbolically, the statutes were public testaments to American women's slowly expanding legal rights. Concretely, more wives than ever before acquired at least a rudimentary contractual capacity and a measure of legal visibility. Nevertheless, the adjudication process, not likely to be scrutinized closely by the public, diminished the possibility of a thorough readjustment in the legal relationship of husband and wife. The economic dependence of most wives on their husbands, regardless of legal ground rules, undoubtedly inhibited a thorough readjustment as well, but the courts diminished even the limited gains wives had acquired by statute. Furthermore, the public was relatively unaware of this reversal. Popular attention was riveted on the changes wrought by the Legislature; the continuities maintained by the judiciary were ignored. A survey of more than 200 relevant cases tried between 1848 and 1880 in the New York Court of Appeals, the highest appellate court in the state, and the New York Supreme Court, the second highest, reveals an astounding array of situations in which the old disabilities of coverture prevailed.

The judiciary limited the impress of the statutes in three basic ways. First, by declaring sections unconstitutional and void, they narrowed the applicability of the statutes. Second, by relying on equity precedents that required the delineation of the married woman's estate to be clear and unambiguous, they limited the number of estates affected. Third and most important, by professing their faith in the propriety and the desirability of the old common law fiction of marital unity, and by applying that fiction

[2]Johnston, "Sex and Property," pp. 1061–75, 1090–91; Kanowitz, *Women and the Law,* pp. 35–99; Warren, "Husband's Right," pp. 421–39; Blanche Crozier, "Marital Support," *Boston University Law Review* 15 (1935):25–58; Robert C. Brown, "The Duty of the Husband to Support the Wife," *Virginia Law Review* 18 (1932):823–24; Paul Sayre, "A Reconsideration of Husband's Duty to Support and Wife's Duty to Render Services," *Virginia Law Review* 29 (1943):857–75; Monrad G. Paulson, "Support Rights and Duties between Husband and Wife," *Vanderbilt Law Review* 9 (1955–56):709–42. For a chronological list of cases in the New York appellate courts, see Norma Basch, "In the Eyes of the Law: Married Women's Property Rights in Nineteenth-Century New York," Ph.D. dissertation, New York University, 1979, pp. 364–71.

to the countless situations the statutes did not spell out, they eviscerated the spirit and intent of the legislation.

Constitutional considerations created the first stumbling block to the statutes. Early opinions on the constitutionality of the 1848–49 acts often involved litigants who were trying to apply the acts retrospectively. Judicial resistance was unanimous. New York Supreme Court Justice Ira Harris, for example, insisted in one of the earliest tests, in 1848, that the courts must operate on the presumption that new law is prospective, not retrospective. The problem was Section 2 of the 1848 act, whose broad wording applied equally to women who had married before and after the passage of the act. Yet all judges at the higher appellate levels refused to attach its provisions to property acquired before that date, and Harris was no exception. And the exclusion included interest, rents, and profits that continued to accrue after 1848 from property acquired earlier. Harris, however, warned that there was no constitutional question about the right of women married earlier to enjoy the benefits of the statutes with respect to property acquired after 1848.[3]

Yet this question arose. Harris was undoubtedly sensitive to the restrictive implication of considering Section 2 an impairment of contractual obligations. If marriage was a contract like any other, the husband's marital rights were part of the contract and could not be abrogated by an act of the Legislature after the contract had been made. This kind of reading would have excluded all women married before 1848, a result clearly antithetical to the objectives of the statute. Yet the impairment-of-contractual-obligations argument was employed by Supreme Court Justice Seward Barculo in *Holmes v. Holmes,* an 1848 case that permitted a wife to prevent her husband from acquiring her legacy on older equity principles rather than under the new statute. Since her husband violated the marriage contract by his cruel and inhuman treatment of her, the court, having jurisdiction over equity as well, could fulfill its traditional role of protecting the property of the helpless, victimized wife. Barculo, however, declared Section 2 of the 1848 act "unconstitutional and void." He included among his citations Joseph Story's dissent in *Dartmouth College v. Woodward,* the famous 1819 Supreme

[3]Snyder v. Snyder, 3 Barb. 621, 623 (1848).

Court case in which the issue of the constitutional limits of state divorce laws arose tangentially. Reviewing marriage as a contract, Story unequivocally had asserted, "A man has as good a right to his wife as to *the property* acquired under a marriage contract. He has a legal right to her society and her fortune."[4]

In the following year Justice Charles Mason, after respectfully citing Story, pointed out that impairment of contractual obligations was a weak foundation on which to establish the limitations of Section 2 because the power of state legislatures "to control and modify the marriage relation" already was firmly established. Section 2, he argued, was unconstitutional because it violated due process by taking the property the husband had acquired by marriage and bestowing it upon the wife without his consent. In *White v. White,* a wife who had been married in 1819 and had inherited realty in Otsego County in 1828 filed to restrain her husband from interfering with her rents and profits after 1848; the court found that the husband's rights were vested, and that the 1848 statute was not applicable.[5]

Appeals to due process which suggested that overly zealous reformers had imperiled sacred constitutional rights ignored the feminist position on marriage and due process. More than a decade earlier Thomas Herttell had argued that marriage deprived women of property and rights that they had had when they were single. Since marriage was obviously not a contract like any other, but an essential relationship in nature and therefore an inalienable right, the state was depriving women of due process by depriving them of their property after marriage. The wife's assent to the contract was spurious; her only alternative was to remain single.[6]

Still, violation of due process constituted a less restrictive judicial approach than impairment of contract. On the surface the two rationales for finding the statute unconstitutional seemed to lead down the same path. Violation of due process, however, permitted Section 2 to apply to property acquired after 1848 by wives who had married earlier. Citing his former line of reason-

[4]Holmes v. Holmes, 4 Barb. 295, 300–301 (1848); Dartmouth College v. Woodward, 17 U.S. 518, 596–97 (1819).

[5]White v. White, 5 Barb. 474, 477–79 (1849). Story's remarks were also cited in Yale v. Dederer, 18 N.Y. 265, 277–78 (1858).

[6]Thomas Herttell, *Argument in the House of Assembly,* p. 40.

ing in *White v. White,* five years later Justice Charles Mason delivered the opinion for the court in a case that allowed a wife to sell realty she had acquired after 1848.[7] Generally it was on this distinction of vested rights and due process as opposed to impairment of contract that later cases were decided.[8]

The constitutional limits on the married women's acts, then, were temporary. Nevertheless, they prevented a large number of wives with a diversity of assets from gaining any benefit from the acts for a long period of time. Consider the case of Elizabeth Rider, an enterprising farm wife who apparently assumed that she came within the purview of the statutes. As late as 1862 her husband was able to break her will because of the nature of her assets. Wives could not bequeath property acquired before 1848, interest that accrued from it after 1848, or earnings received before 1860. Elizabeth's assets seemed to fit each of these categories. Her small estate came from three sources: money she brought to her marriage in 1831, cash from her mother's estate received before 1848, and butter and poultry money earned from their Suffolk County farm. Elizabeth put her money to work by making small loans. Shortly before her death she made out a will leaving her cash plus eighteen promissory notes valued at $1,645 to a female friend, a Miss Hulse. James Rider was successful in recovering the promissory notes because they were choses in action (in this case uncollected debts) and were deemed vested in him as his marital right.[9] The exclusion of Elizabeth Rider from the effects of the statutes is a good example of the trend toward restrictive interpretation. In the gray area of choses in action, the court could just as easily have decided that since the notes were not reduced to the husband's possession at her death, they were part of her estate and she was empowered to bequeath or convey them.

[7]Blood v. Humphrey, 17 Barb. 660 (1854).

[8]For decisions discussing the constitutional limitations of the statutes, see Holmes v. Holmes, 4 Barb. 295 (1848); Perkins v. Cottrell, 15 Barb. 446 (1851); Smith v. Colvin, 17 Barb. 157 (1853); Blood v. Humphrey, 17 Barb. 660 (1854): Sleight v. Read, 18 Barb. 159 (1854); Westervelt v. Gregg, 12 N.Y. 202 (1854); Thurber v. Townsend, 22 N.Y. 517 (1860); In the Matter of Reciprocity Bank, 22 N.Y. 9 (1860); Ryder (Rider in the Supreme Court) v. Hulse, 24 N.Y. 372 (1862); Knapp v. Smith, 27 N.Y. 277 (1863). Buckley et al. v. Wells, 33 N.Y. 518.

[9]Ryder v. Hulse, 24 N.Y. 372 (1862). For a similar decision on choses in action, see Woodworth v. Sweet, 51 N.Y. 8 (1872).

In delineating the constitutional limits of the 1848–49 acts, the judiciary was often frankly skeptical of the legislation on both social and legal grounds. Early decisions reveal apprehension about the future of marriage as a social institution. If the common law fiction of marital unity was the principal bulwark of marital stability, the statutes menaced the entire social structure. Reformers, went this line of reasoning, had been insensitive to or oblivious of the larger social costs of legal equality. Justice Seward Barculo noted somewhat wistfully that the safeguards once considered essential to the inviolability of marriage were "crumbling and falling before the batteries of modern reformers."[10] Justice Charles Mason depicted the court as the defender of ancient constitutional rights against the excesses of well-intentioned but misguided legislative tinkerers. Acknowledging the critical juncture in domestic relations law represented by these decisions, he proclaimed:

> We are called upon to declare an important statute of the state unconstitutional and void; a statute deeply affecting the most important and delicate of the marital rights; a statute, it is said, passed to repeal the common law and substitute the civil law in its stead, a law called for, it is alleged, by the popular voice of the state, and demanded by the onward progress of society.[11]

Mason's allusion to the French civil law was bound to arouse fear in the hearts of those who espoused the common law. It was misleading as well. The Legislature's model was unquestionably the long-established precedents of English and American equity. Mason, however, implied that the court was preserving the rights of Englishmen against foreign influence and legislative ignorance. The court was obligated, under the circumstances, to do its duty, "and I trust," he announced, "the court will always be found to possess independence enough to do that."[12]

The Earnings Act precipitated a new wave of judicial skepticism, and one judge predicted it "very likely will prove to be very mischievous and pregnant with much evil."[13] So flagrant was the

[10]Holmes v. Holmes, 4 Barb. 295, 298 (1848).
[11]White v. White, 5 Barb. 474, 485 (1849).
[12]Ibid.
[13]Barton v. Beer, 35 Barb. 78, 80 (1861).

hostility of some jurists that one member of the Court of Appeals admonished his colleagues to apply the statutes less prejudicially. "It has become the duty of the courts," he said, "to execute the law, both in letter and spirit, and they are not to see how not to do it." Another member of the court in this instance asserted that the goal of the statutes "was, doubtless, to obliterate all those common law doctrines by which the husband was enabled to acquire any of his wife's estate through his marital relations."[14]

Was it the intention of legislators to obliterate "all those common law doctrines," or was it their intention to weaken them only to the extent that it became possible to place the wife's assets in certain cases beyond the reach of her husband's creditors? This was the central issue the judiciary confronted. The unmistakable predilection of the judiciary was to preserve the old common law prototype as fully as possible. Most litigation in the appellate courts, moreover, involved commercial relations between spouses and third parties, thereby reducing the significance of the wife's powers relative to the husband's.

Furthermore, after 1860, organized feminist pressure to improve the legal status of New York wives evaporated. An 1862 amendment of the Earnings Act, for example, returned legal guardianship of children to the father and left the wife with a kind of veto power to prohibit the husband from binding a child out as an apprentice or creating a testamentary guardian other than the mother without her consent. It also erased the clauses of the 1860 act which made spouses equal in intestacies with respect to realty.[15] In a letter to Lydia Mott, Susan B. Anthony found New York feminists asleep on the whole subject and occupied with abolitionist and Civil War commitments. "All our reformers have suddenly grown politic," she noted, and were urging a hiatus in women's rights activities until the national crisis was over.[16] The ideology evolved from the earlier drive

[14]Justices Leroy Morgan and William H. Leonard, Gage v. Dauchy, 34 N.Y. 293, 296, 298 (1866). See also the statement of Justice Platt Potter in Billings v. Baker, 28 Barb. 343, 361 (1859).

[15]For guardianship, see *LNY, 1862,* chap. 172, sec. 6; for intestate succession of realty, see ibid., sec. 2.

[16]This undated letter was probably written shortly after April 10, 1862, the date of the major amendment to the Earnings Act. Section 3 of the 1860 act was also amended to eliminate the necessity of the husband's signature when a married woman conveyed realty. Other sections delineated more clearly the hus-

continued to animate the women's movement after the Civil War, but the New York married women's acts were history. Plagued with its own internal divisions, the women's movement was in the process of narrowing its focus to national political goals. Although Myra Bradwell went to court to test the right of women to be admitted to the bar and Susan B. Anthony went to court to test the right of women to vote, it appears that no prominent feminists organized or financed judicial tests of the New York statutes for which they had battled so vigorously.[17]

One reason for feminists' failure to scrutinize the adjudication process lies in the essentially political rather than legal nature of their drive for married women's property rights. Satisfactory statutes were viewed as building blocks to full equality between the sexes. Another possible reason, however, may lie in the virtual exclusion of women from the legal profession. Such an exclusion not only closed off the possibility of woman-oriented advocates but also contributed to feminists' excessive confidence in the efficacy of statutory reform. Even in the postwar era feminist expertise in the law was still at best protoprofessional. The women's movement needed a cadre of female lawyers who were schooled enough to understand the complexities of the legal system and who were at the same time political enough to expose its inherent sexism.

Given the circumstances—statutory gaps and a post-1860 diminution in reforming zeal—and given the participants—a judiciary that was essentially a conservative all-male elite eager to preserve the status quo and litigants who were essentially bourgeois property owners eager to manipulate the statutes for their own financial advantage—the limitations of the statutes are not surprising. As one would expect, working-class women, clearly empowered by the Earnings Act, appear only occasionally in the appellate court records. The middle class is well represented. Even the Court of Appeals was within its reach. The passage of the statutes and the reorganization of the courts prompted an army of middle-class spouses which encompassed

band's insulation from the liabilities of his wife's estate. More significant was the dropping of Sections 10 and 11, which equalized intestate succession in realty between spouses. See *HWS, 1:748; LNY, 1862*, chap. 172.

[17]This impression is based on *HWS*.

shopkeepers, farmers, artisans, and small-scale entrepreneurs to try to enjoy the financial advantages associated with the married woman's separate estate.

The appellate cases between 1848 and 1880 often mirrored the situations in older chancery cases which arose in disputes over trusts and antenuptial agreements. These older devices, incidentally, continued (and continue) to be favored by families that wish to fix the separation of their assets with reliability and precision. The wife's new legal estate precipitated problems similar to those associated with her equitable estate.

Very much in evidence was the old conflict between principles in equity and principles at law. In equity a married woman was regarded as if she were single with respect to her separate estate. Now at law she was to be regarded in the same way. At the same time she was to be regarded in all other situations as if she were *sub poteste viri,* under the power of her husband.[18] One rationale for the existence of the wife's estate in equity was to protect her in special situations from her husband, from his immense common law powers and his immense common law liabilities. The legal estate, as the language of the statutes declared, was also "for the more effectual protection of married women." Yet like the equitable estate, it allowed her to place her assets at her husband's disposal. And so the old theoretical dilemma persisted. Against what and from whom was the wife being protected? Nevertheless, the principle of protection continued to permeate judicial decisions and to structure legal thinking about the status of married women.

In practice many wives placed their legal estates, as they had their equitable ones, at the disposal of their financially imperiled husbands by signing notes, mortgaging realty, purchasing farm stock, and even buying businesses for husbands. Jane Cawley, for example, brought to her marriage with Samuel Cawley a house and lot in Queens and a ships' chandlery business in New York City. Rosana Branigan presented her husband with a liquor store in New York City. Eliza Douglas bought her husband a glass factory in Lockport. With his wife's legacy from her

[18]See Graham v. Van Wyck, 14 Barb. 531 (1851), where this principle worked to protect the dower of Caroline Van Wyck after she had released it to her husband for the sum of $1.

mother, Edwin Smith, a bankrupt, opened up a dry goods store in Rensselaer County.[19] All these were businesses nominally owned by the wife and managed by the husband.

In a stable marriage one would expect the husband and wife to pool resources. Furthermore, the right of the husband to act as his wife's agent was a fundamental common law assumption; it operated in equity, and it continued to operate with respect to the wife's legal estate. As Justice John K. Porter pointed out, it could not have been the object of the Legislature "to introduce discord in the marital relation, or to disable husband and wife from interchanging offices of mutual service and affection."[20] Inevitably married couples used the new statutes to establish the husband's lack of liability or they relied on the common law to establish the wife's lack of liability.[21]

Thus in each of the four examples of a wife who brought property to her husband, the court had to determine whether or not the couple was committing a fraud against a third party. In the case of the Douglas glass factory, Eliza and her husband made the fatal mistake of changing the name of the company and holding it out as his. Judge Sanford Church of the Court of Appeals asserted that when Douglas substituted his name for his wife's, he bought and sold on his own credit. Jane Cawley, the owner of the chandlery, was ordered to pay attorneys hired for matters concerning her business on the grounds that she could not hide behind her coverture in this instance. Similarly Rosana Branigan, owner of the liquor store, could not evade her responsibility for promissory notes her husband had signed after she gave him power of attorney. The store Edwin Smith ran for his wife, however, could not be seized for judgments against him.

If the courts had not been cautious in this area, the statutes would have thrown debtor-creditor relations into chaos. Couples could not have it both ways, although they certainly tried. Hus-

[19]Owen v. Cawley, 36 N.Y. 600 (1867); Freiberg v. Branigan, 18 Hun. 344 (1879); Hamilton v. Douglas, 46 N.Y. 218 (1871); Buckley et al. v. Wells, 33 N.Y. 518 (1865).

[20]Buckley et al v. Wells, 521. The husband's right of management was also affirmed in Knapp v. Smith, 27 N.Y. 277 (1863); Smith v. Sweeny, 35 N.Y. 291 (1867); Draper v. Stouvenel, 35 N.Y. 507 (1867): and Abbey v. Deyo, 44 Barb. 374 (1863).

[21]See In the Matter of Reciprocity Bank, 22 N.Y. 9 (1860), and Bodine et al. v. Killeen, 53 N.Y. 93 (1873).

bands and wives often attempted precipitous transfers of assets to foil creditors. Sometimes they held themselves out to the world in one light and attempted to have their liabilities viewed in another. Sarah B. Conway and her husband, for example, operated a theater in Brooklyn called "Mrs. F. B. Conway's." They attempted to dismiss a suit for the cost of billboards on the grounds that the action was against the wife alone, but they were not successful.[22]

Because of the statutes a husband could make provisions for his wife as he had in equity and create a legal estate for her as long as the size of the provisions was commensurate with his financial condition. If it appeared that he had no fraudulent purpose, the estate would be recognized as his wife's. In *Carr et al. v. Breese,* a husband who was doing well in business settled property on his wife. Subsequently he sold his own realty to invest in some lots and a saloon in Lansingburgh, and then went bankrupt. The court decided that the amount of his gift was not disproportionate to his assets and liabilities at the time he made it and that he could not have anticipated his bankruptcy. Consequently the wife's assets were beyond the reach of his creditors.[23] Insolvency remained a persistent possibility in the lives of most businessmen, and the statutes were designed to reduce its risks somewhat.

One problem was the tendency of the courts to apply to the married woman's legal estate the same criteria it had applied to her equitable estate. Application of equity principles to the married woman's new legal estate created special difficulties. A married woman's estate, pronounced one Supreme Court judge, was no less separate because it was legal rather than equitable.[24] This was not really true. The best of the devices to create a separate estate marked out the estate clearly and empowered the wife specifically so as to leave little room for ambiguities. But in attempting to offer to the many by statute what had been available to the few by custom and judicial precedent, the Legislature left

[22]Scott v. Conway, 58 N.Y. 619 (1874). See also Sammis v. McLaughlin, 35 N.Y. 647 (1866).

[23]Carr et al. v. Breese, 81 N.Y. 584 (1880). See also Babcock v. Eckler et al., 24 N.Y. 623 (1862). But the husband could not cast "the hazard of his speculation" on his creditors. See Carpenter v. Roe, 10 N.Y. 227 (1851).

[24] Colvin v. Currier, 22 Barb. 371 (1856).

a great deal of room for judicial discretion. Since couples habitually intermingled their assets as well as the fruits of their labor, it was difficult to determine what was his, what was hers, and what was theirs. When was a wife acting in the capacity of a feme covert and when was she acting as a feme sole? To answer this question, one had to delineate first what was the wife's estate. Faced with the question of what constituted the wife's separate estate, the courts tended to consider ambiguous or intermingled assets to belong to the husband. By viewing the requirements of the separate estate stringently, the courts were able to base many decisions on common law principles. If the wife had no separate estate, she reverted to her old common law status.

The case of Caroline Switzer exemplifies this trend. The wife of a New York carpenter, Caroline Switzer operated boardinghouses in the city during the 1850s. She leased houses in her own name, placed a brass nameplate reading "Mrs. A. Switzer" on each door, contracted independently with the boarders, cooked and cleaned for them with the help of her daughter Harriet, and collected the rents. In the course of expanding her business, she signed a note for a loan and secured it with a chattel mortgage on furniture. When she failed to pay at the specified time, her creditor foreclosed and took the furniture. Her husband sued the creditor, claiming his wife had no authority to execute the mortgage. The court decided that the boardinghouse in question was the husband's business because it was used for the support and well-being of the whole family, and the statutes in no way impinged on this situation. Do the statutes, asked the court, "authorize a married woman . . . to become a general trader and make valid contracts in respect to any business which she may be disposed to undertake, or in respect to any speculations in which she may choose to engage?" The answer was that they did not.[25]

It should be noted that the court upheld Switzer's suit. It did not recognize the boardinghouse as the wife's separate estate, and it did not even recognize the validity of her contract on the

[25]Switzer v. Valentine, 10 How Pr. Rep. 109, 116 (1854). Women's legal status with respect to the boardinghouses they ran were a common source of litigation in this period.

old grounds that she acted as her husband's agent. The concept of a wife's separate estate continued to be based on easily identified gifts and legacies either brought to marriage or acquired afterward. Such enterprises as boardinghouses and farms, businesses frequently operated in the family's place of residence and closely related to women's customary domestic duties, were often construed as belonging to the husband.

From the Switzers' point of view, the technicalities of ownership were irrelevant. Undoubtedly they used both incomes to support their family and were eager to defeat the creditor by any available means. But this type of construction seriously impaired the property rights of married women by restricting their ability to get personal credit and assume personal liabilities. Sylvia Bell of Monroe County purchased realty on credit without her husband's consent. Since she was a married woman without a separate estate, her contract was deemed "a mere nullity" in the eyes of the law. The Legislature, explained Judge Thomas Johnson in an 1862 decision, did not authorize a married woman without an estate to purchase land on credit. "Indeed, it is quite apparent," he continued, "that they never contemplated giving a married woman the power to speculate in real estate upon her own credit, whether she had a separate estate or not."[26] Obviously Sylvia Bell was a poor credit risk, but if the creditor were willing to assume that risk, the contract should have been binding. Such a decision seems antithetical to the Earnings Act.

The ability of wives to incur personal liabilities was crucial if they were even to begin to approach legal equality with their husbands. The whole principle of protection underpinning coverture precluded wives from assuming these liabilities. The married women's acts did not overturn this principle. The courts continued to place the wife under the husband's power and protection while regarding her separate estate as the buffer against special circumstances.

Even married women with clearly defined estates had difficulties. The issue of how a married woman with a separate estate made a binding contract plagued the courts throughout the

[26]Rose v. Bell, 38 Barb. 25 (1862). Glann v. Younglove, 27 Barb. 480 (1858), stipulated that when a married woman purchased property on personal credit, the title became vested in her husband.

period under consideration. Decisions varied as to whether her intentions to bind her estate could be implicit or had to be explicit. Decisions tended toward the position that if her contract did not bind her estate explicitly, then the contract had to be for the benefit of her separate estate or herself personally, and not for any other purpose. Not all judges agreed. "In order to carry out the spirit of this statute," advised one jurist, "it will become necessary for the courts to adopt, to its full extent, the equity rule, that a wife having a separate estate, shall be taken to have bound it to the payment of debts contracted by her."[27]

Yale v. Dederer, the era's leading decision on binding a separate estate, was quite restrictive. Ann Eliza Dederer, who owned three farms in Chenango County and whose husband owned two, contracted together with her husband for the purchase of thirty-three cows to be used interchangeably on all the farms. The Court of Appeals decided her signature on a note as her husband's surety did not bind her. Only two modes existed for charging such an estate, pointed out Justice Ira Harris: an appropriate instrument or circumstances that left no reasonable doubt. The purpose of the legislation, said Harris, was "to protect [the wife's] weaknesses against the husband's power and to provide a maintenance against his dissipation."[28]

In the eyes of the law, married women remained in a special and separate category. A husband who wished to sign a note merely signed his name; a wife in similar circumstances, if she wanted to make her signature binding, was well advised to spell

[27]Van Allen v. Humphrey, 15 Barb. 555, 559 (1853). This case hinged on Betsy Van Allen's antenuptial agreement, which empowered her to sell and dispose of her estate. It was decided on equity precedents, which Judge William Shankland urged the courts to adopt with respect to legal estates.

[28]On two subsequent occasions this case came before the Court of Appeals with similar results, so that the note Eliza Dederer signed in 1852 was debated as late as 1877. See Yale v. Dederer, 18 N.Y. 265, 284 (1858), 22 N.Y. 450 (1860), 68 N.Y. 329 (1877). For similar cases, see Barnett v. Lichtenstein, 39 Barb. 194 (1863); White v. McNett, 33 N.Y. 371 (1865); Corn Exchange Insurance Co. v. Babcock, 42 N.Y. 613 (1870); Shorter v. Nelson, 4 Lans. 114 (1870). Maxon v. Scott, 55 N.Y. 250 (1874), recognized an oral contract as binding on a separate estate. Quassaic National Bank of Newburgh v. Waddell, 1 Hun. 125 (1874), found that when the debt was for the benefit of the wife's estate, the charge was implicit. Conlin v. Cantrell, 64 N.Y. 217 (1876), recognized special circumstances such as a separation as implicitly binding the wife's estate. For leaseholds, see Vandevoort v. Gould, 36 N.Y. 639 (1867). See also "The Liabilities of Married Women as Sureties," *Albany Law Journal* 1 (1870):225.

out her marital status and her intention to charge her separate estate. Emily Anderson, a Westchester wife who signed a note with seven others, stated: "I, Emily Anderson, one of the makers of this, the above note, being a married woman, do hereby charge my separate estate with payment of the above note."[29]

The courts' tendency to require such specificity seriously limited the married woman's contractual capacities. An agreement between Hannah Sahler and Sally Manchester, according to which Sally was to nurse Hannah's ailing father, was ruled to be neither valid nor binding in 1866 because Hannah had not contracted to bind her separate estate.[30] Mary McEnany had the same sort of problem. Her family had run up a large bill with the local butcher and he refused further credit until it was paid. Mary promised that if he extended more credit to her, he would "not get cheated out of it." Her promise was deemed invalid. The contract, said the court, was not for her personal benefit, nor did she specifically charge her estate. Since she was living with her husband and ten children and he continued to support the family, nothing in her circumstances suggested her reference was to her personal property. Nor could she be considered her husband's agent, since the sale had been made to her and credit had already been withheld from the husband. The butcher was without a remedy.[31]

Although Hannah Sahler and Mary McEnany must have been pleased with the results of these suits, it should be pointed out that without the ability to bind their property and incur liabilities as readily as their husbands, they were not likely to have corresponding legal rights and financial options. Their continued insulation from liability placed them under the power and protection of their husbands. One can imagine that perspicacious creditors regarded married women circumspectively, and that without credit it was difficult to function with any degree of financial assertiveness in the modern commercial world. Generally in suits involving the contracts of married women, the burden fell on the third party to prove the wife was capable of making the contract.[32]

[29]Treadwell v. Archer et al., 76 N.Y. 196–97 (1879).
[30]Manchester v. Sahler, 47 Barb. 155 (1866).
[31]Salmon v. McEnany, 23 Hun. 87 (1880).
[32]Nash v. Mitchell, 71 N.Y. 199 (1877).

By 1880 the law on binding the wife's estate was not, as one judge pointed out, "fully settled." Noting the restrictive trend, however, Justice Joseph Barnard found most decisions antithetical to the wording of the statutory stipulation that in relation to her separate estate, a married woman should be considered as if she were single. It was more reasonable and in keeping with the statutes, he insisted, that she ought to "be left free to determine when to make a contract, and that she should be able to enforce it, and be bound to have it enforced against her."[33]

Earnings presented the courts with similar issues. How were the courts to differentiate the wife's earnings from the husband's? Should the 1860–62 statutes extend to butter-and-egg money, rent from boarders, or labor spent nursing a terminally ill in-law? In cases of this type tested in the appellate courts, generally they did not; most extra work done at home and closely associated with the household tasks that nineteenth-century wives did anyway were excluded. These customary ways in which women earned extra money that their husbands often allowed them to keep did not meet the legal requirements of a separate estate.

An 1876 Court of Appeals case exemplifies the refusal of the courts to consider this type of labor applicable. Peter Reynolds brought an action against the heirs of James Hill for services rendered by his wife, Lovella, in nursing Hill in their home over the course of eight years. One issue in the case was Reynolds' right to sue for his wife's wages. The court noted that the services took place in the house and were part of Lovella's regular household duties. When a husband "takes boarders into his house or converts his house into a hospital for the sick," ran the argument, "all her services and earnings belong to the husband." Her work was a discharge of her marital duties; the husband, therefore, was the proper person to sue.[34]

When a wife worked for a third party outside of the home and received "her husband's express approval" to keep her earnings as her own, there was no problem. Emily Snow was able to sue her employer for her wages as a housekeeper and collect be-

[33]Murphy v. Carpenter, 22 Hun. 15 (1880).
[34]Reynolds v. Robinson, 64 N.Y. 589, 593 (1876).

cause her husband "permitted her to engage in the defendant's service for herself, on her own account, and in her own right."[35] It appears a married woman could sue for her earnings after 1860 if she made a separate contract with a third party and if the separation of her earnings from those of her husband were clear.[36]

Nevertheless, the Earnings Act, the clear recognition of women's entry into the work force—especially the industrial work force—did not place working wives on an equal legal footing with their husbands. A married woman could not establish a separate estate without her husband's consent. The fact that a wife worked for a third party in a factory did not necessarily mean she performed her labor on her separate account. In fact, in most situations she did not. Unless the wife specifically elected such an option, it was permissible for a husband to sue for her wages as his marital right.[37]

In *Birbeck v. Ackroyd,* an 1878 Court of Appeals case in which a husband sued a woolen mill for the wages of his wife plus those of several children, the court ruled it was his right to recover for the labor and services of his wife. When the husband and wife were living together, working together in this case, and contributing their labor to a common purpose, and when the wife never claimed her earnings as her separate property, it was assumed that they came under the husband's control. "The bare fact that she performs labor for third persons, for which compensation is due," stated the decision, "does not necessarily establish that she performed it under the act of 1860, upon her separate account."[38]

Birbeck v. Ackroyd raised serious doubts about the improvement in the legal status of working wives. Other kinds of earnings remained controversial also. Even earnings from rent on separately owned realty were questioned. The supervision of

[35]Snow v. Cable, 19 Hun. 280–81 (1879).

[36]Adams v. Curtis, 4 Lans. 164 (1870).

[37]In Brooks v. Schwerin, 54 N.Y. 343 (1873), the court permitted a domestic who occasionally earned $1.25 a day to sue for the loss of her wages after she was hit by a horse and wagon. Her loss of services in her house, however, belonged to her husband. See also Beau v. Kiah, 4 Hun. 171 (1875); Caswell v. Davis, 58 N.Y. 223 (1874).

[38]Birbeck v. Ackroyd, 74 N.Y. 356, 358 (1878).

lands, declared the Court of Appeals, was "not the carrying on of a separate trade or business," and did not come under the statutes. "The disabilities of a married woman are general," argued Judge William Allen in this 1877 case, "and exist at common law. The capabilities are created by statute, and are few in number, and exceptional."[39]

Allen's statement illuminates the formal rationale used by the judiciary. While some reformers perceived the statutes as a complete recasting of the laws of husband and wife, much of the judiciary viewed them as particularized exceptions to the general common law structure. What, then, were third parties—creditors, debtors, retailers, employers—to assume? That in the absence of indications that the wife filled this exceptional category, one must assume she was under the disabilities of the common law.

Another restrictive factor was the static quality of the husband's status. A corollary of the wife's common law disabilities was the husband's extensive common law rights. Nothing in the statutes stipulated that the husband was no longer entitled to her services or to sue third parties for his loss of those services.[40] Yet in these situations, the wife remained an extension of the husband. Injuries to her were injuries to him. His deprivation of her services because of her injury was "a wrong done to his rights and interests."[41]

Furthermore, since the statutes did not relieve the husband of his duty of support regardless of the size of the wife's estate, judges inured to the common law equipoise of rights and duties refused to strip the husband of his common law rights. One basic tenet of common law relationships was that individuals who had large obligations ought to have large powers. The husband's obligations continued. As one judge put it, "The husband is bound to provide for her and them whatever is necessary for their suitable clothing and maintenance according to his and

[39]Nash v. Mitchell, 71 N.Y. 199, 203–4 (1877).

[40]Minick v. City of Troy, 19 Hun. 253 (1879). After 1860, a wife could sue and recover for personal injuries, but not for her loss of services to her husband.

[41]Cregan v. Brooklyn Crosstown Railroad, 75 N.Y. 192 (1878). Sloan v. New York Central and Hudson River Railroad, 1 Hun. 540 (1874), allowed a husband to sue for the loss of his wife's services after she had collected for injuries to her person.

their situation and condition in life."[42] If the husband had to continue to pay for his wife's "necessaries," then he had to retain his right to enjoy her services and earnings, and to enjoy other common law prerogatives. He had a right to enjoy her consortium (her company, affection, and sexual favors in addition to services), to elect a place of domicile, and to chastise her within the bounds of modern mores. Wife beating was an offense in New York and most other states, but implicit in the husband's and wife's respective common law positions was his need to control the woman who came so totally under his direction.

Even in many situations that appeared to come within the reach of the statutes, the courts reaffirmed the husband's common law rights. The husband retained certain rights with respect to his wife's personal property. When a wife owned personal property and failed to dispose of it before her death or by will, all that was left went to the husband. Thus the statute that empowered a wife to dispose of her personal property in any way she chose did not in every case strip the husband of his common law rights. In intestacies marriage was still a "gift to the husband" of her "goods and chattels and personal property."[43] The statutes might prevent him from acquiring her property during coverture, said the court, but not from administering it after her death. In cases involving the correct person to be sued, the court was quick to uphold the old doctrine of marital unity and husbandly control. When a wife's personal belongings were lost by a railroad, the court decided that the husband controlled them and had a right to sue for them.[44]

If the wife did not avail herself of the right to convey or bequeath realty under the statutes and died intestate after the 1862 amendment, the husband had complete management of all of it if there were children, a situation considerably more favorable than her dower right and precisely the same as his old

[42]Keller v. Phillips, 39 N.Y. 351, 354 (1868). The husband was still liable for the personal torts of his wife. See Rowe v. Smith, 45 N.Y. 230 (1871); Baum v. Mullen, 47 N.Y. 351 (1872); Fiske v. Bailey, 51 N.Y. 150 (1872).

[43]Barnes v. Underwood, 47 N.Y. 351 (1872), and Leach v. Leach, 21 Hun. 381 (1880), both of which were similar to Ransom v. Nichols, 22 N.Y. 110 (1860), a pre-1860 intestacy.

[44]Curtis v. Delaware, Lackawanna and Western Railroad Co., 74 N.Y. 116 (1878).

common law right of curtesy. The marital equation in which one plus one equaled one by virtue of the wife's invisibility continued to operate in other situations involving realty. Land conveyed to a husband and wife together made them tenants by entirety, leaving the survivor with the whole. But while they were both living, the husband enjoyed complete control of it as well as the ownership of the rents and profits. Nothing in the statutes changed this rule, averred the court. "Those statutes operate only upon property which is exclusively the wife's, and were not intended to destroy the legal unity of husband and wife."[45] So, too, a lease executed to husband and wife, even when she had a separate estate, was considered the husband's. The leasehold and its obligations were his.[46]

When a contractor sought to institute action on a mechanic's lien against a married woman in Buffalo who owned the house in which she and her family lived, it was deemed improper to sue her instead of her husband because the husband lived in the house and supported the family.[47] Similarly a husband had a right to maintain a trespass action on a farm owned by his wife since he was "the head of the family." The fact that she resided there was an indication not of her possession, but of her compliance with her marital duties.[48] A wife who had lived with her husband in New Orleans could not sue him for divorce in New York. She could acquire a separate domicile by judicial decree or separation, but until that time "the theoretic identity of person and interest between the husband and the wife in the eye of the law" was assumed, and it was her duty to dwell with him.[49]

Underlying the old common law fiction was a distinct quid pro quo. The husband enjoyed his powers by virtue of his extensive obligations. The husband's obligations, moreover, accurately reflected nineteenth-century economic realities. Except for the very rich and the very poor, most wives depended on husbands for financial support. Ostensibly the perpetuation of common

[45]Beach v. Hollister, 3 Hun. 519 (1875). See also Farmers' and Mechanics' Bank of Rochester v. Gregory, 49 Barb. 155 (1867).

[46]Goelet v. Gori, 31 Barb. 314 (1860); Eustaphieve v. Ketchum, 6 Hun. 621 (1876).

[47]Jones v. Walker, 63 N.Y. 612 (1875).

[48]Alexander v. Hard et al., 64 N.Y. 228 (1876).

[49]Hunt v. Hunt, 72 N.Y. 217 (1878). In Hunt v. Hunt, 131 U.S. app. clxv, the U.S. Supreme Court dismissed the appeal on jurisdictional grounds.

law principles also represented the ongoing protection of the vast majority of wives. Courts insisted that "on the husband only lies the obligation to support."[50] The husband's support duties, however, did not automatically make him liable for all of his wife's purchases, especially those to which he had not consented and which were not necessaries.

Incidents of wifely extravagance were legendary, but the ultimate power to curb expenditures and even to rule them out completely was always with the husband. Consider the position of the Binghamton wife whose right to a bonnet was scrutinized by the courts and whose spending habits were discussed in a variety of jurisdictions until they received the distinguished attention of the New York Supreme Court. Binghamton milliner Mary Ogden, insolvent by the time she got to the Supreme Court, sued the husband for the price of his wife's winter and summer bonnets, a sum totaling $16.50. The defendant owned a well-stocked 130-acre farm and held several notes on loan. Thus his ability to pay was never in question. Testimony showed he had refused to let his wife charge a pair of shoes or a black silk dress on earlier occasions with other retailers. The main issue was whether bonnets of this type were worn by persons in similar conditions of life. It was an issue that the jurists admitted they were ill suited to determine. Finally the court decided that since the husband had seen her wearing the first bonnet and did not express disapproval, his consent to the purchase of that bonnet as well as the second one was implied.[51]

The ability of a wife with a tight-fisted husband to make ordinary purchases was problematic. It was almost impossible for a wife who lived with her husband to compel support at a particular level. Although the husband's assent to most purchases was presumed, he could destroy the presumption by giving notice that he was withholding his credit. When someone sold the wife goods in the face of such a notice, the burden fell on him to prove that the husband failed to supply necessaries. In *Keller v. Phillips*. when the husband expressed his prohibition to the seller and the seller allowed the wife to make purchases on credit, the seller was left without a remedy. Modern legislation had not yet

[50]Beau v. Kiah, 4 Hun. 171 (1875).
[51]Ogden v. Prentice, 33 Barb. 160 (1860).

reached such a point, proclaimed the court, "as to invest the wife with a discretion which the husband cannot control and enable her to spend his property, or involve him in debt against his will."[52]

This statement illustrates the plight of all those wives who brought no separate estate to marriage and created none during coverture, and whose lifelong services to husband and family continued to be regarded by the law as part of the husband's marital rights. The value of those services constituted the only conceivable assets they could have owned. Only some kind of property system that made the wife a full legal and financial partner in the assets of the marriage could have benefited them. The dominant culture, however, never viewed all of the wife's vital services as work, and neither did the law.

To be sure, court records reveal that some wives bought and sold, borrowed and loaned, built and invested. This pattern seems to have been especially marked in rural areas, where there was no separation between home and work and less segregation by sex in work roles. Added to this group was the smaller one of urban women who ran boardinghouses, small retail businesses, and even a few factories. The women who appear to have benefited most extensively from the statutes, however, were those who brought property to marrigae or received it afterward. Those women and their husbands began to try to take advantage of the exceptions to the common law that equity had traditionally provided. Most working-class couples had neither the assets nor the legal resources to use the appellate courts in this way.

In some ways the statutes fulfilled one main legislative intention. They legitimized and democratized the exceptions recognized in equity by placing them in statutory form and making them at least theoretically available to everybody. The judiciary, although it worked to limit the legislation, could not wipe out its democratizing elements. From a women's rights point of view—and legislative intent in this area is less clear—the results were disappointing. The greatest improvement was procedural. The statutes made wives full legal entities, capable of suing, and being sued in their own names. Substantively, however, much of

[52]Keller v. Phillips, 39 N.Y. 351 (1868).

what American feminists had referred to as "the old Blackstone code" survived legislative assaults, and its survival was in large measure due to the judiciary.

Whatever the weaknesses in the legislation, and there were many, the statutes carried the possibility of readjusting the legal relationship of wives and husbands and of beginning to shatter the legal outlines of the patriarchal family. The judges of New York did not permit this to happen. Their restrictive decisions in the third quarter of the nineteenth century diminished the legal status of the women of New York for decades to come and represented a lost opportunity in the cause of women's rights.

CHAPTER 8

In the Eyes of the Law

> Metaphor is the traditional device of persuasion. Eliminate metaphor from the law and you have reduced its power to convince and convert.
>
> —Lon L. Fuller

> Whereas . . . the state's compensatory and ameliorative purposes are as well served by a gender-neutral classification as one that gender-classifies and therefore carries with it the baggage of sexual stereotypes, the state cannot be permitted to classify on the basis of sex.
>
> —*Orr v. Orr,* U.S. Supreme Court, 1979

Modern textbooks in American history, newly sensitive to the dynamics of change in the lives of women, have depicted the married women's property acts as a watershed in the struggle for equality between the sexes. Some legal scholars view the statutes as the "silent revolution" that legitimated the erosion of the patriarchal family without extensive controversy.[1] The New York experience, however, suggests that the process was neither silent nor revolutionary.

New York continued for the balance of the nineteenth century to make additions and adjustments to the legal status of married women. An 1884 statute gave the married woman power to make contracts as if she were single, and her separate estate was to be liable for all of her contracts whether or not she specified such liability.[2] Since full contractual capacity was surely implicit in the wording of the 1860 Earnings Act, the need for the 1884 statute merely reflects the narrowness of the judicial interpretation of the older statute. Essentially the 1860–62 statutes remained the foundation of the married woman's legal status to

[1]Lawrence Friedman uses this phrase, pointing out that the statutes ratified changes that had already taken place in equity (*History of American Law,* p. 186).
[2]*LNY, 1884,* chap. 381.

the end of the century and after. The principal changes, then, took place between 1848 and 1862 and comprise New York's experience with that constellation of laws known as the married women's property acts.

Further state-by-state research is needed, but there is little reason to suspect that the New York experience was significantly anomalous. Some New York statutes were more liberal than those of many other states and provided the model for new western states.[3] Their influence had international dimensions as well. When such English reformers as John Stuart Mill urged Parliament to pass a married women's bill, they drew on the New York Earnings Act as their model.[4] Yet many of the changes wrought by the New York Legislature were illusory. The evolution of the legal status of New York wives in the nineteenth century was marked more by continuities than by changes. How are we to understand the persistence of these continuities in the face of what looked for all the world like a social and legal revolution?

One obvious source of married women's continued disabilities was their total exclusion from the legal process. The law, the most effective instrument of social control in a modern society, was in all of its manifestations male. It was created, shaped, disseminated, altered, and adjudicated by men. Men fashioned disabilities for women, subsequently devised ways of remedying them for women, and ultimately determined how far concessions to women should go. Few social institutions offer a clearer view of the way men delineated the boundaries of women's lives than the law.

Yet explaining away the limitations of the married women's property acts exclusively in terms of the male arrogation of power is reductive if not somewhat ahistorical. To ignore the women who exerted their "force" in public and private ways is to ignore the caveats Mary Beard issued to historians of women in 1946. Such an explanation demeans the intellectual resource-

[3]See Warbasse, "Changing Legal Rights," pp. 237–46, for an overview of the statutes.

[4]*Speeches of Mr. Jacob Bright, M.P., Right Hon. Robert Lowe, M.P., Mr. J. S. Mill, M.P., and Mr. G. Shaw Lefevre, M.P.; In the Debate on the Second Reading of the Bill to Amend the Law with Respect to the Property of Married Women, June 10, 1858* (Manchester, 1858), p. 21.

fulness with which antebellum feminists extended the liberal philosophy of the Enlightenment to the family itself, and it demeans the financial resourcefulness with which New York wives invested their butter-and-egg money regardless of how the law defined their roles. Furthermore, it precludes an analysis of why male legislators wanted to change the law in the first place. That men have controlled women through the law and that some women have resisted that control overtly or covertly while others have acquiesced is not at issue. Patriarchy has assumed many shapes and so has resistance to it. What is at issue is a surprising amount of legal continuity in the midst of social and economic upheaval.

One way to understand this continuity within the dynamics of social change is to consider the law as a derivative phenomenon that reflects larger social needs and conditions. In this context, it is apparent that legislative motivation for changing the law restricted the scope of the changes. The statutes would have been more comprehensive if the primary legislative motive had been the improvement of the legal status of married women.

One legislative motive was to adapt the legal system to structural changes in the economy. By the middle decades of the nineteenth century a clarification of the relationship between the married couple and the commercial world was essential. Coverture, after all, had been designed to fit the requirements of a medieval agricultural society whose economic focus had been descending scales of tenancy in land. Although equity had fashioned substantial readjustments in the law, by the 1830s the wife's equitable estate was riddled with ambiguities. Precipitous dips in an increasingly complex economy encouraged legislators to pass statutes that insulated the wife's property. From the creditor's perspective, clarity was preferable to ambiguity. Forewarned is forearmed. Furthermore, new developments such as life insurance, the growth of savings banks, the increase in corporate stock, and the appearance of a female wage-earning class all prompted a redefinition of the legal position of the wife.

A second legislative motive was clearly political and took the form of extending the redistributive advantages of the wife's equitable estate to the middle class. The failure of married women's bills to emerge from numerous legislative judiciary committees and the overturn of the married women's clause at the constitutional convention of 1846 suggests that powerful interests were reluctant to extend the advantages of the separate estate to a new group. Reformers attacked trusts and antenuptial agreements and the courts of equity that recognized and adjudicated them because such devices fostered two legal models of marriage, one for the wealthy and legally sophisticated and one for everyone else. While equity precedents recognized marriage as an individual bargain in which the contracting parties set their own terms, the common law depicted marriage as a monolithic institution in which the state imposed uniform rules for marital property. Resentment toward this two-level system, which took shape in the Jacksonian era, coalesced in the codification movement. The Revised Statutes of 1828 were the first step in codification; the merger of law and equity in 1846 was the second. New York legislators passed the married women's acts in order to offer to the many by statute what the few had enjoyed by custom and judicial precedent.

The third motive for change was the woman question, which emerged from the nation's failure even to begin to apply the principle of equality before the law to its women. Juxtaposed against the emergence of universal white male suffrage and the egalitarian rhetoric and reforming zeal of the antebellum period, the legal disabilities of married women were all the more striking. While the cult of domesticity elevated and empowered the wife within the domestic sphere, the common law reduced her to the status of a child. The 1848 statute improved the status of married women incidentally in comparison with economic and political objectives; by contrast, the 1860 statute was designed to meet some feminist demands. But although the woman question was a strong catalyst for legal change, few legislators envisioned or desired the fundamental changes demanded by such women as Stanton, Anthony, and Rose. When feminist pressure ebbed in 1862, women lost some of their gains. Statutes that met limited feminist goals functioned as significant instruments of social stability by making some accommodations for women without significantly overturning the pyramid of male power.[5] Adjudication, which took place when judicial hos-

[5]For the place of legal accommodation, see Thurman Arnold, *The Symbols of Government* (New Haven, 1935), p. 35.

tility to the legislature was high, diminished some of these limited gains.

When we view the law as a derivative phenomenon, a rational response to economic exigencies and social change, it becomes apparent that the married women's property acts were weak because they represented the juncture of conflicting demands. Some amelioration of the wife's legal disabilities was necessary, but to give her full equality with her husband threatened to make her competitive rather than cooperative. The image of amazons in the marketplace was both economically and psychologically disturbing to nineteenth-century men. Thus wives were granted limited rights when all other aspects of the dominant culture excluded them from the marketplace. Ironically, the very social changes that spurred the development of the women's movement in the nineteenth century also buttressed the sex-segregated world in which most women lived.[6] The process of industrialization and urbanization and the separation of home and work at least temporarily impelled the vigilant protection of the nuclear family. The common law supported that structure with powerful legal sanctions. The wife's dependency at common law ensured her sexual fidelity, guaranteed that her children's legitimacy would be beyond question, and nourished the sexual division of labor. Theorists as disparate as William Blackstone and Frederick Engels recognized these functions in marital property law.

Certainly jurists, legislators, and judges had little reason to transform or imperil the nuclear family, that indissoluble unit of psychological loyalty and economic cooperation, the institution contemporaries viewed as the remaining source of stability in an atomistic world.[7] Women, acculturated to view their role in marriage as advantageous and to be grateful for the support that marriage laws granted them and their children, undoubtedly played no small part in their own subjugation. Jurisprudence merely mirrored this larger hierarchy of values. Joel Prentice Bishop, one of the nineteenth century's most prominent specialists in domestic relations law, proclaimed that the wife made a "bargain" that "freed her . . . from that yoke of toil and

[6] William H. Chafe, *Women and Equality:: Changing Patterns in American Culture* (New York, 1977), p. 40.

[7] Stone, "Rise of the Nuclear Family," pp. 24–25.

that burden of care for a future support under which God placed all his children."[8] The wife's yoke of toil in service to family never received legal recognition.

It is a mistake, however, to view the law exclusively as a derivative phenomenon. The law in all of its manifestations is more than a battlefield for competing interests, and it is more than a barometer of social change. Law has an autonomy of its own and is capable of asserting its influence over legislators, jurists, and the public. The ability of the common law tradition to inhibit and diminish statutory change is an intriguing example of what Eugene Genovese has termed "the hegemonic function" of the law.[9] The conservative pull of centuries of jurisprudence that relegated wives to an inferior status dwarfed the ambiguous stipulations of legislative tinkerers. Legislators did not begin with a tabula rasa.

One example of the pull of older law was the influence of equity. The legislative model for change was dubious because it was rooted in the precedents of Anglo-American equity, a system that recognized the wife as the husband's subordinate while it protected her from the problems created by her subordination. In correcting simplistic notions about the legal status of women, Mary Beard overestimated the ameliorative qualities of American equity and failed to distinguish the ways in which equity maintained the legal subordination of women. In fact, by contravening some basic common law assumptions about marriage, equity became the handmaiden of the common law, easing its rigidities and removing the obstacles in its path. With equity as a model, the rights granted to nineteenth-century wives were a far cry from the rights that underpinned the United States Constitution. The married women's property acts did not grant wives the same right to property and its protection that had been synonymous with individual liberty in the eighteenth century. By immuring women as wives within the household and by defining their legal status exclusively in relation to their husbands, the

[8]Joel Prentice Bishop, *Commentaries on the Law of Married Women . . .*, 2 vols. (Boston, 1873), 1:680.

[9]Eugene Genovese has applied the concept of legal hegemony to southern slave codes in *Roll, Jordan, Roll: The World the Slaves Made* (New York, 1974), pp. 25–27. For the hegemony of legal language, see Pollack and Maitland, *History of English Law*, 2:87.

common law tradition also deprived them of political status as individuals. Equity merely carved out exceptions; it did not overturn the basic common law model.

The whole common law tradition, as one practitioner put it, was a "mighty conservative spirit" over the English and American bars.[10] This same spirit informed judicial resistance to statutory changes. With its emphasis on precedents and its reliance on fictions, the common law discouraged the lawyer from overturning the time-honored canons of coverture. Maxims, learned and repeated, were part of every lawyer's education and experience. It was his function "to understand them, with all their inconsistencies, their verbal distinctions, their scholastic refinements." Therefore, argued David Dudley Field, the lawyer came to regard these rules to which he applied his reason daily "as natural and true."[11]

Not to be forgotten was the prescriptive influence of older legal forms on the nonprofessional public, which saw the common law with few ameliorating distinctions and in its harshest and most repressive form. The assignment of rights and duties mandated by marital property laws was one way to prescribe behavior appropriate to wives and husbands. What was hers and what was his constituted a statement about what she should be as a wife, what he should be as a husband, and what marriage should be as a social institution. Court records, to be sure, reveal an enormous gap between this legal ideal and day-to-day reality. Widows who protested they had been duped by uncaring husbands, husbands who asserted they had been shamed by adulterous wives, one spouse who underscored the deviant behavior of the other simply suggest that common law outlines of appropriate sex roles were recognized if not closely adhered to. By creating an ideal, abstract wife and husband, the law imposed a fictitious unity on a heterogeneous culture. These abstractions, moreover, had a degree of autonomy all their own.

The evidence found in treatises, legislative debates, and appellate cases suggests that these abstractions survived and that the old common law fiction of marital unity inhibited the reform of marital property law. It suggests that the legal fiction was so pervasive in the language and literature of the law that it af-

[10] Anthon, *Law Student,* pp. 6–7.
[11] *NYAD,* 1842, vol. 5, no. 81, p. 30.

fected as well as reflected attitudes toward women and marriage. In one context judges consciously selected this richly suggestive and readily available metaphor for wifely subservience for their own purposes. This was a matter of thought dominating language. But in another context, especially a legal one, language dominated thought. Furthermore, the adaptability and flexibility for which the common law tradition is famous helped the legal fiction to survive. Thus while the doctrine of marital unity underwent some alterations in the antebellum period, it simultaneously tempered substantial changes.

The evolution of married women's property rights in New York suggests that the inherently conservative processes of law embodied in the power and legitimacy of the ancient legal fiction blunted the inherently radical possibilities of dismantling the legal foundations of the patriarchal family. When nineteenth-century American feminists attacked common law categories, they at least dimly perceived that language orders and classifies, and contains the existing conceptual apparatus for creating new law. When they registered their rage and humiliation at being lumped together with infants and lunatics, they were groping toward a fundamental restructuring of power and readjustment of gender roles that those in power—jurists, legislators, and judges—would not and could not permit as long as they held to the fiction of marital unity.

For innumerable reasons, New York failed in the nineteenth century to recast marital property laws into a code that was truly equitable. Was such a code even theoretically possible? It was more possible than Mary Beard implied it was. Legislators are only beginning to prove it is possible for the law to apply gender-free language to spouses in a variety of circumstances and to recognize the contributions in labor and services made by the spouse who remains at home without automatically disabling the wife who works. This legislative trend represents profound changes in the support patterns of the nuclear family since World War II.[12]

Nevertheless, despite the presence of women in unprecedented numbers in the work force, a high divorce rate, and a spate

[12]Chafe, *The American Woman: Her Changing Social, Economic, and Political Roles, 1920–1970* (New York, 1972). Chafe sees economic change as the precondition for women's equality.

of constitutional test cases on sexual discrimination, remnants of coverture remain.[13] Although modern jurists no longer invoke the one-flesh doctrine, they still exhibit a tendency to view woman's primary role as wife and mother and her work as an addition to her primary role. As Susan Moller Okin has pointed out, the modern judiciary at both state and federal levels still defines women by the functions they serve in relationship to men. It is coverture, she suggests, that has provided a firm basis for depriving women of legal personhood, and its disabilities have been extended in practice to all women, married and single.[14] It is coverture that has informed the assumption that harmony in the family can prevail only at the expense of full legal equality for women. And coverture, with its promise of protecting and compensating women as nurturers, has proved to be less than genuinely protective or compensatory.

Finally the question implicit throughout this discussion is the relation of women's legal status to their overall status in society. To be more precise, what was the cost of failing to give wives formal legal equality in the nineteenth century? Equality before the law was not a panacea. The absence of legal disabilities failed to relieve nineteenth-century men of the social and economic disabilities of class and race. Similarly, legal equality for married women could not have relieved them of the social and economic disabilities of sex. But at least the law could have removed its sanctions from those disabilities. Nobody suggested that the condition of nineteenth-century men could be improved by a return to the deference and protection of feudal statuses. Their legal equality was, in fact, a precondition for their understanding of the larger inequities of their society.

Antebellum feminists' emphasis on coverture as the source of crippling sexual discrimination was neither naive nor misguided; it was essential to an exploration of the conflict between motherhood and citizenship, the critical first stage in bridging the world of domesticity and the world of politics, and an integral part of that larger and enduring drive for women's liberation.

[13]Kanowitz, *Women and the Law,* pp. 41–59; on legal trends in recent sexual discrimination cases, see Nancy S. Erickson, "Equality between the Sexes in the 1980's," *Cleveland State Law Review* 28 (1979):591–610.

[14]Okin, *Women in Western Political Thought,* pp. 247–73.

APPENDIX

Married Women's Property Acts, 1848–62

Laws of New York, 1848, Chapter 200

§1. The real and personal property of any female who may hereafter marry, and which she shall own at the time of marriage, and the rents issues and profits thereof shall not be subject to the disposal of her husband, nor be liable for his debts, and shall continue her sole and separate property, as if she were a single female.

§2. The real and personal property, and the rents issues and profits thereof of any female now married shall not be subject to the disposal of her husband; but shall be her sole and separate property as if she were a single female except so far as the same may be liable for the debts of her husband heretofore contracted.

§3. It shall be lawful for any married female to receive, by gift, grant devise or bequest, from any person other than her husband and hold to her sole and separate use, as if she were a single female, real and personal property, and the rents, issues and profits thereof, and the same shall not be subject to the disposal of her husband, nor be liable for his debts.

§4. All contracts made between persons in contemplation of marriage shall remain in full force after such marriage takes place.

Laws of New York, 1849, Chapter 375

§1. The third section of the act entitled "An act for the more effectual protection of the property of married women," is hereby amended so as to read as follows:

§3. Any married female may take by inheritance or by gift, grant, devise or bequest, from any person other than her husband and hold to her sole and separate use and convey and devise real and personal property, and any interest on estate therein, and the rents, issues and profits thereof in the same manner and with like effect as if she were unmarried, and the same shall not be subject to the disposal of her husband nor be liable for his debts.

§2. Any person who may hold or who may hereafter hold as trustee for any married woman, any real or personal estate or other property under any deed of conveyance or otherwise, on the written request of such married woman accompanied by a certificate of a justice of the supreme court that he has examined the condition and situation of the property, and made due enquiry into the capacity of such married woman to manage and control the same, may convey to such married woman by deed or otherwise, all or any portion of such property, or the rents, issues or profits thereof, for her sole and separate use and benefit.

§3. All contracts made between persons in contemplation of marriage shall remain in full force after such marriage takes place.

Laws of New York, 1860, Chapter 90

SECTION 1. The property, both real and personal, which any married woman now owns, as her sole and separate property; that which comes to her by descent, devise, bequest, gift or grant; that which she acquires by her trade, business, labor or services, carried on or performed on her sole or separate account; that which a woman married in this state owns at the time of her marriage, and the rents, issues and proceeds of all such property, shall, notwithstanding her marriage, be and remain her sole and separate property, and may be used, collected and invested by her in her own name, and shall not be subject to the interference or control of her husband, or liable for his debts, except such debts as may have been contracted for the support of herself or her children, by her as his agent.

§2. A married woman may bargain, sell, assign and transfer her separate personal property, and carry on any trade or business, and perform any labor or services on her sole and separate account, and the earnings of any married woman, from her trade, business, labor or services, shall be her sole and separate property, and may be used or invested by her in her own name.

§3. Any married woman possessed of real estate as her separate property, may bargain, sell and convey such property, and enter into any contract in reference to the same, but no such conveyance or contract shall be valid without the assent, in writing, of her husband, except as hereinafter provided.

§4. In case any married woman possessed of separate real property, as aforesaid, may desire to sell or convey the same, or to make any contract in relation thereto, and shall be unable to procure the assent of her husband, as in the preceding section provided, in consequence of his refusal, absence, insanity, or other disability, such married woman may apply to the county court in the county where she shall at the time reside, for leave to make such sale, conveyance or contract, without the assent of her husband.

§5. Such application may be made by petition, verified by her, and setting forth the grounds of such application. If the husband be a resident of the county, and not under disability, from insanity or other cause, a copy of said petition shall be served upon him, with a notice of the time when the same will be presented to the said court, at least ten days before such application. In all other cases the county court to which such application shall be made, shall, in its discretion, determine whether any notice shall be given, and if any, the mode and manner of giving it.

§6. If it shall satisfactorily appear to such court, upon such application, that the husband of such applicant has willfully abandoned his said wife, and lives separate and apart from her, or that he is insane, or imprisoned as a convict in any state prison, or that he is an habitual drunkard, or that he is in any way disabled from making a contract, or that he refuses to give his consent, without good cause therefor, then such court shall cause an order to be entered upon its records, authorizing such married woman to sell and convey her real estate, or contract in regard thereto without the assent of her husband, with the same effect as though such conveyance or contract had been made with his assent.

§7. Any married woman may, while married, sue and be sued in all matters having relation to her property, which may be her sole and separate property, or which may hereafter come to her by descent, devise, bequest, or the gift of any person except her husband, in the same manner as if she were sole. And any married woman may bring and maintain an action in her own name, for damages, against any person or body corporate, for any injury to her person or character, the same as if she were sole; and the money received upon the settlement of any such action, or recovered upon a judgment, shall be her sole and separate property.

§8. No bargain or contract made by any married woman, in respect to her sole and separate property, or any property which may hereafter come to her by descent devise, bequest or gift of any person except her husband, and no bargain or contract entered into by any married woman in or about the carrying on of any trade or business under the statutes of this state, shall be binding upon her husband, or render him or his property in any way liable therefor.

§9. Every married woman is hereby constituted and declared to be the joint guardian of her children, with her husband, with equal powers, rights and duties in regard to them, with the husband.

§10. At the decease of husband or wife, leaving no minor child or children, the survivor shall hold, possess and enjoy a life estate in one-third of all the real estate of which the husband or wife died seized.

§11. At the decease of the husband or wife intestate, leaving minor child or children, the survivor shall hold, possess and enjoy all the real estate of which the husband or wife died siezed, and all the rents, issues and profits thereof during the minority of the youngest child, and one-third thereof during his or her natural life.

Appendix

Laws of New York, 1862, Chapter 172

SECTION 1. The third section of the act entitled "An act concerning the rights and liabilities of husband and wife," passed March twentieth, eighteen hundred and sixty, is hereby amended so as to read as follows:

§3. Any married woman possessed of real estate as her separate property, may bargain, sell and convey such property and enter into any contract in reference to the same, with the like effect in all respects as if she were unmarried, and she may in like manner enter into such covenant or covenants for title as are usual in conveyances of real estate, which covenants shall be obligatory to bind her separate property, in case the same or any of them be broken.

§2. The fourth, fifth, sixth, ninth, tenth, and eleventh sections of the said act are hereby repealed.

§3. The seventh section of the said act is hereby amended so as to read as follows:

§7. Any married woman may, while married, sue and be sued in all matters having relation to her sole and separate property, or which may hereafter come to her by descent, devise, bequest, purchase, or the gift or grant of any person in the same manner as if she were sole; and any married woman may bring and maintain an action in her own name, for damages, against any person or body corporate, for any injury to her person or character, the same as if she were sole; and the money received upon the settlement of any such action or recovered upon a judgment, shall be her sole and separate property. In case it shall be necessary in the prosecution or defence of any action brought by or against a married woman, to enter into any bond or undertaking, such bond or undertaking may be executed by such married woman with the same effect in all respects as if she were sole, and in case the said bond or undertaking shall become broken or forfeited the same may be enforced against her separate estate.

§4. The eighth section of the said act is hereby amended so as to read as follows:

§8. No bargain or contract made by any married woman, in respect to her sole and separate property, or any property, which may hereafter come to her by descent, devise, bequest, purchase, or the gift or grant of any person (except her husband), and no bargain or contract entered into by any married woman in or about the carrying on of any trade or business, under any statute of this state, shall be binding upon her husband, or render him or his property in any way liable therefor.

§5. In an action brought or defended by any married woman in her name, her husband shall not neither shall his property be liable for the costs thereof, or the recovery therein. In an action brought by her for an injury to her person, character or property, if judgment shall pass against her for costs, the court in which the action is pending shall have jurisdiction to enforce payment of such judgment out of her separate estate, though the sum recovered be less than one hundred dollars.

§6. No man shall bind his child to apprenticeship or service or part with the control of such child or create any testamentary guardian therefor, unless the mother if living, shall in writing signify her assent thereto.

§7. A married woman may be sued in any of the courts in this state, and whenever a judgment shall be recovered against a married woman the same may be enforced by execution against her sole and separate estate in the same manner as if she were sole.

Selected Bibliography

Manuscripts and Special Collections

New-York Historical Society
- Beekman Family Papers
- Amelia Jenks Bloomer Letters
- De Peyster Chancery Papers
- De Peyster Family Papers
- Rebecca Anne Smith Janney Letters
- Vanderbilt Family Papers

New York Public Library
- Smith Family Papers (Gerrit Smith and Elizabeth Smith Miller)
- Uncatalogued pamphlets, women's legal status

Vassar College Library
- Alma Lutz Collection
- Elizabeth Cady Stanton Papers

Westchester County Archives
- Surrogate's Office, Probated Wills, 1825, 1850, 1875

Public Documents

Laws of New York, 1830–62.

New York Assembly Documents, 1830–62.

New York Senate Documents, 1830–62.

Journal of the New York Assembly, 1830–62.

Journal of the New York Senate, 1830–62.

Journal of the Convention of the State of New York Begun and Held at the Capital in the City of Albany, on the First Day of June, 1846. Albany: Carroll & Cook, 1846.

The Revised Statutes of the State of New York as Altered by the Legislature . . . From 1828 to 1835 Inclusive. 2d ed. 3 vols. Albany: Packard & Van Benthuysen, 1836.

The Revised Statutes of the State of New York as Altered by Subsequent Legislation. 7th ed. 3 vols. New York: Banks & Bros., 1882.

The Revised Statutes of the State of New York Passed during the Years 1827 and 1828. 3 vols. Albany: Packard & Van Benthuysen, 1829.

Chancery Reports

Barbour, Oliver L. *Reports of Cases Argued and Determined in the Court of Chancery of the State of New York.* 3 vols. Albany: Banks & Gould, 1847–49.

Edwards, Charles. *Reports of Chancery Cases Decided in the First Circuit of the State of New York, 1831–1850.* 4 vols. Albany: Gould, Banks & Co., 1837–87.

Hopkins, Samuel M. *Reports of Cases Argued and Determined in the Court of Chancery of the State of New York, 1823–1826.* Albany: William A. Gould, 1837.

Johnson, William. *Reports of Cases Adjudged in the Court of Chancery of New York . . . 1814–1823* 2d ed. 7 vols. Albany: Banks & Bros., 1816–87.

Paige, Alonzo C. *Reports of Cases . . . Determined in the Court of Chancery of the State of New York, 1828–1845.* 11 vols. New York: Banks & Bros., 1858–87.

Nineteenth-Century Legal Treatises and Manuals

Amos, Sheldon. *Difference of Sex as a Topic of Jurisprudence and Legislation.* London: Longman, Green, 1870.

Anthon, John. *An Analytical Abridgement of the Commentaries of Sir William Blackstone.* New York: Isaac Riley, 1809.

———. *The Law Student, or Guides to the Study of the Law in Its Principles.* New York: Appleton, 1850.

Bentham, Jeremy. *A Comment on the Commentaries: A Criticism of William Blackstone.* Ed. Charles Warren Everett. London: Oxford University Press, 1928.

Bishop, George. *Every Woman Her Own Lawyer.* New York: Dick & Fitzgerald, 1858.

Bishop, Joel Prentice. *Commentaries on the Law of Marriage and Divorce and Evidence in Matrimonial Suits.* Boston: Little, Brown, 1852.

———. *Commentaries on the Law of Married Women under the Statutes of the Several States and at Common Law and in Equity.* 2 vols. Boston: Little, Brown, 1873–75.

Blackstone, Sir William. *Commentaries on the Laws of England, in Four Books.* Ed. Thomas M. Cooley. 4th ed. 2 vols. Chicago: Callaghan, 1899.

Bright, John Edward. *A Treatise on the Law of Husband and Wife as Respects Property . . . with Copious Notes and References to The American Decisions, by Ralph Lockwood.* 2 vols. New York: Banks & Gould, 1850.

Hall, Benjamin F. *The Land Owner's Manual.* Auburn, N.Y.: J. C. Derby, 1847.

Hand-Books for Home Improvement Comprising How to Write, How to Talk, How to Behave, How to Do Business. New York: Fowlers & Wells, 1857.

Jenkins, John S. *The New Clerk's Assistant or Book of Practical Forms.* Auburn and Buffalo, N.Y.: Miller, Orton, & Mulligan, 1853.

Kent, James. *Commentaries on American Law.* Ed. George F. Comstock. 11th ed. 4 vols. Boston: Little, Brown, 1867.

Kinne, Asa. *The Most Important Part of Kent's Commentaries Reduced to Questions and Answers.* 3d ed. New York: Asa Kinne, 1844.

Proffat, John. *Woman before the Law.* New York: G. P. Putnam's Sons, 1874.

Reeve, Tapping. *The Law of Baron and Femme.* 3d ed. Albany: William Gould, 1862.

Story, Joseph. *Commentaries on Equity Jurisprudence.* 2 vols. Boston: Little, Brown, 1839.

Wright, David. *Executor's, Administrator's, and Guardian's Guide.* 3d ed. Auburn, N.Y.: Derby & Miller, 1852.

Pamphlets, Diaries, Commentaries, Reminiscences

Beecher, Henry Ward. *Woman's Influence in Politics: An Address Delivered at the Cooper Institute, Feb. 2, 1860.* Boston: C. K. Whipple, 1860.

Bishop, William G. and William H. Attree. *Report of the Debates and Proceedings of the Convention for the Revision of the Constitution of the State of New York.* Albany: Bishop & Attree, 1846.

Bloomer, Dexter C. *Life and Writings of Amelia Bloomer.* New York: Arena Press, 1895.

Butler, Benjamin Franklin. *Outline of the Constitutional History of New York, an Anniversary Discourse Delivered at the Request of the New-York Historical Society in the City of New York, November 30, 1847.* New York: New-York Historical Society, 1847.

Butler, William Allen. *The Revision of the Statutes of the State of New York and the Revisors: An Address Delivered before the Association of the Bar of the City of New York.* New York: Banks & Bros., 1889.

Carlier, August. *Marriage in the United States.* 1867; reprinted New York: Arno Press, 1972.

Codification of the Common Law: Report of the Commissioners Appointed to Consider and Report upon the Practicability and Expediency of Reducing to a Written and Systematic Code, the Common Law of Massachusetts. Law Reform Tracts. New York: John S. Voorhies, 1852.

Cooper, James Fennimore. *The American Democrat.* 1836; reprinted New York: Minerva Press, 1969.

Croswell, Sherman, and Sutton, Richard. *Debates and Proceedings in the New York State Convention for the Revision of the Constitution.* Albany: Albany Argus, 1846.

Dall, Caroline, *Woman's Rights under the Law.* Boston: Walker, Wise, 1861.

——. *The College, the Market, and the Courts: A Woman's Relation to Education, Labor, and Law.* Boston: Lee & Shephard, 1867.

D'Arusement, Frances Wright. *Course of Popular Lectures as Delivered by Frances Wright in New York, Philadelphia, Baltimore.* New York: Free Enquirer, 1830.

Davis, Paulina Wright. *A History of the National Woman's Rights Movement, for Twenty Years.* New York: Journeymen Printers' Co-operative Association, 1871.

Evidence on the Operation of the Code: Obtained by the English Law Amendment Society and Chancery Commission, and Published in England. Law Reform Tract. New York: John S. Voorhies, 1852.

Field, David Dudley. *The Reorganization of the Judiciary: Five Articles Originally Published in the Evening Post.* New York, 1846.

——. *The Administration of the Code.* Law Reform Tract. New York: John S. Voorhies, 1852.

——. *Legal Reform: An Address to the Graduating Class of the Law School of the University of Albany.* Albany: W. C. Little, 1855.

——. *A Short Manual of Pleading under the Code.* Law Reform Tract. Albany: W. C. Little, 1856.

——. *Speeches, Arguments, and Miscellaneous Papers of David Dudley Field.* Ed. A. P. Sprague. 2 vols. New York: D. Appleton, 1884.

The First Convention Ever Called to Discuss the Civil and Political Rights of Women, Seneca Falls, New York, July 19, 20, 1848. N.p., n.d.

Foster, R. W. *Women's Rights and Servants' Rights According to the Bible.* Corning, N.Y., 1854.

Grimké, Sarah M. *Letters on the Equality of the Sexes and the Condition of Woman.* Boston: Isaac Knapp, 1838.

Hankins, Mary Louise. *City Sketches: Original, Curious and Truthful Episodes in Female Society.* New York: M. Gaunt, 1862.

Herttell, Thomas. *Remarks on the Law of Imprisonment for Debt Showing Its Unconstitutionality and Its Demoralizing Influence on the Community.* New York: Gould & Banks, 1823.

——. *Speech of the Hon. Thomas Herttell of New York in Assembly, January 3, 1833, on the Resolution for the Appointment of Chaplains.* Ballston Spa, N.Y., 1833.

——. *Argument in the House of Assembly of the State of New York in the Session of 1837 in Support of the Bill to Restore to Married Women "The Right of Property" as Guaranteed by the Constitution of This State.* New York: Henry Durell, 1839.

Hone, Phillip. *The Diary of Phillip Hone, 1828–1851.* Ed. Allan Nevins. 2 vols. New York: Dodd, Mead, 1927.

Hurlbut, Elisha P. *Essays on Human Rights and Their Political Guaranties.* New York: Fowlers & Wells, 1850.

Lefevre, G. Shaw. *Speech for "The Bill to Amend the Law with Respect to the Property of Married Women" in the House of Commons, April 21, 1868.* Manchester, 1868.

May, Samuel Jay. *The Rights and Condition of Women: A Sermon Preached in Syracuse, Nov., 1845*. 3d ed. Woman's Rights Tract no. 1. N.p., n.d.

Mill, Harriet Taylor. *Enfranchisement of Women: An Essay by Mrs. John Stuart Mill, Reprinted from the Westminster and Foreign Quarterly Review, for July, 1851*. New York: Office of the Revolution, 1868.

Mott, Lucretia. *Discourse on Woman, by Lucretia Mott, Delivered at the Assembly Building, December 17, 1849*. Philadelphia: T. B. Peterson, n.d.

Nichols, Thomas Low. *Forty Years of American Life*. 2 vols. London: John Maxwell, 1864.

Osgood, Samuel. *The Hearth-Stone: Thoughts upon Home-Life in Our Cities*. New York: Appleton, 1854.

Ossoli, Margaret Fuller. *Woman in the Nineteenth Century*. 1845; reprinted New York: Norton, 1971.

Parton, Sarah Payson (Willis). *Fern Leaves*. 2d ser. Auburn and Buffalo, N.Y.: Miller, Orton, & Mulligan, 1854.

———. *Fresh Leaves*. New York: Mason Bros., 1857.

Patterson, John. *The Philosophy of Woman's Rights and the Dress Reform: The Means and Conditions of Woman's Freedom*. Tracts for Thinkers, no. 1. N.p., n.d.

Phillips, Wendell. *Speech of Wendell Phillips, Esq. at the Convention, Held at Worcester, October 15 & 16, 1851*. Woman's Rights Tracts no. 2. N.p., n.d.

Proceedings of the National Women's [*sic*] *Rights Convention Held at Cleveland, Ohio, on Wednesday, Thursday, and Friday, October 5th, 6th, and 7th, 1853*. Cleveland: Gray, Beardsley, Spear, 1854.

Proceedings of the Ninth National Woman's Rights Convention Held in New York City, Thursday, May 12, 1859. Rochester, N.Y.: A. Strong, 1859.

Proceedings of the Seventh National Woman's Rights Convention Held in New York City at the Broadway Tabernacle, Tuesday and Wednesday, Nov. 25th and 26th, 1856. New York: Edward Jenkins, 1856.

Proceedings of the Tenth National Woman's Rights Convention Held at the Cooper Institute, New York City, May 10th and 11th, 1860. Boston: Yerrinton & Garrison, 1860.

Proceedings of the Woman's Rights Convention Held at Akron, Ohio, May 28 and 29, 1851. 1851; reprinted New York: Burt Franklin, 1973.

Proceedings of the Woman's Rights Convention, Held at the Broadway Tabernacle in the City of New York on Tuesday and Wednesday, Sept. 6th and 7th, 1853. New York: Fowlers & Wells, 1853.

The Proceedings of the Woman's Rights Convention, Held at Syracuse, September 8th, 9th, and 10th, 1852. Syracuse: J. E. Masters, 1852.

The Proceedings of the Woman's Rights Convention, Held at Worcester, October 15th and 16th, 1857. New York: Fowlers & Wells, 1857.

Smith, Elizabeth Oakes. *Woman and Her Needs*. New York: Fowlers & Wells, 1851.

———. *The Sanctity of Marriage*. Woman's Rights Tracts, no. 5. Syracuse, 1853.

Speeches of Mr. Jacob Bright, M.P., Right Hon. Robert Lowe, M.P., Mr. J. S. Milll, M.P., and Mr. G. Shaw Lefevre, M.P.; In the Debate on the Second Reading of the Bill to Amend the Law with Respect to the Property of Married Women, June 10, 1858. Manchester: A. Ireland, 1858.

The Speech of Wendell Phillips [and Abby Kelley Foster] to the Convention in Worcester, October 1851. Woman's Rights Tracts, no. 2. N.p., 1853.

Stanton, Elizabeth Cady. *Address to the Legislature of New York Adopted by the State Woman's Rights Convention Held at Albany, Tuesday and Wednesday, February 14 and 15, 1854.* Albany: Weed, Parsons, 1854.

———. *Appeal to the Women of New York.* New York State Woman's Right Committee, 1860.

———. *Eighty Years and More: Reminiscences, 1815–1897.* 1898; reprinted New York: Schocken, 1971.

———. *Elizabeth Cady Stanton as Revealed in Her Letters, Diary, and Reminiscences.* Ed. Theodore Stanton and Harriot Stanton Blatch. 2 vols. New York: Harper, 1922.

———, Susan B. Anthony, Matilda Joslyn Gage, and Ida Husted Harper, eds. *History of Woman Suffrage.* 6 vols. New York: Fowlers & Wells, 1881–1922.

Stanton, Henry B. *Random Recollections.* New York: Harper, 1887.

Swisshelm, Jane Grey. *Half a Century.* Chicago: Jansen, McClurg, 1880.

Trollope, Frances. *Domestic Manners of the Americans.* 1832; reprinted New York: Alfred A. Knopf, 1949.

The Woman's Rights Almanac for 1858. Worcester, Mass.: Z. Baker, 1858.

Advice Manuals

Abbot, John Stevens Cabot. *The Mother at Home; or the Principles of Maternal Duty Familiarly Illustrated.* New York: Harper, 1852.

Alcott, William A. *The Young Wife, or Duties of Woman in the Marriage Relationship.* 1837; reprinted New York: Arno, 1972.

Arthur, Timothy Shay. *Advice to Young Ladies on Their Duties and Conduct in Life.* Boston: Barton, 1848.

Beecher, Henry Ward. *Lectures to Young Men.* New York: Derby & Jackson, 1860.

Chapin, Edwin Hubbell. *Duties of Young Women.* Boston: Putnam, 1856.

Child, Lydia Maria. *The American Frugal Housewife.* 1829; reprinted New York: Harper & Row, 1972.

Cobbett, William. *Advice to Young Men, and (Incidentally) to Young Women in the Middle and Higher Ranks of Life.* New York: John Doyle, 1833.

Coggeshall, William T. *Cash and Character: A Lecture on High Life.* Cincinnati: Moore, Wilstack, & Keys, 1855.

Eliot, William G. *Lectures to Young Women.* 11th ed. Boston: American Unitarian Association, 1890.

Farrar, Eliza. *The Young Lady's Friend.* New York: Samuel & William Wood, 1849.

Morris, Robert. *Courtship and Marriage.* Philadelphia: T. B. Peterson, 1858.

Sedgwick, Catherine Maria. *Means and Ends: or Self Training.* Boston: Marsh, Capen, Lyon, & Webb, 1839.

Sigourney, Lydia H. *Letters to Young Ladies.* New York: Harper, 1837.

———. *Whisper to a Bride.* 2d ed. Hartford, Conn.: William James Hamersley, 1850.

Sprague, William B. *Letters on Practical Subjects to a Daughter.* 4th ed. New York: Appleton, 1835.

Titcomb, Timothy. *Titcomb's Letters to Young People.* 26th ed. New York: Charles Scribner, 1861.

Secondary Sources on Legal History and the History of Marriage

Beard, Mary Ritter. *Woman as Force in History: A Study in Tradition and Realities.* New York: Macmillan, 1946.

Bergold, Laurel R. "The Changing Legal Status of American Women." *Current History* 70 (May 1976):206–11, 230.

Billson, William W. *Equity with Relations to Common Law.* Boston: Boston Book Co., 1916.

Blake, Nelson Manfred. *The Road to Reno.* New York: Macmillan, 1962.

Bloomfield, Maxwell. *American Lawyers in a Changing Society, 1776–1876.* Cambridge, Mass.: Harvard University Press, 1976.

Boorstin, Daniel. *The Mysterious Science of the Law: An Essay on Blackstone's Commentaries.* Cambridge, Mass.: Harvard University Press, 1941.

Brown, Robert C. "The Duty of the Husband to Support the Wife." *Virginia Law Review* 18 (1932):823–49.

Buckstaff, Florence Griswold. "Married Women's Property in Anglo-Saxon and Anglo-Norman Law and the Origin of the Common-Law Dower." *Annals of the American Academy of Political and Social Science* 4 (1893–94):233–64.

Bullock, William E. *A Treatise on the Law of Husband and Wife in the State of New York Including Chapters on Divorce and Dower.* Albany: H. B. Parsons, 1897.

Carroll, Berenice. "Mary Beard's *Woman as Force in History:* A Critique." In *Liberating Women's History: Theoretical and Critical Essays,* ed. Berenice Carroll, pp. 21–41. Urbana: University of Illinois Press, 1976.

Chester, Alden, ed. *Legal and Judicial History of New York.* 3 vols. New York: National Americana Society, 1911.

Chroust, Anton-Herman. *The Rise of the Legal Profession in America.* 2 vols. Norman: University of Oklahoma Press, 1965.

Clark, Charles E. "The Union of Law and Equity." *Columbia Law Review* 25 (1925):1–10.

Coleman, Peter J. *Debtors and Creditors in America: Insolvency, Imprison-*

ment for Debt, and Bankruptcy, 1607–1900. Madison: State Historical Society of Wisconsin, 1974.

Crozier, Blanche. "Marital Support." *Boston University Law Review* 15 (1935):25–58.

Deen, James W., Jr. "Patterns of Testation: Four Tidewater Counties in Colonial Virginia." *American Journal of Legal History* 16 (1972):154–76.

Degler, Carl N. "*Woman as Force in History* by Mary Beard." *Daedalus* 103 (1974):67–73.

———. *At Odds: Women and the Family in America from the Revolution to the Present.* New York: Oxford University Press, 1980.

Donahue, Charles, Jr. "What Causes Fundamental Legal Ideas?: Marital Property in England and France in the Thirteenth Century." *Michigan Law Review* 78 (1979):59–88.

Dowd, Morgan. "The Influence of Story and Kent on the Development of the Common Law." *American Journal of Legal History* 17 (1973):221–22.

Eller, Catherine Spicer. *The William Blackstone Collection in the Yale Law Library: A Bibliographic Catalogue.* New Haven: Yale University Press, 1938.

Engels, Frederick. *The Origin of the Family, Private Property and the State in the Light of the Researches of Lewis H. Morgan.* New York: International Publishers, 1972.

Friedman, Lawrence M. "Patterns of Testation in the 19th Century: A Study of Essex County (New Jersey) Wills." *American Journal of Legal History* 8 (1964):34–53.

———. *A History of American Law.* New York: Simon & Schuster, 1973.

Friedmann, Wolfgang. *Law in a Changing Society.* 2d ed. New York: Columbia University Press, 1972.

Fuller, Lon L. *Legal Fictions.* Stanford, Calif.: Stanford University Press, 1967.

Goebel, Julius, Jr. *Cases and Materials on the Development of Legal Institutions.* Brattleboro, Vt.: Vermont Printing Co., 1946.

———. "The Common Law and the Constitution." In *Chief Justice John Marshall: A Reappraisal,* ed. W. Melville Jones. Ithaca: Cornell University Press, 1970.

Grossberg, Michael. "Law and the Family in Nineteenth Century America." Ph.D. dissertation, Brandeis University, 1979.

Haar, Charles M., ed. *The Golden Age of American Law.* New York: George Braziller, 1965.

Holdsworth, William S. *A History of English Law.* 14 vols. London: Methuen, 1903–26.

Holt, Wythe, ed. *Essays in Nineteenth-Century American Legal History.* Westport, Conn.: Greenwood Press, 1976.

Horwitz, Morton J. *The Transformation of American Law, 1780–1860.* Cambridge, Mass.: Harvard University Press, 1977.

Howard, George Eliot. *A History of Matrimonial Institutions.* Vol. 3. Chicago: University of Chicago Press, 1904.

Hurst, J. Willard. *Law and the Conditions of Freedom in the Nineteenth Century United States.* Madison: University of Wisconsin Press, 1956.

Johnston, John D., Jr. "Sex and Property: The Common Law Tradition, The Law School Curriculum and Developments toward Equality." *New York University Law Review* 47 (1972):1033-93.

Jones, Gareth, ed. *The Sovereignty of the Law: Selections from Blackstone's Commentaries on the Laws of England.* Cambridge, Mass.: Harvard University Press, 1941.

Kanowitz, Leo. *Women and the Law: The Unifinished Revolution.* Albuquerque: University of New Mexico Press, 1969.

———. *Sex Roles in Law and Society: Cases and Materials.* Albuquerque: University of New Mexico Press, 1973.

Kenny, Courtney Stanhope. *The History of the Law of England as to the Effect of Marriage on Property and on the Wife's Legal Capacity.* London: Reeves & Turner, 1879.

Kutler, Stanley G., ed. *John Marshall.* Englewood Cliffs, N.J.: Prentice-Hall, 1972.

Lévi-Strauss, Claude. *The Elementary Structures of Kinship.* Trans. James Harle Bell and Rodney Needham. Boston: Beacon, 1969.

Lincoln, Charles Z. *The Constitutional History of New York.* 5 vols. Rochester: Lawyers' Co-operative Publishing Co., 1906.

Loeb, Isador. "The Legal Property Relations of Married Parties: A Study in Comparative Legislation." In *Studies in History, Economics, and Public Law,* vol. 13, no. 1. New York: Columbia University Press, 1900.

McWalters, Keith G. "Marriage as a Contract: Towards a Functional Redefinition of the Marital Status." *Columbia Journal of Law and Social Problems* 9 (1972-73):607-45.

Maitland, Frederic William. *Equity.* Cambridge, Eng.: Cambridge University Press, 1926.

Miller, Perry. *The Life of the Mind in America from the Revolution to the Civil War.* New York: Harcourt Brace & World, 1965.

———, ed. *The Legal Mind in America.* Garden City, N.Y.: Anchor, Doubleday, 1962.

Morris, Richard B. *Studies in the History of American Law with Special Reference to the Seventeenth and Eighteenth Centuries.* New York: Columbia University Press, 1930.

Nelson, William E. *Americanization of the Common Law: Impact of Legal Change on Massachusetts Society, 1760-1830.* Cambridge, Mass.: Harvard University Press, 1975.

Ostrogorski, M. *The Rights of Women: A Comparative Study in History and Legislation.* New York: Scribner, 1893.

Paulson, Monrad G. "Support Rights and Duties between Husband and Wife." *Vanderbilt Law Review* 9 (1955-56):709-42.

Pierce, Christine. "Natural Law Language and Women." In *Women in Sexist Society: Studies in Power and Powerlessness,* ed. Vivian Gornick and Barbara K. Moran, pp. 242-58. New York: New American Library, 1972.

Pollack, Sir Frederick, and Frederic William Maitland. *The History of English Law.* 2d ed. 2 vols. 1898; reprinted London: Cambridge University Press, 1968.

Pound, Roscoe. "Common Law and Legislation." *Harvard Law Review* 21 (1908):389–407.

———. *The Spirit of the Common Law.* Francestown, N.Y.: Marshall Jones, 1921.

———. *The Formative Era of American Law.* New York: Peter Smith, 1950.

Rabkin, Peggy A. "The Origins of Law Reform: The Social Significance of the Nineteenth-Century Codification Movement and Its Contribution to the Passage of the Early Married Women's Property Acts." *Buffalo Law Review* 24 (1974–75):683–760.

Salmon, Marylynn. "The Property Rights of Married Women in Early America: A Comparative Study." Ph.D. dissertation, Bryn Mawr College, 1980.

Sayre, Paul. "A Reconsideration of Husband's Duty to Support and Wife's Duty to Render Services." *Virginia Law Review* 29 (1943):857–78.

Stevenson, Charles E. "Influences of Bentham and Humphreys on the New York Property Legislation of 1828." *American Journal of Legal History* 1 (1957):155–69.

Thurman, Kay Ellen. "The Married Women's Property Acts." L.L.M. dissertation, University of Wisconsin Law School, 1966.

Vernier, Chester G. *American Family Laws.* Vol. 3. Stanford, Calif.: Stanford University Press, 1935.

Warbasse, Elizabeth Bowles. "The Changing Legal Rights of Married Women, 1800–1861." Ph.D. dissertation, Radcliffe College, 1960.

Warren Charles. *A History of the American Bar.* Boston: Little, Brown, 1911.

Warren, Joseph. "Husband's Right to Wife's Services." *Harvard Law Review* 38 (1925):421–39.

Westermarck, Edward. *A Short History of Marriage.* New York: Humanities Press, 1968.

Zainaldin, Jamil S. "The Emergence of a Modern American Family Law: Child Custody, Adoption, and the Courts." *Northwestern University Law Review* 73 (1979):1038–89.

Miscellaneous Secondary Sources

Barker-Benfield, G. J. *The Horrors of the Half-Known Life: Male Attitudes toward Women and Sexuality in Nineteenth-Century America.* New York: Harper & Row, 1975.

Benson, Lee. *The Concept of Jacksonian Democracy: New York as a Test Case.* Princeton: Princeton University Press, 1961.

Berg, Barbara J. *The Remembered Gate: Origins of American Feminism. The*

Woman and the City, 1800–1860. New York: Oxford University Press, 1978.

Blackwell, Alice Stone. *Lucy Stone: Pioneer of Woman's Rights.* Norwood, Mass.: Alice Stone Blackwell Committee, 1930.

Brown, Richard D. "Modernization: A Victorian Climax." *American Quarterly* 27 (1975):533–48.

Brownlee, W. Eliot, and Mary M. Brownlee, eds. *Women in the American Economy: A Documentary History, 1675–1929.* New Haven: Yale University Press, 1976.

Carr, Lois Green, and Lorena S. Walsh. "The Planter's Wife: The Experience of White Women in Seventeenth-Century Maryland." *William and Mary Quarterly,* 3d ser., 34 (1977):542–71.

Chafe, William H. *The American Woman: Her Changing Social, Economic, and Political Roles, 1920–1970.* New York: Oxford University Press, 1972.

———. *Women and Equality: Changing Patterns in American Culture.* New York: Oxford University Press, 1977.

Cochran, Thomas C., and William Miller. *The Age of Enterprise: A Social History of Industrial America.* New York: Harper & Row, 1961.

Cott, Nancy. *The Bonds of Womanhood: "Woman's Sphere" in New England, 1780–1835.* New Haven: Yale University Press, 1977.

Cross, Whitney. *The Burned-Over District: The Social and Intellectual History of Enthusiastic Religion in Western New York, 1800–1850.* Ithaca: Cornell University Press, 1950; reprinted 1982.

Daly, Mary. *The Church and the Second Sex.* New York: Harper & Row, 1975.

Ditzion, Sidney. *Marriage, Morals, and Sex in America: A History of Ideas.* New York: Octagon Books, 1969.

Donavan, Herbert D. A. *The Barnburners.* New York: New York University Press, 1925.

Dorfman, Joseph. *The Economic Mind in American Civilization, 1606–1865.* Vol. 2. 1946; reprinted New York: August M. Kelley, 1966.

Dorr, Rheta Childe. *Susan B. Anthony: The Woman Who Changed the Mind of a Nation.* 1928; reprinted New York: AMS Press, 1970.

Douglas, Ann. *The Feminization of American Culture.* New York: Alfred A. Knopf, 1977.

DuBois, Ellen Carol. "The Radicalism of the Woman Suffrage Movement: Notes toward the Reconstruction of Nineteenth-Century Feminism." *Feminist Studies* 3 (1975):63–71.

———. *Feminism and Suffrage: The Emergence of an Independent Women's Movement in America.* Ithaca: Cornell University Press, 1978.

———, Mary Jo Buhle, Temma Kaplan, Gerda Lerner, and Carroll Smith-Rosenberg. "Politics and Culture in Women's History: A Symposium." *Feminist Studies* 6 (1980):26–64.

Flexner, Eleanor. *Century of Struggle: The Woman's Rights Movement in the United States.* 1959; reprinted New York: Atheneum, 1971.

Flick, Alexander C., ed. *History of the State of New York.* 10 vols. 1934; reprinted Port Washington, N.Y.: Ira J. Friedman, 1962.

Foner, Philip S., ed. *Frederick Douglass on Women's Rights.* Westport, Conn.: Greenwood Press, 1976.

Genovese, Eugene. *Roll, Jordan, Roll: The World the Slaves Made.* New York: Random House, 1974.

Gordon, Linda. *Woman's Body, Woman's Right: A Social History of Birth Control in America.* New York: Grossman, 1976.

Gordon, Michael, ed. *The American Family in Social-Historical Perspective.* 2d ed. New York: St. Martin's Press, 1978.

Hartman, Mary S., and Lois Banner, eds. *Clio's Consciousness Raised: New Perspectives on the History of Women.* New York: Harper & Row, 1974.

Hartz, Louis. *Economic Policy and Democratic Thought: Pennsylvania, 1776–1880.* Cambridge, Mass.: Harvard University Press, 1948.

Howe, Daniel Walker: "American Victorianism as a Culture." *American Quarterly* 27 (1975):507–32.

Kerber, Linda K. *Women of the Republic: Intellect and Ideology in the American Revolution.* Chapel Hill: University of North Carolina Press, 1980.

Lane, Ann J., ed. *Mary Ritter Beard: A Sourcebook.* New York: Schocken, 1977.

Lasch, Christopher. *Haven in a Heartless World: The Family Besieged.* New York: Basic Books, 1977.

Lerner, Gerda. "The Lady and the Mill Girl: Changes in the Status of Women in the Age of Jackson." *Midcontinent American Studies Journal* 10 (1969):5–15.

———. *The Majority Finds Its Past.* New York: Oxford University Press, 1979.

Lutz, Alma. *Created Equal: A Biography of Elizabeth Cady Stanton, 1815–1902.* New York: John Day, 1940.

———. *Susan B. Anthony: Rebel, Crusader, Humanitarian.* Boston: Beacon, 1959.

Melder, Keith E. *Beginnings of Sisterhood: The American Woman's Rights Movement, 1800–1850.* New York: Schocken, 1977.

Meyers, Marvin. *The Jacksonian Persuasion: Politics and Belief.* Stanford, Calif.: Stanford University Press, 1957.

Miller, Casey, and Kate Swift. *Words and Women.* Garden City,N.Y.: Anchor, Doubleday, 1977.

Miller, Douglas T. *Jacksonian Aristocracy: Class and Democracy in New York, 1830–1860.* New York: Oxford University Press, 1967.

Millett, Kate. *Sexual Politics.* New York: Avon Books, 1970.

North, Douglas C. *The Economic Growth of the United States, 1790–1860.* New York: W. W. Norton, 1966.

Norton, Mary Beth. *Liberty's Daughters: The Revolutionary Experience of American Women, 1750–1800.* Boston: Little, Brown, 1980.

Okin, Susan Moller. *Women in Western Political Thought.* Princeton: Princeton University Press, 1979.

Peal, Ethel. "The Atrophied Rib: Urban Middle-Class Women in Jacksonian America." Ph.D. dissertation, University of Pittsburgh, 1970.

Pessen, Edward. *Jacksonian America: Society, Personality, and Politics.* Homewood, Ill.: The Dorsey Press, 1969.

———. "The Wealthiest New Yorkers of the Jacksonian Era: A New List." *New-York Historical Society Quarterly* 54 (1970):145–72.

———. *Riches, Class, and Power before the Civil War.* Lexington, Mass.: D. C. Heath, 1973.

———. "The Marital Theory and Practice of the Antebellum Urban Elite." *New York History* 55 (1974):389–410.

Peterson, Merrill D., ed. *Democracy, Liberty, and Property: The State Constitutional Conventions of the 1820's.* Indianapolis: Bobbs-Merrill, 1966.

Riegel, Robert. *American Feminists.* Lawrence: University of Kansas Press, 1963.

———, ed. "Woman's Rights and Other Reforms in Seneca Falls: A Contemporary View." *New York History* 46 (1965):41–59.

Riley, Glenda Lou Gates. "From Chattel to Challenger: The Changing Image of the American Woman, 1808–1848." Ph.D. dissertation, Ohio State University, 1967.

Roberts, Ellis Henry. *New York: The Planting and the Growth of the Empire State.* Vol. 2. Boston: Houghton Mifflin, 1904.

Ryan, Mary. *Womanhood in America: From Colonial Times to the Present.* 2d ed. New York: New Viewpoints, 1979.

Sklar, Kathryn Kish. *Catharine Beecher: A Study in American Domesticity.* New Haven: Yale University Press, 1973.

Smith, Page. *Daughters of the Promised Land.* Boston: Little, Brown, 1970.

Smith-Rosenberg, Carroll. "Beauty, the Beast, and the Militant Woman: A Case Study in Sex Roles and Social Stress in Jacksonian America." *American Quarterly* 23 (1971):562–84.

Stone, Lawrence. "The Rise of the Nuclear Family in Early Modern England: The Patriarchal Stage." In *The Family in History,* ed. Charles Rosenberg, pp. 19–31. Philadelphia: University of Pennsylvania Press, 1975.

Suhl, Yuri. *Ernestine L. Rose and the Battle for Human Rights.* New York: Reynal, 1959.

Taylor, George Rogers. *The Transportation Revolution, 1815–1860.* New York: Rinehart, 1951.

Taylor, William R. *Cavalier and Yankee.* New York: Harper & Row 1961.

Thomas, Keith. "The Double Standard." *Journal of the History of Ideas* 20 (1959):195–216.

Tyler, Alice Felt. *Freedom's Ferment: Phases of American Social History from the Colonial Period to the Civil War.* 1944; reprinted New York: Harper & Row, 1961.

Welter, Barbara. "The Cult of True Womanhood: 1820–1860." *American Quarterly* 18 (1966):151–74.

Welter, Rush. *The Mind of America, 1820–1860.* New York: Columbia University Press, 1975.

Wood, Gordon S. *The Creation of the American Republic, 1776–1787.* Chapel Hill: University of North Carolina Press, 1969.

Index

In the Eyes of the Law

Designed by Richard E. Rosenbaum.
Composed by The Composing Room of Michigan, Inc.
in 10 point Baskerville V.I.P., 2 points leaded,
with display lines in Baskerville.
Printed offset by Thomson/Shore, Inc. on
Warren's Number 66 Antique Offset/50 pound basis.
Bound by John H. Dekker & Sons, Inc.
in Holliston book cloth
and stamped in Kurz-Hastings foil

Library of Congress Cataloging in Publication Data

Basch, Norma.
In the eyes of the law.

Bibliography: p.
Includes index.
1. Married women—New York (State)—History.
2. Husband and wife—New York (State)—History.
3. Property—New York (State)—History. I. Title.
KFN5124.B37 346.74701'6 82-2454
ISBN 0-8014-1466-0 347.470616 AACR2